Measuring the Dynamics of Technological Change

Measuring the Dynamics of Technological Change

Edited by Jon Sigurdson

Pinter Publishers,
London and New York

© Jon Sigurdson and Contributors, 1990

First published in Great Britain in 1990 by
Pinter Publishers Limited
25 Floral Street, London WC2E 9DS and
PO Box 197, Irvington, NY 10533

British Library Cataloguing in Publication Data

A CIP catalogue record for this book is available from the
British Library
ISBN 0 86187 842 6

**A CIP catalog record for this title is available
from the Library of Congress**

Typeset by GCS, Leighton Buzzard, Beds.
Printed and bound in Great Britain by Biddles Ltd.

Contents

Part III ORGANIZING TECHNICAL CHANGE

List of Figures

List of Tables

List of Contributors

Jon Sigurdson, Professor of Research Policy, is director of the Research Policy Institute (RPI) at the University of Lund, Sweden. His research work covers various areas concerning R&D systems. His main present focus is on globalization of R&D in large multinational companies. Current activities include studies of corporate R&D in Japan and preparing the Longman Guide on Science and Technology in Japan.

Rikard Stankiewicz, PhD, is Associate Professor of R&D Policy and Management at the Research Policy Institute (RPI) at the University of Lund, Sweden. His research activities have ranged across several fields including the organization and leadership of academic research units, interactions between universities and industry and the R&D dynamics of new basic technologies. At present he is engaged in a major study of Sweden's Technological System.

Fumio Kodama as Director-in-Research of National Institute of Science and Technology Policy (Science and Technology Agency) and Professor at the Graduate School of Policy Science at Saitama University, Fumio Kodama is responsible for research and education on innovation processes, innovation policy, and mathematical modelling. He also serves on several advisory committees for MITI.

Hariolf Grupp is Head of the Technological Change Department at Fraunhofer Institute for Systems and Innovation Research (ISI), FRG. He is editor of the series of books *'Future for Technology'*, six volumes published. Grupp received his PhD in semiconductor physics and biophysics at Heidelberg university 1978. In the beginning of the 1980's he served as senior researcher at the Scientific Service of the FRG Parliament, and at the FRG Federal Ministry for Research and Technology.

Anders Granberg, PhD, is Research Fellow at the Research Policy Institute (RPI) at the University of Lund, Sweden. His main field of interest comprises the cognitive and institutional structure and developmental dynamics of science-based technologies. Current activities include studies, in a comparative international perspective, of Swedish efforts in factory automation, powder technology, and superconductivity.

Beatrix Schwitalla received her diploma in National economy from Freiburg University. Since 1987 she has been at the Fraunhofer Institute for Systems and Innovation Research (ISI), FRG preparing her PhD thesis on multi-factorial approaches to measuring innovation.

Ulrich Schmoch is head of the research section "Development of Science and Technology Indicators" at the Fraunhofer Institute for Systems and Innovation Research (ISI), FRG. Schmoch graduated as mechanical engineer in 1977 and has a PhD in social sciences from Hanover University in 1983. Before joining ISI in 1985 Schmoch was patent engineer at a large patent attorney's office. His publications cover issues related to international economy and mechanical engineering as well as patent analysis and technology genesis.

Masayuki Kondo of the Ministry of International Trade and Industry (MITI), Japan is presently Director of General Affairs Division at the Chubu Bureau. He joined MITI in 1976. Kondo has a MSc degree in Engineering-Economic Systems from Stanford University (1981). During 1984–86 he was Associate Professor at the Graduate School for Policy Science, Saitama University.

Helmar Krupp was until 1989 Director of the Fraunhofer Institute for Systems and Innovation Research (ISI), FRG. He has a PhD in Engineering and is Professor at Karlsruhe University. He is presently visiting professor at the University of Tokyo, Komaba (until 1992) working on a project dealing with present Japanese energy policies.

Preface

In a discussion of science and technology policy there is no way of avoiding Japan which has emerged as a technological superpower. This book is no exception, although it primarily thrashes out analytical approaches to understanding technological change. However, the research on which the present book draws saw its beginning at a luncheon at Saitama University. Professor Toru Yoshimura, Dean of the Graduate School of Policy Science, Mr Göran Friborg and Mr Jan Olof Carlsson, from the Swedish Board for Technical Development (STU), decided that it would be worthwhile to carry out a comparative study of technological policies in Japan and Sweden.

Researchers from Sweden and Japan were soon joined by colleagues in Germany, and a three-country comparative study group was formed at a first meeting in Stockholm in the autumn of 1984, sponsored by STU. A tentative research plan was hammered out in subsequent meetings. Seminars to discuss research findings were organized by the Fraunhofer Institute for Systems and Innovations Research in Karlsruhe, by the Institute for Policy Science at Saitama University in Urawa and finally by the Research Policy Institute at the University of Lund in June 1989. The last meeting provided the opportunity for suggesting final changes to the contributions which are included in this volume. The research at the three places has also resulted in numerous other papers, publications and a volume of seminar proceedings.[1]

The Research Policy Institute has emphasized primary R&D activities rather than advanced systems integration and general diffusion of technologies. The Fraunhofer Institute for Systems and Innovation Research has developed a new indicator which promises to fill the gap between basic technologies analysis and trade analysis of success in the market-place for high technology products. The Institute for Policy Science at Saitama University and the National Institute of Science and Technology Policy (NISTEP), the present intellectual base of Kodama, have contributed to interesting and challenging insights on how to assess and understand changes in the R&D system.

In the seminars we have been joined by many research colleagues who have prepared presentations from which we have benefited. In the process of carrying out the research we have also enjoyed close interaction with researchers from other countries.

We want to thank the sponsoring organizations which have made the research possible. These include the Bundesministerium für Forschung und Technologie (BMFT) in Bonn, the Ministry of Education (Monbusho) in Tokyo and the Swedish Board for Technical Development (STU) in Stockholm.

We hope that this volume, aside from being the results of an enjoyable period of international comparative research, will also provide new insights into the exciting and changing field of science and technology policy studies and stimulate new research.

Finally, I want in particular to thank my research assistant, Ms Yael Tågerud, without whose unfailing support and hard work this volume would have never reached the readers.

Note

1. Grupp, H. (ed.) (1986), *Problems of Measuring Technological Change*, Verlag TüV Rheinland GmbH, Köln.

Jon Sigurdson
Saitama and Lund
January 1990

1 Challenge and new analytical methods in science and technology policy— an introduction

Jon Sigurdson

Background

The following nine chapters in this volume offer insights into the generation, diffusion and integration of knowledge based on R&D activities. It has a strong methodological body which puts forth analytical approaches for both R&D actors and systems. It also attempts to measure R&D efficiency—based on partly new methodological tools. Finally, it also suggests a new system for R&D which can encompass broad and long-term societal needs.

Science and technology inputs have become crucial inputs for many new goods and services which are demanded in world markets. The national and regional trading patterns are increasingly influenced through differential rates in commercializing new technologies. Consequently, nations, in particular the highly industrialized ones, are nervously extending their participation in the support of science and technology activities. Such measures include national R&D programs in microelectronics, biotechnology and new materials in a host of countries. Other approaches include multi-disciplinary research centres, mainly in engineering, or science-based technologies, with an explicit or implicit objective to serve national economic development.

Many such efforts are no longer national in character but extend beyond the national borders in linking global companies and various national actors. Thus, it has become natural to refer to techno-globalism—moving away from techno-nationalism—with techno-regionalism as an intermediate stage where the European Commission in Brussels is taking over some of the national responsibilities. The changing global situation in science and technology requires new insights and improved analytical tools in order to provide relevant policy guidance on various thematic issues. One emerging theme is the changing relationship between nations and global companies and another, related one, is the growing capability of companies in developing and controlling resources for R&D.

There are several factors underlying these changes, a couple of which are covered in some detail in this volume. First, the technological change or rather the innovation process is now characterized by 'scientification' which signifies a need to have a relevant and substantial science basis in order to achieve technological progress. Second, there is a growing heterogeneity and complexity for almost all advanced technologies which prompts a broadening of the technological base in order to remain successful. The scientification and the broadening of the base for technological change creates tensions within the R&D system. The strains appear among firms, among nations, among regional blocks and also among the actors within each national R&D system.

One example of intensification in regional or supra-national conflicts in technology is the attempts to form regional research and production cartels in Europe and in the US in order to challenge the hegemony of Japanese manufacturers in the technology for the manufacture of integrated circuits. Such a changing situation poses a number of questions for those involved in research and technology policy. Is more funding needed? In which scientific and technological fields? Who should fund and who should perform R&D in the new fields? In which stages of the process is more activity required? Which organizational forms and linkages among various actors are beneficial? Those responsible for formulating and implementing science and technology policy are increasingly facing an array of alternatives and combinations.

This volume attempts to analyze some of the significant changes in the R&D system and suggests ways of using various quantitative indicators to study the shifts, rather than providing answers to such questions. On this basis the role of different actors and various organizational forms for technological change becomes more transparent. The volume includes three distinct tacks. The first includes two papers which analyze and indicate major changes in the innovation process. The second part, providing the main body, is centred on quantitative analysis of technological change. The third part consists of two papers which address issues in organizing technological change—one with a focus on corporate globalism and the final one with an ecological future-oriented scenario.

Ways of understanding the innovation process

In an introductory paper Rikard Stankiewicz notes that basic technologies have been less conspicuous in technological development of the past. A major reason is that the rate of innovation in those technologies tended to be rather low and the relevant knowledge practical and based on common sense rather than systemic. Basic technology is a set of physical insights, heuristic principles and manipulative skills which enables one to control and exploit the properties of natural objects and processes.

Basic technologies are typically identified not by their functions but by their character of the natural phenomena which are exploited. Thus it is natural to talk about laser technology and protein engineering. Most basic technologies are highly generic in character which means that they can be used as the main or auxiliary means of achieving many different functions or objectives, but are on the other hand strongly identified with a special class of natural phenomena.

Stankiewicz emphasizes that the research by himself and colleagues at the Research Policy Institute shows that the character and structure of a national system for science and technology have a deep influence on the orientation and strength of a national capability in basic technologies. The environment of basic research is originally important but later on it becomes critical that various scientifc-technological environments become active. A vigorous development of several parallel attacks tends to foster a rapid growth of pertinent knowledge, an early evaluation of options and an effective integration with other technologies.

This interpretation supports the accepted fact that Japan has become accustomed to a rapid succession of different technologies by anticipating and rapidly entering into new technological fields. Stankiewicz also suggests that another important factor for the technological success of Japan lies in the weakness of its public R&D system. Thus, the relative weakness of the university and the absence of large military R&D programs have forced the industrial firms to engage not only in advanced engineering development but also in long-term exploratory research. The conclusion is that the national systems in the US and Europe should restructure in order to become more integrative—both at the level of company and nation. This would then decrease the 'high level of segmentation and linear division of labour', in the words of Stankiewicz, and facilitate an early diffusion of basic technologies.

Fumio Kodama, in his first chapter, identifies technological fusion as another major new phenomenon in organizing research, which supports the earlier conclusion that the integrative character of a national R&D system is important. He argues that mechatronics as the combination of mechanics and electronics is an example of technological fusion in which several different industries are involved. He suggests that such technological fusion is of equal importance with breakthrough innovations exemplified by the transistor. Kodama argues strongly for a dichotomy between technological breakthrough innovations and technology fusion with the transistor belonging to the former. The significance of fusion-type innovations, he says, is that they contribute to the gradual growth of all companies within relevant industries rather than to the revolutionary growth of certain companies.

The basis for his research is the rich R&D statistics available in Japan which makes it possible to identify the R&D expenditure of one industrial sector into R&D of other sectors. His research clearly indicates an increasing level of cross-financing among sectors which leads to higher levels of technological fusion. This interpretation is also supported by studies on multi-technology companies in the Japan, the USA and Europe, carried out by other researchers. Many Japanese companies appear very prominently as multi-technology companies which contrast sharply with the situation in Sweden and in the USA. Kodama's research shows, as an interesting example, the emergence already in 1974 of a triple connection of industries in food, drugs and medicines, and industrial chemicals. Kodama says that this can be interpreted as the emergence of biotechnology. The dual connection between the first two appeared already in 1971 while only the later connection with industrial chemicals established biotechnology as a new high technology arena in Japan.

The two different analytical approaches—by Kodama and Stankiewicz —both indicate a changing role for firms and governments in the innovation process. 'Who should be responsible for strategic research?' emerges as a central question. Subsequently, it is necessary to clarify to what extent universities and government agencies/institutes should be involved in technological development. Without being able to provide any definite answers it has already become obvious that today's innovations require new ways for organizing industrial and technological development. These are amply exemplified by various types of joint research and strategic alliances and the reorganization of industrial companies/groups into networks.

Measuring technological change[1]

A major part of this volume is related to measuring technological change. In doing so the analysis has been narrowed down to a few technological fields—laser technology, robot technology and genetic engineering— although research within our network has also covered several other technological fields.

The analysis is in the main limited to three countries—Japan, West Germany and Sweden. The countries were chosen as they are the native countries of the researchers involved. However, the countries are also highly industrialized and technologically advanced countries with a high involvement of international trade. For reference it may be mentioned that the total R&D expenditure in the three countries is approximately 25, 12 and 2 per cent, respectively, of total R&D expenditure within the OECD group. An interesting characteristic is that privately funded R&D dominates in all three countries. At the same time, the R&D systems of these countries show great differences which makes it possible to relate the research findings to a discussion on the interaction between science and technology policy and the institutional characteristics of the national R&D systems.

It is common knowledge that indicators provide an easy way of comparing alternatives. The fuel efficiency and the maximum torque of a car engine can easily be compared by using indicators. The comparison becomes more complex when comparing passenger capacity, operational range, and maintenance costs for a modern large passenger aircraft. The complexity and problems are equal or even greater when attempting to gauge the results and efficiency of various parts of a national or a company's R&D system. It is still hotly debated as to what extent science and technology indicators can be used to assess scientific performance. However, counting publications and citations have spread from the domain of scientific papers to patents to become widely used as a tool for assessing the efficiency of individuals to aggregates such as R&D units, industrial sectors or whole nations.

The increasing use of S&T indicators has led to the appearance of scientific cartography which together with qualitative analysis may provide an increasingly accurate understanding of the results of what takes place inside a system of R&D activities. Input indicators such as R&D personnel and expenditure are familiar to everyone in the field which is equally true for the citation of scientific papers and patents.

During the 1980s the analysis of foreign trade in R&D-intensive products has brought about new indicators even though they suffer from many shortcomings. It is apparent that the indicators are still not sufficient or relevant in assessing efficiency and choices among alternatives. However, devising intelligent variations in the basic data available may in fact provide us with new indicators.

It is generally accepted that most of the established R&D indicators are relatively precise but isolated which mean that they can rarely be used for any consistent evaluation of the output from the science and technology system. By combining different indicators, of which the technometrics approach promises a major contribution, it may be possible to have an evaluative type of indicator.

Technometrics provides a new and badly needed indicator to measure the phase between industrial development measured by patent activity and the full commercialization measured in the foreign trade statistics. The concept, which has been developed since 1984 by Hariolf Grupp and his group at the Fraunhofer Institute for Systems and Innovations Research in Germany, takes as its point of departure the difficulty in measuring the results of R&D expenditure. Thus technometrics indicators are established in direct relation to the technological trade figures as well as patent and literature statistics.

Grupp and his colleagues have noted that the results of industrial development are rarely published in scientific journals and there is no chance of filing a patent by imitating existing innovation, anywhere in the world, though companies may be very successful in the market-place. The starting-point is to select those technological specifications which are essential for competing in the market-place. Grupp and his colleagues maintain that it is important to use various science and technology indicators selectively depending on the type of R&D activity to be studied. Technometrics indicators are aggregated figures which are composed of specifications for certain physical units. Thus, the figures specify the state of the art for either a product or a process and different functional characteristics have to be used if the product or process serves different purposes.

Grupp and his research group argue that more case studies have to be made in order to provide a coupled system of science, technology and innovation indicators. Further, it is suggested that using different classification systems with the emphasis on various indicators will provide a bonus. It will allow 'for comparisons between different R&D-performing institutions, and for comparisons between input and output measures and thus opens the door for efficiency deliberations'.

It is testified that the technometrics indicator is well suited to studying R&D and innovation dynamics as the technometrics data may be combined with anticipated market shares in order to assess the importance of the technology factor embodied within new and successful innovations. This type of analysis unfolds a rich and diverse spectrum so that the ranking becomes quite complex and differentiated. Thus the leadership in laser technology is shown to be more complex and varying than would normally have been assumed. The findings support the basic notion that the technological quality of R&D-intensive products is primarily deciding the competitiveness in world markets.

As a major task in his contribution Granberg explores the differential involvement of the three national R&D systems in the development of new strategic fields of technology and identifies two major aims. The substantive aim is to clarify and compare the overall dynamics and institutional structure of the national R&D efforts in certain science-based fields of technology. The methodological aim is to assess the possibilities and limitations of bibliometric methods in the mapping of development patterns and institutional actors. Granberg shows that scientific research in laser technology has over a period of twelve years been, in relative terms, expanding in Japan, diminishing in Germany while remaining fairly constant in Sweden. The analysis of laser technology patents reveal a similar change.

In studying the role of institutional actors, it is revealed that Sweden is the country—in every field of technology—where academic institutions are most important as a source of published contributions. Japan, on the other hand, is the country in which the company sector is most important. When comparing Japan and Germany it becomes evident that the company sector has increased in the former country while it has decreased in the latter. The opposite is true for the academic sector in the two countries.

The strength of this bibliometric approach, according to Granberg, lies primarily in the performance of two closely interrelated functions. First, it is a scanning device for the development of an initial sketch map of the evolving R&D landscape with a focus on the overall dynamics and the major institutional characteristics of the national efforts. Second, the bibliometric surveys also generate a set of questions and hypotheses which will guide further enquiry.

Two contributions describe and analyze the development of industrial robot technology and how the results are revealed in various indicators based on bibliometric data sources. Thus they provide in-depth examples of the new methodological approaches which have been described earlier in the volume. Grupp and his colleagues are utilizing the so-called Revealed Comparative Advantage (RCA) as an indicator of competitiveness. The RCA values indicate the extent to which export surpluses in a product group deviate from the average for manufactured industrial products. The analysis shows that patent and publication numbers correlate strongly. It is of considerable interest to find that in a field like robotics, where patents play a weighty role, scientific publications in related research do not appear earlier but rather later.

Kondo covers similar ground for both robotics and genetic engineering although with less attention to methodological considerations. He also notes that original papers on robotics were, in Japan, published after patents were applied for, which suggests a close relation between R&D and patent application. However, original papers on genetic engineering precede patents which suggests that R&D in this field has a more academic orientation. Furthermore, information diffusion preceded patent application in genetic engineering. It is suggested that the enthusiasm for new scientific fields precede both research results and patent applications.

In chapter 8 Kodama introduces a new tool for mapping the changing patterns of industrial development. He suggests a new way for tracing the development of technological fields or the accomplishment of technical tasks—through mobilization of R&D resource efforts within national programs, joint research projects or similar type of organizational arrangements. In proposing a new method for analysing national R&D efforts he suggests that such efforts should, initially, be considered as a learning process. The aim, according to Kodama, is to establish which industrial technologies are relevant and which ones are irrelevant in terms of interaction between national R&D programs and industrial development. He argues that the best way to formulate national R&D efforts is to draw them up as a process of reducing the uncertainty existing in the fluid stage of innovation. Such programs should be based on performance criteria aiming at identifying the best technological option through a trial and error process.

The concept of entropy—which is the measurement of uncertainty—plays a central role in his speculative and rich chapter. The establishment of time series for entropy values will tell us how searches are progressively narrowed down as uncertainty decreases or how they are enlarged as uncertainty increases—as national efforts progress. It is possible to identify two major types of national efforts which are (1) mission-type activities as exemplified by environmental protection and (2) generic-type research as exemplified in information technologies. The entropy generally decreases in the former as problems are being solved, while entropy increases in the latter type which aims at exploring relevant industrial technologies as widely as possible. Thus, the growing entropy in generic programs should not necessarily be seen as a program failure. The launching of a generic national program influences industrial R&D behaviour in expanding research towards developing products which would otherwise not have been created.

With reference to the analysis of the Japanese situation and examples Kodama indicates that this method can be used not only to trace the overall industry pattern of involvement in common activities but also to explore such patterns within industrial sub-sectors. Kodama suggests that a recognition of entropy dynamics will lead to an improved understanding of the role of national R&D efforts in the identification process of critical industrial technologies. It is implied that national programs should be terminated when the entropy level stabilizes. Kodama ends his paper by discussing the policy conclusions at the international level by suggesting ways of organizing joint research efforts in the early fluid stage of R&D.

Structural changes in the R&D system

The R&D scene is constantly shifting with regard to funding in disciplines, actor composition and their relations. During the 1980s concepts such as joint research and strategic alliances have become keywords in the S&T policy debate. There is little doubt that the diversity and extent of R&D networks are constantly increasing. It is also obvious that the networks, particularly among companies, extend far beyond the national borders. Sigurdson offers a description of an international R&D system in process of becoming global.

The expansion of joint research (national programs) and strategic alliances are discussed in terms of R&D globalization with the national control decreasing, at least for small and medium-sized countries while increasing for companies. Although difficult to quantify, the papers offer the suggestion that R&D strategies of global companies require considerable more attention in order to identify relevant national policies.

The paucity of the data bases still prevents the quantitative approach on which the earlier chapters have been based. Important policy issues also arise from the changing geographical location and control of R&D resources in which multinational companies are major actors. The changes discussed by Sigurdson are only vaguely covered in data bases which indicates the need to assess the information and develop methods to analyze the revealed changes.

Sigurdson argues that the structural changes require new S&T indicators which clearly reveal structural changes in various parts of an S&T spectrum. The use of data bases on patents and scientific publications clearly testify that structural changes can be revealed through bibliometric analysis as shown by Anders Granberg in an earlier chapter. Given the increasing importance of structural changes in which companies are involved it appears highly desirable to establish data bases which cover in considerable detail company-specific activities in science and technology.

In discussing the dynamics in research and technology policy it is a natural temptation to assume that the present overall situation will prevail while collecting the data and analyzing their significance. Helmar Krupp in the final chapter takes a very different approach. He argues that the actors which have a major role in the use and direction of R&D resources are dominated by companies and interest groups which generally lack a long-term perspective of societal needs and technological possibilities. His observations are based on the German situation but have in all likelihood a much wider relevance. Krupp argues that the short-term perspective of the industry-research relationship has the effect of shifting R&D resources away from more urgent—although long-term—needs of society.

Consequently, it is essential to analyze the dynamics of technological change in relation to needs which are still only vaguely articulated. In simplistic terms, it may be argued, that, while science and technology have in a major way served the needs for warfare and are presently serving economic warfare among nations or regions, nations, regions or the world must now find ways of making S&T serve more whole-heartedly environmental and broad societal needs.

The chapter outlines some of the major societal needs where—in many situations—technological change is making the situation worse. This is particularly true in the transportation sector and in the use of power and transportation. Krupp discusses the present system of interest groups and structures which change only slowly. However, he suggests that a re-orientation is possible even if the identified obstacles are extra-ordinarily great. He envisages that an 'ecologizing' of the economy is, at least in principle, possible. He notes that the system of R&D is able to identify risks to the environment and to develop ecologically sound technologies. Thus, it would be possible to regulate the utilization of technologies through 'context conditions' so that ecologically beneficial technologies would prevail over those which are ecologically harmful.

Considering the complexity of large systems which prevail in sectors such as energy and transportation, Krupp suggests that the time required to develop alternative technologies and/or systems would involve an introductory phase of roughly one to two generations, 25–50 years. The process may be speeded up, or at least not delayed, through the emergence of single-issue citizen groups which are able to challenge the government-industrial complexes and force a paradigmatic change. However, the tenacity of entrenched paradigms, as opposed to new ones, should not be underestimated, as the interest groups supporting the former ones are better able to assert themselves than those in an early formative stage.

Note

1. This introductory chapter does not provide references either to research of relevance or influence for the contributions contained in the volume. However, I would like to mention that the work of Francis Narin served as an inspiration. Dr Narin also participated in one of the research seminars in Japan. Furthermore, the early research on patent statistics by Professor Keith Pavitt is also highly pertinent in this context. Finally, I would in the Swedish context also like to mention the bibliometric research done by Olle Persson at INFORSK, Umeå University.

Part I
Dimensions of Technical Change

2 Basic technologies and the innovation process

Rikard Stankiewicz

Introduction

Until relatively recently the predominant image of technology was one of an historically accumulated cornucopia of techniques and artefacts ordered roughly by field of application. Despite some important earlier efforts by scholars such as Gilfillan and Schumpeter, it was only during the last few decades that a coherent image of the structure and dynamics of technology began to emerge. Today we recognize that unless the various dimensions of technical change are clearly differentiated and analyzed each in their own right, many of the classical questions—such as those about the relative importance of the radical versus incremental changes, the role of systemic versus disjointed innovations or the 'technology-push' versus 'demand-pull'—will continue to evade a satisfactory answer. The above questions are not merely 'academic'; in fact they correspond to some of the recalcitrant policy dilemmas.

Today's technology is characterized by two fundamental trends: one towards increasing 'scientification' and the other towards growing heterogeneity and complexity. The first of these trends manifests itself in the rapid development and diffusion of new 'basic technologies' which revolutionize the very foundations on which systems technologies are based. The second can be seen in the rapid broadening of the technological base on which these systems depend. These trends give rise to contradictory pressures in the R&D systems on the firm level as well as national and, to a growing extent, international levels.

The 'scientification' of basic technologies is rapidly making the conventional patterns of division of labor in research and development obsolete. This, in turn, leads to a number of important consequences. The extent to which strategic research should become a responsibility of firms, and technology development a concern for universities and governments, is a major policy issue in many countries as is the question of the right mechanisms for the appropriation and transfer of generic technical knowledge. The technological and scientific 'free rider' problem has emerged as an important concern both among companies and among nations.

The increasing complexity of technologies has a similar unsettling effect on the established policies and institutions. On the one hand, it prompts growing specialization among the actors on the economic and technological scene; this is reflected, among others, in the tendencies towards 'vertical disintegration' in industry. On the other, it demands the introduction of countervailing mechanisms to achieve the necessary degree of system integration. These pressures lead to innovations in industrial and technological organization including new kinds of groups and networks (Imai, 1989). The strategies for coping with the problem of technological complexity are enormously important in the context of S&T policy. There are considerable variations in the ways in which that problem is dealt with in different countries. The increasing complexity of technology also plays a very important role in the internationalization of science and technology.

This paper will focus on one of the dimensions of technical change mentioned above: the emergence and rapid evolution of new basic technologies. Several such technologies have been the subject of studies at the Research Policy Institute over the last few years.[1] A paper by Granberg, in this volume, reports in detail the results of the study of laser technology. The present paper is more theoretical in character. I will:

1. attempt to set basic technologies in a general context of the theory of technological change;
2. define the demands which the development of these technologies makes on the R&D systems (both at the national and firm level); and
3. discuss the ways in which these demands are handled in different national systems.

It will be argued that the approach to basic technologies taken by most decision-makers in Europe and the United States reflects an *implicit belief* in the *overtly rejected* linear model of technological innovation. The policies and organizational structures derived from that model tend to be inefficient. This, I will claim, might be the chief reason why Japan, in spite of its relative weakness in basic research, has been able to close the development gap in several basic technologies and is positioning itself for leadership in such areas as superconductivity.

Basic technologies and the evolution of technical systems

What are basic technologies and what is their place in the overall process of technical change? In order to answer this question it is necessary to start with a discussion of certain broad features of technology. To begin with, let us distinguish between two levels at which technology can be analyzed: (i) the technical systems-in-use; and (ii) the technological knowledge associated with them.

Technical systems-in-use (the actually existing products and production processes) can be analyzed in terms of (i) the *functions* they are designed to perform; (ii) the nature of the *subsystems* of which they consist; and (iii) the *design concepts* linking these subsystems into a functioning whole. The subsystems can, in their turn, be analyzed into their constitutive elements until we arrive at an ultimate set of technical procedures using which we manipulate, and thus purposefully exploit, certain natural objects and processes. The bodies of insights and skills associated with those procedures are defined here as *basic technologies* (Granberg and Stankiewicz, 1981).

Technological knowledge-systems consist of (i) the insights into the functional requirements of various technical systems, (ii) the knowledge of the possibilities, limitations and manipulability of various natural processes and structures which might be utilized in technical practice, as well as (iii) a wide range of design concepts through which such processes and structures are harnessed to the performance of various functions. Technology-as-knowledge can be compared to a biological 'gene pool' which when 'expressed' takes the form of technical systems-in-use.

Technical innovations are defined as changes in technical systems-in-use. The nature and significance of innovations is therefore largely a function of the character and structure of the systems within which they take place. These systemic aspects of technological innovation have, in recent years, been strongly stressed by a number of writers. Concepts such as 'technological trajectory' (Nelson and Winter, 1977), or 'technological guide-posts' (Sahal, 1985) reflect an implicit recognition of the fact that technical systems possess a certain internal developmental logica. Technological change is increasingly seen as a result of a complex series of trade-offs between external economic and internal technological considerations.

The existence of the internal developmental logic in technology can be interpreted in two complementary ways: cognitively and structurally. Perhaps the best articulated cognitive interpretation has been offered by Dosi (1982 and 1988) who suggested that technological praxis at any given time is guided by certain broad 'technological paradigms'. These paradigms determine the ways in which technical problems are posed and the nature of the solutions which are sought. There is a general tendency towards close correlation between the major technical systems in use and the dominant technological paradigms. The latter guide the development of the former by channeling the creative activities of scientists and engineers in certain favoured directions. Paradigms in technology have a similar function as in science, i.e. they make the learning process effective by making it cumulative.

The structural interpretations come in several variants but they all share the emphasis on the *systemic* character of technologies. A technical system is a system of elements (*structures* and *processes*) linked by *design* into a whole with certain desired *functional* properties. Rosenberg (1976) has pointed out that certain elements in a technical system can function as restrictions on the effective utilization of others. The need to eliminate these bottle-necks channels the inventive activity in certain directions. Sahal (1985) has drawn attention to the tendency of technical systems to increase in size and complexity. These quantitative changes cannot, however, continue for a long time without significant structural changes in the system. There is therefore a certain inherent sequence of developmental crises in each evolving technical system. The search for the means of overcoming these crises determines largely (though not exclusively) the agenda for the scientists and engineers.

Abernathy and Clark (1985) emphasize, in their interpretation of technology dynamics, the hierarchical nature of technical systems. The idea has been articulated in an earlier paper by Clark (1983) as follows:

It is useful ... to think of the product as a set of design concepts, that is, particular approaches to basic functional parameters. ... Within the overall set of concepts, there is what I shall call the core concept. This is the concept which is particularly trenchant in its effects on other design choices. The core concept is fundamental in the sense that change in it requires significant change in most other aspects of the product. In effect, selection of a core concept establishes the development agenda for the other technical systems and thus requires priority in the evolution of the product.

In the early 'fluid' phase of system's development, there are often several alternative core concepts and the direction of their evolution is uncertain. With time, however, one or a few concepts become dominant and their developmental direction fixed. What follows then is a rapid evolutionary change, the pace of which eventually slows down as the system achieves technological maturity.

The structuralist theories account well for the evolutionary development of technical systems along certain trajectories. But what about the more revolutionary shifts in technology, shifts which lead to the starting of new technological trajectories and new dominant design concepts? Broadly speaking, one can distinguish three main mechanisms which, usually in combination, bring about such changes: (i) abrupt shifts in the nature of demand and prices; (ii) exhaustion of the developmental potential of the dominant design concepts; (iii) unanticipated emergence of new basic technologies.

A technological trajectory, as noted earlier, is determined as a trade-off between, on one hand, the technical potential and opportunities of a given system and the structure of demand and relative prices, on the other. In the notion of 'demand' are included even non-market factors such as regulations. A stable dominant design can only emerge when the economic environment is also relatively stable and changes only gradually. This is normally the case. Occasionally, however, a major shift in, for instance, prices can radically upset the balance between the technological and economic factors. It may then prove difficult to cope with the situation within the framework of the current dominant designs. A search for alternative solutions is initiated which might either lead to a rapid development of some pre-existing design concepts (which have earlier been 'shelved' for one reason or used to satisfy other functions) or to the development of entirely new design concepts.

A search for radical alternatives can also become attractive when the development potential of the dominant design has been exhausted while the demand for enhanced performance (or reduced costs) continues.

The third cause of revolutionary change in design concept is the emergence of new basic technologies which totally change the fundamental premises of the system in question and offer potential performance far in excess of what can be obtained with the traditional set of basic technologies. In fact, the new technologies may revolutionize not only the concept of the design but also that of function giving rise to new technical systems satisfying new configurations of needs.

Clark (1985) gives the following illuminating description of the design process:

Design is a search for understanding of what the object or product is, and ought to be, given the context in which it must function. The working out of a design involves a process of analysis, of identifying the components of the form, the major systems and sub-systems, and then grouping them in different ways to illuminate their interrelations. Not all elements or components of a system are of equal significance in function or in concept.

What is implied, but not expressly stated in this description, is the fact that the process of design takes place in the context of a certain set of basic technologies. Functional insights are always intimately linked with physical insights. An engineer relies on a certain instrumental knowledge of materials and natural processes and of the procedures using which these materials and processes can be controlled and manipulated. An engineer's education consists, to a considerable extent, in learning a set of basic technologies as related to certain functions and applications. He acquires the knowledge of a set of fundamental design concepts intimately linked to these basic technologies and the problem-solving skills necessary for the development and optimization of systems based on these technologies.

Engineering traditions or 'paradigms' can, in fact, be defined as distinct configurations of functional insights, design concepts and basic technologies. Major changes in functional requirements represent a challenge to a technical 'paradigm'. A successful response means that new or modified design concepts meeting the new requirements, can emerge within the paradigm. If not, an incentive is created to search for solutions based on other types of basic technologies—already existing in other engineering fields or newly discovered.

If the above argument is correct, then the pace and character of technological change is strongly conditioned by the availability/supply of new basic technologies. During periods in which the supply is low, the technological change will be guided by relatively stable technological paradigms, irrespective of economic fluctuations. Rapid introduction of new basic technologies, on the other hand, is likely to have an unsettling influence on the established traditions, and could create a powerful technology-push effect.

We are living in a period when new basic technologies revolutionizing technical systems-in-use are being introduced at a very rapid pace. Developments in materials technologies, information technologies, electronics and in biotechnologies are widely recognized as major factors behind the stream of innovations which change the structure of our economies at both the national and global level. And yet, the systematic study and analysis of the mechanisms involved has been largely neglected. This neglect is probably the result of the fact that the role of basic technologies in the past was far less dramatic than it is today. Another contributing factor may have been the simplistic fashion in which basic technologies have been treated in the theories of technical change.

The changing role and character of basic technologies

By 'basic technology'—let us repeat—we mean a set of physical insights, heuristic principles and manipulative skills which enables one to control and exploit the properties of natural objects and processes. Basic technologies are typically identified not by their functions but by the character of natural phenomena they exploit. Thus we talk about *laser* technology, *nuclear* technology, *protein* engineering and so on. Most basic technologies are highly generic in character, i.e. they can be used as the main or auxiliary means of performing many different functions.

The most prototypical of basic technologies are, perhaps, the material technologies. The ability to identify, extract, process and handle the naturally occurring materials has been the foundation of technological praxis from time immemorial. In fact, the major epochs in the history of mankind are named after the dominant materials, from the 'stone' to the 'silicon age'. The materials technologies and the sciences associated with them have been the foundation of other technologies—structural, mechanical, electrical, as well as chemical and biological ones.

In spite of their fundamental significance, the basic technologies have been less conspicuous in the previous technological development, largely because the rate of innovation in those technologies tended to be quite low and the relevant knowledge practical and common sense rather than systematic. Indeed, until the emergence of modern science, the accumulation of knowledge regarding various basic technologies had been almost exclusively empirical and very closely linked to specific technological practices. The technologies tended to be codified as rigid 'recipes' and procedural rules which were restricted to certain, often narrow, areas of application.

The above situation changed dramatically in the course of the nineteenth century as several fields of physical science started exercising strong impact on certain basic technologies. These impacts were first felt in the areas of metallurgy, electrical phenomena and chemical synthesis. They were soon to be followed by developments in other fields.

Initially, the impact of science was confined to restricted areas of technology. There emerged 'islands' of science-based technologies in the chemical and electrical industries. Those islands formed very dynamic but relatively self-contained technical clusters linked to a few well-defined fields of scientific knowledge. Today, the technological map looks quite different. The islands of science-based technology have become both larger and more numerous, and they have started coalescing into veritable continents. For that reason they have become increasingly visible in the overall process of technological change. The 'scientification' of basic technologies has a number of profound consequences:

1. To the extent that the natural phenomena underlying the basic technologies are understood scientifically, the *pace* of their development can be greatly enhanced. Science *informs* the otherwise empiricist heuristics of technological search making it more efficient and effective.
2. Scientification allows the physical insights underlying a technology to be *generalized* thus increasing the range of its applicability and adaptability (i.e. its *generic* character).
3. The new science-based technologies tend to emerge in *families* rather than as isolated events. This is often overlooked since the popular image of the emergence of science-based technology is one of a dramatic 'breakthrough'. In fact, what often happens is that a whole area of science becomes ripe for technological exploitation and this results in a whole cluster of related technical developments. The current situation in biotechnology is a good illustration of this phenomenon. This tendency means that new basic technologies often have broad systemic impacts.

4. The fourth property of science-based technologies is what one might call their *cognitive convergence* or homogenization. While the major basic technologies of the past rested on highly divergent cognitive foundations, today there is a trend towards a remarkable degree of convergence. This trend seems to be a consequence of the fact that many science-based technologies rely on the knowledge and methodology of the molecular and submolecular sciences which themselves are increasingly unified from the theoretical standpoint. Today many of the most exciting technical developments occur precisely in the areas where the basic technologies begin to converge as, for instance, in optelectronics, bioelectronics or in parts of biotechnology. This trend appears to be so strong that it has led to some futuristic speculation about the possibility of developing a unified basic technology—a 'nano-technology'—using technical systems which could be designed and built atom-by-atom and molecule-by-molecule (Drexler, 1988). Irrespective of what one might say about such an ambitious project, the fact is that certain multidisciplinary submicron programs are already under way—including the Swedish '*mikronik*' program.[2] Speaking of essentially the same phenomenon, Sahal (1985) predicts:

> Beginning from the twenty-first century, we may expect an accelerating trend towards what may be called the 'fusion' of certain important technologies based on intermingling of knowledge from a wide variety of fields. In this respect, Kodak's new camera, an outcome of joint efforts of photochemists and electronics experts, seems a good pointer to the shape of things to come.

The above listed properties of contemporary basic technologies would lead one to expect that:

i. Technological innovation in general will increasingly depend on exogenous factors—such as basic research. This poses a number of institutional and organizational problems.

ii. The rate of radical technical changes should increase. If so, the ability to effect rapid switches between generations of technology should become an important prerequisite of competitive success.

iii. The growing adaptability and fusability of basic technologies should result in: (a) greater technological instability of technical systems and their development trajectories; (b) increasing complexity and heterogeneity of technical systems; and, at the same time, (c) increasing technological commonalities between divergent functional areas of technology.

The broad developmental tendencies in contemporary technology tend to confirm these expectations. Let us now briefly discuss the conditions under which basic technologies develop and diffuse.

Developmental dynamics of new basic technologies

The origins and developmental histories of basic technologies are diverse. It is therefore difficult to propose a single well-specified model of the dynamics of these technologies. A looser analytical framework outlining the main developmental stages of basic technologies has been offered by Granberg and Stankiewicz (1981). There is no room here to present the model in any degree of detail. Instead I will focus on certain critically important aspects of the dynamics of basic technologies including (i) their relationship to science, (ii) the crucial importance of the processes of diffusion and integration and (iii) the roles of various 'incubator' environments in these processes. Each of these aspects highlights certain dilemmas which reflect the ambigous status of the basic technologies.

Basic technologies and science

As repeatedly emphasized in the preceding sections, many (perhaps most) of the new basic technologies are closely linked to certain developments in basic sciences. This leads easily to a notion that the two are largely the same and that, consequently, fundamental science environments can be relied upon to develop new basic technologies. This is a variant of the so-called 'linear model' of technological innovation. Although it has been severely criticized as the basis of science and technology policy in general, the model continues to shape our thinking about basic technologies. This has, I will argue, a number of unfortunate consequences.

An alternative view, which is well supported by our research on basic technologies, is that science and technology constitute two interacting, but very different, cognitive systems each guided by a distinct logic and striving for different goals. A similar attitude has been adopted by several other writers, in particular Derek De Solla Price (1984). They adhere to what one might call the 'parallel development model' of the relations between science and technology. The Model emphasizes two types of impacts of science on technology:

i. Science, in the course of exploring various phenomena, develops technological needs and solutions of *its own*. If generic, the resulting technological insights can then be transferred into other areas of application. Many new basic technologies, such as radio or genetic engineering, originated as experimental techniques or instruments in scientific laboratories.
ii. By analyzing the propeties and modes of functioning of natural objects or systems, fundamental research leads to *physical insights* which, when diffused into receptive environments, can be transformed into *functional insights* and thus lead to new technologies.

The fundamental science environment tends, however, to be highly restrictive as regards the development of basic technologies beyond the needs of science itself. It is therefore of crucial importance that the basic technologies, which originate within science, get widely diffused at the earliest possible stage into a broad range of environments of potential application. Such diffusion can accomplish several things:

1. It can mobilize material and personal resources far beyond those which can be mobilized within the science environment alone.
2. It assures the diversity of effort which helps to identify the developmental niches which are most promising and which therefore lead to an enhanced effort.
3. The high volume and diversity of effort results in simultaneous growth of both generic and user-specific technical knowledge. A balance between these two kinds of knowledge is a necessary precondition for effective growth and utilization of basic technologies.
4. The wide diffusion of a new basic technology creates a broad contract area with other technologies. This permits rapid integration of the new technology into a diversity of systems thus further stimulating its effective evolution.

This last point is particularly important. A new basic technology can hardly ever become important without fusing with a whole range of other new and old technologies. In fact, it is only after it has become an organic part of the dominant 'technological paradigm' that a basic technology can exercise its full impact on the economy and society.

Incubation and diffusion of new basic technologies

The pattern of transfer and diffusion of technologies generally, and of the basic technologies in particular, depends to a large extent on the degree of their development or maturity. Very roughly we can distinguish between three main modes of technology transfer: (i) *experiential*—where technology is transferred as personal knowledge; (ii) *codified*—where technology is transferred as information; and (iii) *embodied*—where technology is transferred in the form of artefacts (consumer or capital goods). The three modes of transfer tend to be present at all stages of a technology's development, but their relative importance changes over time.

A rapid diffusion of basic technologies at an early stage of their development is hampered by the high costs of transferring personal knowledge. Consequently, most of the actors who wish to enter the field are forced to start building up their own competence from a very low level. R&D operations have to be initiated with the aim of creating the experiential knowledge in-house. Activities of this kind offer an actor the chance to get on the technology's learning curve at an early stage and to develop enhanced ability to utilize the external sources of knowledge. Yet, the risks are very high and pay-offs usually far in the future. Only a small proportion of the potential users of a new technology have the insight, motivation and resources to engage in such activities. In these circumstances the philosophy of the 'linear model' is sometimes invoked (explicitly or implicitly) to justify a passive attitude: the technology is said to be still in the domain of science; it has not yet matured to the point at which effective development work can be initiated, etc.

And yet, the early transfer of new basic technologies to many potential user environments is necessary for the simultaneous and balanced development of both the generic capabilities and the application of specific knowledge. The generic knowledge accumulates chiefly as a consequence of solving a series of specific problems. The broader the range of contexts within which the new technology is being applied, the more rapid the evolution of the generic knowledge, which in its turn facilitates the application of the technology to a yet wider range of problems.

This self-reinforcing process presupposes, however, a fairly high level of communication between the actors involved. Hence, the effective development of basic technologies calls for organizational and insti-tutional innovations facilitating the sharing of generic knowledge.

The integration of basic technologies

One of the main arguments for wide diffusion of basic technologies is the need for their integration into a variety of technological systems. The blending of new basic technologies with others (new and old) is a complicated, costly and time-consuming process. One can distinguish at least three different ways in which technological integration can take place: (i) technological fusion; (ii) technological co-evolution; and (iii) standardization.

Technological fusion means that two or more basic technologies are combined into a single one. This sort of development usually requires deep technological competence regarding all the component technologies under a single organizational roof.

Technological co-evolution demands effective mutual adjustment in the development of different parts of a complex technical system based on intensive communication and interaction among the actors involved. This means that basic technologies are developed and applied in the context of specific subsystems but at the same time they are coordinated in relation to the requirements of certain super-systems. Large-scale technology development programs, R&D collaboration, joint ventures, close user-producer interactions are among the mechanisms which can enhance co-evolution of technologies. The super-system context leads to a precise definition of requirements which have to be satisfied by the basic technologies involved. It also focuses and intensifies the research effort at the interfaces of various technologies.

Technological standardization involves formal agreements which regulate interfaces between various systems and technologies with the aim of increasing their compatibility and thus integration. Such agreements can, however, be reached only when at least the most important of core technologies underlying the system have reached a certain degree of maturity and stability. Once achieved, standardization allows very rapid diffusion of technologies in the embodied form.

Effective integration of technologies, similar to their effective generation and diffusion, poses a whole range of complicated economic, institutional, and even political, problems. Different companies and national R&D systems may be better or worse suited to achieve integration or profit from it. Indeed, the development of complex technologies requires a special form of entrepreneurship and organization which both tend to be in short supply.

What then are the roles played in the development and utilization of basic technologies by various types of institutional actors?

Actors in the development of basic technologies

The main types of actors in the development of basic technologies are: universities, companies, institutes and various public/governmental development programs (which as a rule involve several of the above mentioned categories of actors). The individual inventor is of course an important actor too, but today he almost always operates in the context of the organizations and institutions listed above.

There is, of course great diversity within each of the above categories. Consequently, what will be said below is very simplified and indicates only the most general or common features of these environments. In the next two sections I shall consider some more country-specific characteristics of these categories of actors.

Each of the actors presented below will be discussed from the point of view of the role it is likely to play in *generation, diffusion,* and *integration* of basic technologies.

UNIVERSITIES

Universities have functioned as 'incubators' of many science-related basic technologies such as chemical synthesis techniques, nuclear technology, laser technology, and several materials and biotechnologies. Academics have also played important roles in the 'scientification' of many traditional basic technologies such as fermentation technology and ceramics technology. To the extent that new basic technologies of great importance do tend to have their origin in science, the role of universities is likely to become even greater in the future.

Nevertheless, there are certain inherent limitations as far as the role of universities is concerned. As has been pointed out earlier, basic technologies, no matter how similar their character may be to science, are clearly distinct from it. There are serious intellectual, institutional and resource constraints on the amount of effort which an academic institution can be expected to put into the development of new basic technologies without compromising its commitment to a balanced, many faceted and autonomous program of research and training. Some of these difficulties can be mitigated by creating new types of academic units. Unfortunately, many universities, especially in Europe, have been very slow in institutionalizing new fields of technical research.

However, the most important weakness of the academic system as the incubator of new basic technologies is its limited integrative capability. The university system is highly compartmentalized and the programs located in it do not achieve the necessary degree of interdisciplinarity and of systems-expertise. The development of basic technologies tends, furthermore, to proceed with little experience of the actual technological context in which they will be required to function.

From the point of view of transfer and diffusion of basic technologies, it is again easy to point to significant strengths as well as weaknesses of the academic environment. The strength has to do with the educational function of universities. The new technologies can be disseminated through the graduate and undergraduate training programs. Unfortunately, in many cases such programs start late and grow slowly, severely restricting the population of experts in the new fields.

Summing up, we could say that, given the progressive scientification of basic technologies, the role of the academic system in their development will no doubt be intensified, but it will always be a partial role which must be effectively linked to parallel developments in other institutional environments, especially in industry.

COMPANIES

Two categories of companies tend to play particularly important roles in the development of basic technologies: the large R&D intensive multi-technology company and the small high-tech specialist company.

Few companies, large or small, have the sort of long-term science and technology programs which can result in entirely new basic technologies being discovered. However, many companies have played a major role in the early development of several important basic technologies. Firms such as IBM, AT&T, as well as several European and Japanese corporations, scan the scientific horizon in search of new basic technologies which may significantly affect their businesses. This often results in the setting up of long-term research projects which in some instances can result in true breakthroughs. Similarly, there are many small high-tech companies which stake their future on the ability to develop applications of the emerging basic technologies quickly. Such companies are typically spin-offs from large R&D intensive companies or from universities.

Although it is rarely the originator of new basic technologies, the participation of the company sector in the development of these technologies from an early stage is of decisive importance. That participation is, however, very uneven. It varies considerably from sector to sector, from country to country, and over time. In some branches— such as chemicals—there has been a gradual build-up of basic R&D competence within leading companies which, in some areas at least, have become quite independent of the universities in the development of new basic technologies. Similar tendencies may be found in the electronics industry, and many observers predict that it will sooner or later also happen in biotechnology. It is important to note, however, that this sort of massive build-up of long-term R&D tends to occur only at a relatively advanced stage in the development of new technologies. A strong commitment to a new technology in its early developmental stage is less usual.

Perhaps the most important function of the company environments is the integrative one. The multidisciplinary character of the industrial research laboratories, the accumulated practical experience from a large spectrum of old and new technologies, combined with the financial strength and marketing experience provide the necessary context in which effective incorporation of new technologies into more complex systems can take place. The small specialized spin-off companies, while capable of playing a very important role at some points in the development of a technology, usually lack the necessary integrative capacity to maintain their position in a longer run. The recent developments in both electronics and biotechnology illustrate this tendency.

The intense participation of companies in the development of basic technologies has the advantage of greatly increasing the total volume of R&D effort in the field, of exploring a large spectrum of application niches and developmental strategies and of promoting effective technological integration.

NATIONAL LABORATORIES, INSTITUTES, ETC.

National laboratories and free-standing institutes have played significant roles in the development of several basic technologies, especially in connection with military, space, energy and some medical programs. However, in relative terms they appear to have been far less important than the universities or industry—at any rate in civilian technologies. The national laboratories and institutes may have been occasionally superior to the universities in being able to mobilize quickly large resources and to set up multidisciplinary programs. On the other hand they tend to be generally inferior in terms of creativity—especially in the long term—and in the ability to transfer and disseminate technology. Their role as a source of technological know-how and skills tends to decrease as the general R&D sophistication of industry increases. There are, however, signs that national laboratories and institutes may be finding a new role for themselves—one of catalysts and 'honest brokers' in large multilteral technology programs.

MULTIACTOR TECHNOLOGY DEVELOPMENT PROGRAMS AND NETWORKS

Multiactor technology development programs, such as the recent national and international information technology programs, can be potentially important in stimulating the development, dissemination and integration of new basic technologies. In fact, many of them have this as their explicit objective.

In some cases, programs involve setting up special laboratories or centers in which the new technologies are developed. In others the effort is decentralized to the participating companies, university departments and institutes. One advantage of the programs, whether orchestrated by governments or industry itself, is their ability to increase quickly the volume of relevant R&D activity. Even more important, however, is their ability (i) to disseminate the relevant technology to a large number of potential users and (ii) to create networks of actors which facilitate technology integration and the development of new complex systems technologies.

Basic technologies and the national R&D systems

National S&T systems differ in the size and sophistication of their academic systems, the techno-industrial structures, the technical cultures and strategies of companies, the character of the governmental R&D establishments as well as in their S&T policies. These differences might be expected to have conequences for these countries' ability to develop and use new basic technologies and thus to exploit the Schumpeterian 'new economic space' which radical technological innovations open up.

An assessment of the technological strength of a company or a nation is an exceedingly difficult undertaking. To describe and measure competence in basic technologies is particularly hard. We simply lack satisfactory quantitative methods to accomplish these tasks with a high degree of reliability. However, a combination of qualitative (judgmental) and partial quantitative studies allows one to draw a tentative picture of the relative strength and weakness of the national S&T systems as regards basic technologies. This picture could be summarized as follows: During most of the period following the Second World War, the development of new basic technologies was dominated by the United States. This manifested itself in the undisputable US leadership in most science-based industries (the only major exceptions being chemical and pharmaceutical ones), in the high-performance military and space technologies, and in the position of the US as a dominant exporter of high technologies. This position of strength could largely be attributed to (i) the superiority of the American science system (particularly the universities); (ii) the presence of several major sophisticated multi-technology companies (such as AT&T, IBM, as GE) in the US economy; (iii) an economic climate favourable to technological entrepreneurship and to the small high-tech firm; and (iv) the presence of major governmental technology development programs in the strategic fields, i.e. military, space and energy. This was, and still continues to be, a very potent configuration of factors making for technological strength.

The American superiority in technology was, naturally, strongly accentuated by comparison with the European and Japanese economies struggling to recover from the devastation brought about by the Second World War. These countries (and particulary the losers of the war, Japan and Germany) neither could nor wished to engage in a technological race with the United States. They concentrated instead on the task of industrial reconstruction and on the gradual closing up of the technological gaps in the relatively mature fields. They did so largely by importing American technologies and applying them then to the civilian industries.

In the 1960s and 1970s the technological superiority of the United States started gradually to erode. It did so 'from below'. The Europeans and the Japanese have proved very successful in importing American technologies and integrating them into their industrial systems. In many instances they have showed a remarkable ability to squeeze more performance from these technologies than did the US industry. They have also gradually rebuilt their own R&D capability. As a result, many European and Japanese companies established strong positions in the low and particularly in the mid-tech range of industries.

This new pattern of international division of 'technological labor' (the US dominating the suply of new basic technologies and the high-tech sector, and the Europeans and Japanese dominating in the mid and low-tech sectors) proved, however, short-lived. The Japanese industry has soon shown itself capable of challenging the US position in a number of high-tech areas, causing something of a panic both in the United States and in Europe in the 1980s. The former was faced with the possibility of losing the status of undisputed technological leader. The Europeans faced an even bleaker prospect of being excluded from the high-growth high-tech markets and left to fight rear battles against the rapidly developing NICs.

These perceptions have been confirmed by a variety of recent studies and analyses showing Europe losing the ground to Japan and the United States in a large number of strategic technologies, including basic ones.[3] The European industry, it is felt, depends too much on the relatively mature branches and is too weak in the expansive high-tech businesses.

If true, how should these trends be accounted for? The causes are of course multiple and cannot be dealt with in an adequate manner in this chapter. Neither do I wish to claim that the European approach to basic technologies alone was a decisive factor. However, if we accept the theoretical arguments presented in the first part of this chapter about the crucial role of basic technologies in long-term technical development, then we should, at the very least, recognize these technologies as a strategically important objects of study.

In recent years several case studies of basic and strategic technologies have been undertaken at the Research Policy Institute in Lund. (Several of them have been done in the context of the Three Country Programme.) The fields covered have been single-cell protein, biological pest controls, fibre optics, laser technologies, VLSI, parts of robotics, genetic engineering and superconductivity. The object of the studies has been to develop a general conceptual model for the analysis of basic technologies, to formulate some empirically grounded propositions about their dynamics and to learn about the relative ability of various R&D systems to promote the development of basic technologies.

The focus of the studies has been on the 'early' phases in the development of the technologies, i.e. we have emphasized primarily R&D activities rather than advanced systems integration and general diffusion of the technologies. The system integration aspects have, however, also been studied in the context of VLSI technology and robotics.

In most of the studies the empirical approach was two fold. On the basis of literature and expert interviews, the general developmental history of the field was developed in a qualitative manner. This was then supplemented by a bibliometric analysis of the field based on the data on scientific and engineering publications, patent applications and granted patents. Using that data it was possible to give a tentative description of

(i) the dynamics of the technology (increase in the volume of activity over time and changes in its composition), as well as (ii) the degree and character of involvement of various actors within the S&T system. The bibliometric data has then been related to various institutional and policy variables relevant for the studied R&D systems.

The studied technologies varied greatly in character and degree of development. This was clearly reflected in the specific results of the case studies. Nevertheless, we have also identified certain features which showed a remarkable degree of similarity in most of the examined fields. Some of these 'constants' had to do with the general developmental dynamics of science-based technologies (for instance, the role of fundamental science in various stages of technology's development), while others reflected the influence of institutional factors.

Indeed, one of the main conclusions which emerges from our studies is that *the general structure and character of a national S&T system exercises profound impact on the ways in which the basic technology capabilities are established and developed, and that this pattern repeats itself across different fields of technology.*

Three types of differences among countries merit special mention: (i) the balance between the fundamental and applied research relating to basic technologies; (ii) the general rate of growth of the applied activities; and (iii) the cross-sectoral diffusion of the new basic technologies. Let us illustrate these differences using as an example the early development of genetic engineering (GE). (For a more detailed presentation see Stankiewicz, 1986a and 1986b.)

Figure 2.1 shows the *structure of the R&D output* in the field of genetic engineering (GE) in the period of 1974–83 in the United States, Europe and Japan. It indicates the number of papers listed in Chemical Abstracts in the fields of 'recombinant DNA' and 'genetic engineering' as well as the number of patent applications in genetic engineering (as reported by Chemical Abstracts). The three literatures can be taken roughly to correspond to the three main types of R&D activity: basic research, applied research and development work.

The differences between Japan on one hand and both the United States and Europe on the other are quite striking. Despite its apparently weak science base, Japan has shown itself capable of initiating an impressive level of technological activity in the field of GE. The contrast with the US and Europe is stronger the closer we come to the commercial end of the R&D spectrum.

The significance of the above comparisons can be disputed on the grounds that bibliometric data from different countries, especially the patent application data, are not always strictly comparable.[4] Instead of comparing the cumulative levels of R&D output let us therefore consider its *dynamics*. Figure 2.2 describes the growth of patent applications in the field of GE.

We observe that (1) the United States had a head start in the

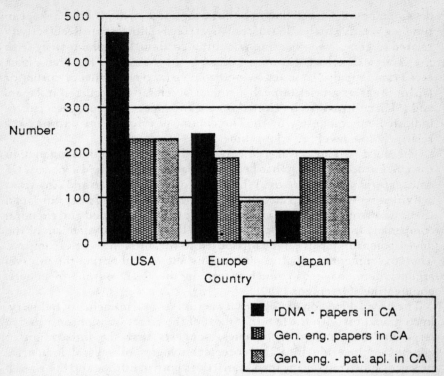

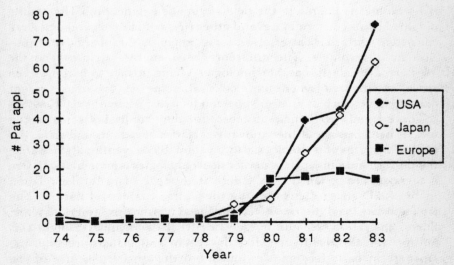

Figure 2.1 GE-related literature and patent applications in Chemical Abstracts

Figure 2.2 Comparable patent applications—companies (Source: Chemical Abstracts)

development of GE relative to both Europe and Japan; (2) the European time-lag relative to the US was, however, fairly short; some R&D activity related to genetic engineering was initiated almost simultaneously with the American effort; (3) once initiated, the American research effort accelerated rapidly, soon achieving a volume far beyond that of Europe or Japan; (4) after a brief inteval, a similar acceleration occurred in Japan; and (5) in contrast to the United States and Japan, the European curves indicated only modest growth. The volume of effort seemed to stay at a relatively low level for a long time.

The third striking difference between the patterns of development in the US, Europe and Japan has been the relatively more rapid *diffusion of GE across different sectors of industry*. While most of the European and American activities were concentrated in the pharmaceutical industry, in Japan there was from the start a strong participation of the food and chemical companies. In fact, it can be argued that the apparent dynamism of the development in Japan can be attributed to this broadness of GE impact. The governmental initiatives (programs, etc.) could not, in the interval studied here, have had much effect on the R&D output in genetic engineering (Orsenigo, 1989).

The broad diffusion of GE activity across several branches of industry, in combination with the fact that most of the effort was concentrated in large multi-technology companies, suggests that the integration of genetic engineering into the core technologies of several industries proceeds more rapidly in Japan than it does both in Europe and the United States.

As already stated, the general pattern of development described above is by no means unique to the field of genetic engineering. The results obtained by us concerning several other fields of basic technology were consistent with that pattern (see, for example, A. Granberg's contribution to this volume. The difference between the Japanese and the Western attitude to basic technologies seems in fact to become even more accentuated when one looks at some of the most recent developments such as that in superconductivity (Robyn *et al.*, 1989).

These trends are remarkable because they contradict some of the established ideas about the innovative abilities of nations and about the general features of technological innovation. By conventional standards, the performance of Japan in new basic technologies is anomalous. There is a tendency to explain it away as derivative or even parasitical in relation to the R&D effort carried out by the United States and Europe. The Japanese are said to *exploit* technologies which the Americans and Europeans *create*. The entire 'free rider' debate revolves around this notion. Yet, the real issue is less the real or anticipated success of the Japanese in basic technologies and more the apparent failure of the Western countries, particularly the European, to utilize their superiority in science.

An interpretation

New basic technologies, we have claimed, are increasingly science-based or at least science-dependent. Consequently, the way in which they will be handled depends to a large extent on the notions about the relationship between science and technology. I would like to suggest that the European, and to a considerable extent also the American, scientists, policy-makers and managers continue implicitly to adhere to the linear model of technological innovation in which basic research is seen as a *phase in the development of technology*. Associated with this view is the idea that a basic technology in its early stages can be satisfactorily handled by academic scientists, public institutes and various governmental programs.

The role of industry is then limited to following the development so that the commercialization can begin when the technology becomes 'ripe' and the risks associated with it calculable. Companies invest significantly in technological capability only or predominantly in the areas where such investments can be justified in terms of products and markets which are directly exploitable. They tend to believe that additional capabilities can be easily acquired when needed by buying people or information. There are of course important exceptions to those tendencies. Some companies run important basic research programs or collaborate with the universities in doing so. Unfortunately, in many cases this merely means that the 'linear model' is internalized within the company R&D system itself.

In terms of the analysis of the dynamics of basic technologies presented earlier in this paper, the assumptions and implications of the linear model are largely incorrect and can lead to wrong policies. The basic research environment, while often very important as an original incubator of a new basic technology, has severe limitations as an institutional locus for the development of these technologies. It is therefore essential that relevant R&D activities rapidly diffuse to environments in which technological values are paramount.

Furthermore, it is important that many different scientific-technical environments become involved and that many parallel approaches to the development and application of the technology are pursued vigorously. Such tactics permit the rapid growth of relevant knowledge, the early evaluation of alternative opportunities and the effective integration of the new technologies with other new or old ones. Early diffusion of the technology assures that a large number of actors start early on their learning curves, which increases technological rivalry and stimulates the overall effort. It also leads to a better balance between the generic and the user-specific technical knowledge.

The European industry's apparent unwillingness (with some important exceptions) to engage in the development of basic technologies at an early stage creates difficulties which cannot be wholly overcome by increasing the corresponding efforts at universities or in public institutes. Basic technologies, especially in the early stages of their development, are difficult to transfer, consequently an in-house learning process is very important as the prerequisite of the effective importing of knowledge from outside.

The situation in the United States is different, but not diametrically different, from that in Europe—at least as far as the attitudes of the established industry are concerned. Even here there is a considerable reluctance to engage in long-term technical R&D activity. However, in the United States there are certain off-setting mechanisms in the form of a number of very large R&D intensive companies, the spin-off firms which often function as a means of transferring new technologies from research to commercial environments and, at least in some fields, military and other strategic R&D programs which, by being located in industrial laboratories, contribute to the diffusion of new basic technologies. Whether these off-setting effects are sufficient is somewhat doubtful. Judging by the differences between the US and the Japanese approach to superconductivity (a technology which promises to revolutionize several major technical systems), one is tempted to conclude that the deeply rooted attitudes and behavior patterns are extremely hard to change (Robyn *et al.*, 1989). In contrast to the massive, open-ended and diversified approach of the Japanese industry to the superconductor technology, the American response has so far been restricted to a few firms, and focused on a narrow set of objectives, predominantly of military character. While still maintaining a significant leadership in the superconductivity science the US might be about to lose out in the superconductivity technology.

How should we account for the evident willingness of the Japanese established companies to experiment with, and invest in, the development of new basic technologies? I have no ready answers to this question. However, I would like to point out to some potentially fruitful hypotheses.

1. In the process of catching up with the United States and Europe, the Japanese have become accustomed to a rather *rapid succession of different technologies*. This might have led to a more dynamic concept of technology in the minds of Japanese management and a greater emphasis on the ability to anticipate technical developments. The Japanese have been building up their technological strength by first mastering the relatively mature technologies and then systematically moving up the technological stream. Since the late 1970s they have begun targeting new basic technologies seen as the foundation of new industrial developments in the 1990s and beyond.

2. Facilitating commitment to new basic technologies is the management system and philosophy in Japan with its emphasis on long-term

growth rather than short-term profitability. The lifetime employment system reinforces this long-term orientation.

3. The skill with which the Japanese companies have learnt to handle technological integration—including technological fusion as discussed by Kodama (1986b) may have made them more prepared to extend their set of core technologies by adding radically new ones. Several authors (including Giget, 1984, Granstrand and Sjölander, 1988 and Granstrand, Sjölander and Alänge, 1989) have recently pointed out that the large Japanese companies tend to be 'multi-technology companies'; they acquire a broad base of technologies which they seek to integrate in relation to a broad spectrum of applications. In doing so they achieve considerable economy of scope—a vital advantage from the point of view of innovation.

4. Similarly, the success of a 'leap-frogging' approach to technological competition adapted by the Japanese companies in many technologically dynamic areas may have taught them the value of being a step or two ahead of competitors in integrating the new developments into their R&D and technical programs. The Japanese management seems more prepared to start R&D activities even in the areas, where their level of skill is low: there is more emphasis on 'learning by doing' (Imai *et al.*, 1985).

5. Another, in my opinion very important, factor explaining the role of the Japanese companies in the promotion of new basic technologies, has been the weakness of the Japanese public R&D system. In particular the relative weakness of universities and the absence of large military R&D programs have forced the industry to accept the responsibility for not only engineering development but also long-term technical research. This might have contributed to the development of a corporate technical culture which is both more receptive to and less awed by the science-derived basic technologies.

6. Finally, one should consider the role of various national initiatives in the promotion of new basic technologies. The distinct feature of most of these programs in Japan has been their emphasis on the support of long-term technical research in company laboratories. They have also contributed to a more rapid diffusion of the R&D capabilities and results between companies. Given the low mobility of technical personnel in Japan, the national schemes can be seen as mechanisms for the sharing of technology which otherwise could become encapsulated in a few leading companies.

All these factors contributed, in my opinion, to a climate in which long-term technical activities could be legitimized and supported in the Japanese companies. This, I believe, offers the Japanese industry a considerable long-term technological advantage over the European and, to a lesser degree, American counterparts.

The Japanese R&D system continues to have considerable short-comings, especially as regards fundamental science. This is a source of serious weakness in the earliest stage of the development of many basic technologies. It also makes the Japanese vulnerable to the accusation of being scientific and technological 'free riders'. However, the basic research gap in Japan is gradually being closed—which means that the Japanese challenge in basic technologies is likely to become even more formidable in the future. In order to meet that challenge the Europeans and Americans will have to modify their approaches to the basic technologies both at the institutional and at the 'philosophical' level. The Western R&D systems—especially the European ones—tend towards a high level of segmentation and linear division of labor. This applies both at the national and the company level. Contrary to what is widely assumed, this does not create optimal conditions for the development of new basic technologies. It needs to be more strongly emphasized that the development of technologies, including basic ones, is very intimately linked to the process of their application. Consequently, the diffusion of these technologies must start at the earliest possible time as the means of accumulating know-how—both specific and generic. Only this kind of broad accumulation can lead to a transformation of the dominant technological paradigm, a transformation which is necessary if an economy is to exploit fully the potential created by the new basic technology.

The tenacity of the linear thinking about the relationship between science and technology might be deeply rooted in our culture. We tend to view technology as an essentially practical activity and science as an essentially intellectual activity and, consequently, we are reluctant to consider technology as an autonomous cognitive system. The result is that the long-term technological R&D falls between the institutional and the intellectual stools. It is possible that the Japanese approach to science and technology is less handicapped by these sort of culture-determined attitudes.

Notes

1. See Granberg (1981, 1986, 1988); Granberg and Stankiewicz (1981); and Stankiewicz (1981, 1986a, 1986b).
2. *Tvärvetenskap för framtiden—forskare om mikronik*, (1986) STU Information no. 532–986, Stockholm.
3. As examples of such evaluations one could mention EC Commission (1989); Macrum (1986); Narin (1986); Uyehara (1988); and Office of Technology Assessment (1984).
4. It is often claimed that the Japanese patent application figures tend to be 'inflated' as compared with the European and Japanese ones. However, the

extent of that inflation seems to differ from field to field and is generally difficult to estimate. The problem with the American figures in our diagram is that the US patent office does not publish applications. The references found in the Chemical Abstracts are based on the US applications in other national and international patent systems. This means that a certain percentage of the American applications has not been included in our statistics. It is likely that, if complete and fully comparable data were available, the Japanese figures would be relatively lower and the American higher. However, it is not likely that the overall pattern would change radically. Patent literature is fairly strongly correlated with 'applied literature' and the latter is not affected by the biases discussed above.

References

Abernathy, W.J. and Clark, K.B. (1985), 'Innovation: mapping the winds of creative destruction' *Research Policy*, vol. 14, pp. 3–22.

Abernathy, W.J. and Utterback, J.M. (1978), 'Patterns of industrial innovation', *Technology Review*, June–July.

Clark, K. (1983), 'Competition, technical diversity, and radical innovation in the U.S. auto industry', *Research on Technological Innovation, Management and Policy*, vol. 1, pp. 103–149.

Clark, K. (1985), 'The interaction of design hierarchies and market concepts on technological evolution', *Research Policy*, vol. 14.

Dosi, G. (1982), 'Technological paradigms and technological trajectories: a suggested interpretation of the determinants and directions of technical change', *Research Policy*, vol. 11.

Dosi, G. (1988), 'The nature of the innovative process', in G. Dosi (ed.), *Technical Change and Economic Theory*, Pinter Publishers, London.

Drexler, K.E. (1988), 'The coming era of nanotechnology', in T. Forester (ed.), *The Materials Revolution*, Basil Blackwell, London.

EC Commission (1989), *Panorama of EC Industry 1989*.

Giget, M. (1984), 'Le bonzai de l'industrie Japonaise', Bulletin CPE, no. 40, Paris.

Granberg, A. (1981), *Biological Pest Control as a Technological Field*, Research Policy Institute, Lund.

Granberg, A. (1986), *A Bibliometric survey of Laser Research in Sweden, Germany and Japan*, Research Policy Institute, Lund.

Granberg, A. (1988), *Fibre Optics as a Technological Field*, Research Policy Institute, Lund.

Granberg, A. and Stankiewicz, R. (1981), 'The development of generic technologies—the cognitive aspects', in O. Granstrand and J. Sigurdson (eds), *Technological and Industrial Policy in China and Europe*, Research Policy Institute, Lund.

Granstrand, O. and Sjölander, S. (1988), 'Some preliminary impressions from Japan', Dept. of Industrial Economics, Chalmers University (mimeo).

Granstrand, O., Sjölander, S. and Alänge, S. (1989), 'Strategic technology management issues in Japanese manufacturing industry', *Technology Analysis & Strategic Management*, vol. 1, no. 3.

Imai, K. (1989), 'Evolution of Japan's corporate and industrial networks', in B. Carlsson, (ed.), *Industrial Dynamics. New Issues in Industrial Economics*, Kluwer Academic Publishers, Dordrecht/Boston/Lancaster.

Imai, K., Nonaka, I. and Takeuchi, H. (1985), 'Managing the new product development process: how Japanese companies learn and unlearn', in K.B. Clark *et al.* (eds), *The Uneasy Alliance. Managing the Productivity-Technology Dilemma*, Harvard Business School Press, Boston, Mass.

Kodama, F. (1986a), 'Japanese innovation in mechatronics technology: a study of technological fusion', *Science and Public Policy*, 13, p. 44.

Kodama, F. (1986b), 'Technological diversification in Japanese industry', *Science*, vol. 233, pp. 291–6.

Macrum, J.M. (1986), 'The technology gap: Europe at a crossroads', *Issues in Science and Technology*, Summer 1986.

Narin, F. (1986), 'Identifying areas of leading edge Japanese science and technology', Japan Briefings (mimeo), Tokyo.

Nelson, R.R. and Winter, S.G. (1977), 'In search of a useful theory of innovation', *Research Policy*, no. 6.

Nevins, J.L. (1988), 'Mechatronics', in C.H. Uyehara (ed.), *US–Japan Science and Technology Exchange. Patterns of Interdependence*, Westview Press, Boulder and London.

Office of Technology Assessment (1984), *Commercial Biotechnology: An International Assessment*, US Government Printing Office, Washington, DC.

Orsenigo, L. (1989), *The Emergence of Biotechnology. Institutions and Markets in Industrial Innovation*, Pinter Publishers, London.

Price, D. de Solla (1984), 'The science/technology relationship, the craft of experimental science, and policy for the improvement of high technology innovation', *Research Policy*, vol. 13, pp. 3–20.

Reich, R.B. (1989), 'The quiet path to technological preeminence', *Scientific American*, vol. 261, no. 4.

Robyn, D. *et al.* (1989), 'Bringing superconductivity to market', *Issues in Science and Technology*, Winter 1988–9.

Rosenberg, N. (1976), *Perspectives on Technology*, Cambridge University Press, Cambridge.

Sahal, D. (1985), 'Technological guideposts and innovation avenues', *Research Policy*, vol. 14.

Stankiewicz, R. (1981), *The Single Cell Protein as a Technological Field*, Research Policy Institute, Lund.

Stankiewicz, R. (1986a), 'Utvecklingsdynamik inom genteknisk FoU i USA, Japan och Europa', in G. Haskå & R. Stankiewicz (eds), *Strategier för Bioteknisk Forskning och Utveckling*, BRF and RPI, Lund.

Stankiewicz, R. (1986b), 'Genetic engineering—international R&D trends', paper presented at the International Symposium on Japanese Technology, Urawa Saitama, Japan.

Uyehara, C.H. (ed.) (1988), *US–Japan Science and Technology Exchange. Patterns of Interdependence*, Westview Press, Boulder and London.

3 Japanese innovation in mechatronics technology*

Fumio Kodama

Japan has certainly been successful in designing products and production systems based on foreign basic technologies. However, it is often said that Japan is still an adapter as much as an innovator. A US National Science Foundation's study is often cited as proof for this view. It found that Japanese scientists developed only two of the 185 innovative technologies studied, from 1953 through to 1961.

However, more than twenty years have passed since then. Therefore, the argument that the Japanese are not innovators is based on outdated evidence. We should ask what has happened since 1961. Were there increases in innovations by the Japanese during the 1960s and 1970s? If there were, what were they and what were their characteristics? Are there differences in types of innovation between those from the West and those from Japan?

Mechatronics revolution in Japan

In 1975, the Japanese created a new word, *mechatronics*, by combining mechanics and electronics. Essentially it implies the following two categories of products:

1. The marriage of electronic technology to mechanical technology resulted in the birth of a more sophisticated range of technological products. Typical examples are Numerically Controlled (NC) machine tools and industrial robots.

*Reprint from *Science and Public Policy*, vol 13, number 1, February 1986. The editor appreciates the permission to reprint Fumio Kodama's original contribution which has been slightly edited for this volume.

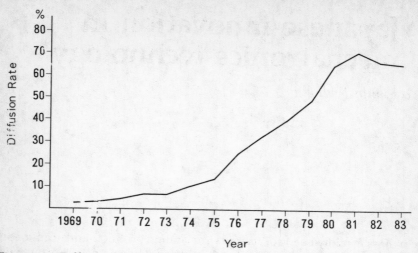

Figure 3.1   Diffusion rate of NC machine tools (ratio of NC to total production of machine tools)

2. Products in which a part, or the whole, of a standard mechanical product was superseded by electronics. Typical examples are digital clocks and electronic calculators.

In order to measure the diffusion of mechatronics technology in the various types of machinery, some indicator should be developed. In the case of machine tools, the diffusion rate can be measured by the ratio of the numerically controlled machine tools to the total production of machine tolls, as shown in Figure 3.1. A marked increase in the diffusion rate, in fact, occurred in 1975.

By the same token, a *mechatronized machine* is defined as a machine with computer control. The diffusion rate can be measured by the ratio of the mechatronized machine to the total production of the machine. On the basis of this measure, the diffusion curves of mechatronics in various categories of machines are obtained as shown in Figure 3.2.

Those categories of machinery whose diffusion rate of mechatronics is above 30 per cent are industrial robots, machine tools, bending machinery and printing and bookbinding machinery. Those categories of machines which are not yet widely mechatronized are woodworking machinery, plastics-processing machinery, packaging machines and food-processing machines.

We also observe a significant difference in the growth rate of production between these two groups. The group of machinery with higher than 30 per cent in diffusion rate of mechatronics has a higher growth rate. On the other hand, the group was less than 30 per cent in the diffusion is lower in growth rate. Thus, there seems to be a positive

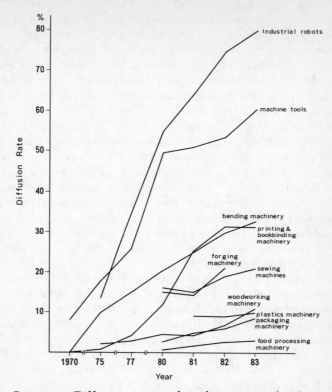

Figure 3.2 Diffusion curves of mechatronics technology

correlation between the diffusion rate and the growth rate. This indicates the possibility that the group of machinery whose growth is stagnating can regain a growth momentum by the introduction of mechatronics technology (MITI, 1984).

There is also a difference in the introduction of mechatronized machines between large enterprises and small and medium ones. While 71.9 per cent of large enterprises introduced the mechatronized machines, only 25.8 per cent of small and medium sized enterprises did. Therefore, the mechatronics technology which is appropriate for the needs of small and medium enterprises will be developed in the near future.

Mechatronics as Japanese innovation

The mechatronics revolution was generated by the fusing of mechanical and electronic technology. Therefore, I would argue that there are two types of innovations: one is *technological breakthrough* and the other is *technological fusion.* A typical example of the former is the transistor revolution, and of the latter the mechatronics revolution.

Breakthrough-type innovation is associated with strong leadership of a particular industry, and fusion-type becomes possible by a concerted effort of the several different industries involved. Developments in the Japanese machine tool industry are a case in point. The mechatronics revolution in this industry has become possible only with the cooperation of three other industries outside the machine tool industry itself.

First, FANUC developed a small and reliable controller which could be produced inexpensively. This made possible the wider use of the NC machine tool, which had previously been used only by special industries like the aeroplane industry. Second, the ball-screw was developed by NSK. This made possible control by servo-motor, which is low in torque, by substantial reduction in the friction coefficient. Third, painting a new material (Teflon) on the sliding bed of the machine tool made low speed and uniform movement possible, an absolute necessity for the operation of a machine tool.

Fusion-type innovation contributes not to the radical growth of certain companies, but to the gradual growth of all companies of the relevant industries. The semiconductor revolution of the late 1950s in the USA brought about a major reshuffle in the relevant industries. Many of the existing vacuum-tube manufacturers went out of business, while some of the new entrants, such as Texas Instruments, Motorola and Fairchild, grew rapidly. In 1966, the market share of the new entrants was 65 per cent, while that of the previous vacuum-tube manufacturers was only 26 per cent (Tilton, 1971). On the other hand, the Japanese production of machine tools has risen from fourth in the world after the USSR to first, in the last five years. However, there was no substantial change of market share of existing machine tool firms during this period.

Fusion-type innovation can be induced by industrial policy, while the breakthrough-type is associated with defense policy. Let us look into the development of industrial policy which induced the mechatronics revolution. Before 1971, the Law on Temporary Measures for the Development of Machinery Industry (enacted in 1956) and the Law on Temporary Measures on the Development of Electronics Industry (enacted in 1957) were enforced independently of each other. In 1971, these two laws were transformed into the Law on Temporary Measures for the Development of Specified Machinery and Electronics Industries.

The Mechatronics Revolution was intended in that law (MITI, 1971). In the Diet (parliament), the Minister of MITI explained the objectives of the law as follows:

In deciding upon an Intensification Plan, the competent minister shall take note of the increased interrelationships among different industries, in particular, between the machinery and the electronic machinery and equipment, and shall pay due consideration to the direction of so-called 'consolidation of machinery and electronics into one' or 'systematization of them'.

Data base for analysis of technological fusion

The process of innovation of the technological fusion type begins with the industry's interests in product fields other than its principal ones. Therefore, the traditional dichotomy between product and process innovation is not helpful in analyzing technology fusion. More relevant is whether or not a sector's industrial R&D is done within or outside its principal product fields.

The industrial R&D by each sector within its principal product fields is supposed to be directed toward either improving existing products or seeking technological breakthroughs. The industrial R&D activity outside its own principal product fields is directed toward creating technology fusion.

The unusually rich Japanese R&D data source collected in the Survey of Research and Development by the Statistics Bureau of the Prime Minister's Office makes it possible for us to implement the conceptualization described above into an empirical study. For all the Japanese companies with a capital of 100 million yen or more (3,803 companies in 1982), intra-mural expenditure on R&D is disaggregated into 31 different product fields.

A company such as Hitachi, is asked under survey instructions to break its R&D expenditure into such categories as chemical products, fabricated metal products, ordinary machines, electric household equipment, communication and electronic equipment, automobiles, precision instruments. This is an alternative to reporting expenditure in one lump assigned to Hitachi's primary industry—electrical machinery manufacturing. Expenses, which are difficult to classify by types of product, are divided proportionally on the basis of the number of researchers.[1]

Since an industrial sector's effort toward technological fusion is defined as the sector's R&D activity outside its principal product fields, we must first distinguish the two types of product fields for each sector: its principal product fields and those which are not principal. This distinction was made among manufacturing industries. In other words, every product field produced by manufacturing industries is to be classified into the principal product fields of one of the 21 manufacturing industrial sectors. The classification table is shown in Table 3.1.

Table 3.1 Classification of principal product fields

Industrial sector	Principal product fields
Food manufacturing	Food products
Textile mill products	Textile products
Pulp and paper products	Pulp and paper products
Printing and publishing	Printing and publishing
Industrial chemicals	Chemical fertilizers and organic and inorganic chemical products
	Chemical fibers
Oil and paints	Oil and paints
Other chemical products	Other chemical products
Drugs and medicines	Drugs and medicines
Petroleum and coal products	Petroleum products
Rubber products	Rubber products
Ceramics	Ceramics products
Iron and steel	Iron and steel
Non-ferrous metals and products	Non-ferrous metals
Fabricated metal products	Fabricated metal products
Ordinary machinery	Ordinary machinery
Electrical machinery, equipment and supplies	Household electrical appliances
	Other electrical equipment
Communication and electronic equipment	Communication and electronic equipment and electric gauges
Motor vehicles	Automobiles
Other transport equipment	Ships
	Aircraft
	Other transportation equipment
Precision equipment	Precision instruments
Other manufacturing	Other manufacturing products

Based on the data available for R&D expenses, we can formulate the technology fusion as follows:

Let

E_{ijt} = i-th industry's R&D expense into j-th industry's principal product fields in t-th year,
($i, j = 1 ,..., N; t = 1 ,..., T$)

D_t = research expenditure deflator of t-th year (the reference year is 1975),

then, the real R&D expenditure for technological fusion can be represented by

R_{ijt} = E_{ijt}/D_t.

Since the data is available every year from 1970 to 1982, we can pool a

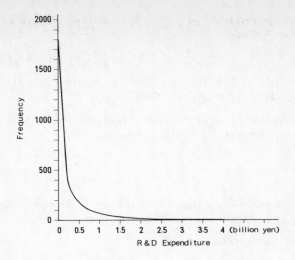

Figure 3.3 Frequency distribution of R&D expenditure for technological fusion

large amount of data and produce a frequency distribution of all the *Rijt*s. As is shown in Figure 3.3, the distribution is exponential. In 80 per cent of all the non-zero *Rijt*s, the expense is less than one billion yen.

The exponential distribution implies that almost all the industry's R&D expenditure outside its principal product fields is for exploratory search and little for advanced development. It also reflects the dynamic process of R&D, where a heavy investment is realized only after many exploratory searches have been conducted for a long time and a good prospect is proven. Furthermore, it indicates the very nature of R&D, that almost all the exploratory research fails and very few projects survive for advanced development.

Dynamics of technological fusion

To construct a dynamic model, we need a dynamic interpretation of the exponential distribution obtained in Figure 3.3. As time passes, an R&D program progresses from an exploratory phase through an advanced development phase. Thus, its annual investment increases with the passage of time, as long as its prospect continues to be favourable. However, at any time when its prospect is found to be unfavourable, it can be cancelled, so an increase in its investment is no longer expected.

On this basis, we can think of a survival type model of an R&D program's investment as follows:

Let

   $R(C)=$ the probability that an R&D program can survive until its annual investment reaches C,

then, the probability that an R&D program is cancelled before it reaches the investment level of C, can be represented by,

   $1-R(C)$

Let

   $f(C)=$ the probability density function of C (the probability that an R&D program is cancelled at the amount of C),

then, $f(C)$ can be represented by,

$$f(C)= \quad d/dC \; [1-R(C)] = -R'(C). \tag{1}$$

Let

   $r(C)=$ the cancelling probability of an R&D program whose investment level is C,

then, $r(C)$ can be formulated as the probability that an R&D program is cancelled, given that it can survive up to the investment level of C, therefore, the probability $r(C)$ can be represented by,

$$r(C)= \quad f(C)/R(C) = -R'(C)/R(C). \tag{2}$$

By assuming that an R&D program's cancelling probability $r(C)$ is independent of its investment level C, we can derive an exponential distribution of an R&D program's annual investment. However, it is not always appropriate to assume that an R&D program's cancelling probability is independent of its investment level. In other words, we have to conceptualize the *cancelling probability* as the probability function of C.

First, exploratory research can be defined as that where the investment C is smaller, and advanced development as that whose C is larger. Second, the cancelling probability of an exploratory research can be supposed to be higher, and that of an advanced development to be lower, because the prospect of an R&D program in the advanced development phase is already proven through the exploratory research which precedes it.

Therefore, generally speaking, we can assume that the cancelling probability function $r(C)$ is a decreasing function of C. On this basis, the cancelling probability function can be represented as an exponential curve as follows:

$$r(C) = a * \exp(-bC). \tag{3}$$

Thus, by substituting (3) into (2), we can calculate the probability density function of C, as follows:

$$f(C) = a * \exp[(a/b) * \exp(-bC) - bC - a/b] \tag{4}$$

For each of 21 industrial sectors, R&D expenses into 20 product fields outside its principal product field are available from 1970 through 1982. Therefore, for each industrial sector, we can use 260 data points for the curve fitting of $f(C)$ in the equation (4). A non-linear least square method, Marquard Method, was used.

The result of the curve fitting is shown in Table 3.2, with the coefficient of determination. In the sector termed 'other manufacturing', we cannot complete the estimation process because convergence conditions are not met.

Table 3.2 Results of curve fitting

Industrial sector	a	b	Coefficient of determination
Food manufacturing	0.4439	0.3955	0.9142
Textile mill products	0.3306	0.1889	0.9197
Pulp and paper products	0.5681	0.5737	0.9965
Printing and publishing	0.5309	0.3236	0.9204
Industrial chemicals	0.0844	0.0102	0.8864
Oil and paints	0.4513	0.3220	0.8967
Drugs and medicines	0.5376	0.6793	0.9889
Other chemical products	0.3840	0.2627	0.9683
Petroleum and coal products	0.4768	0.5200	0.9722
Rubber products	0.4507	0.2681	0.9153
Ceramics	0.2995	0.1478	0.9111
Iron and steel	0.2968	0.2261	0.9451
Non-ferrous metals and products	0.2772	0.1372	0.9388
Fabricated metal products	0.2991	0.1879	0.9571
Ordinary machinery	0.1753	0.1399	0.7894
Electrical machinery	0.3029	0.6336	0.9344
Communications and electronics	0.4460	0.5211	0.9885
Motor vehicles	0.2777	0.1454	0.9643
Other transport equipment	0.3998	0.2680	0.9755
Precision equipment	0.4153	0.4657	0.9813
Other manufacturing	—	—	—

Realization of technological fusion

Considering the dynamics of R&D, we can assume that research reaches the development stage only if the expense exceeds a certain amount.

What is important for this purpose is the demarcation between the exploratory phase and the development phase.

The demarcation can be done on the basis of the cancelling probability. We can define an R&D program in the development phase as one whose cancelling probability is smaller than a specified value r^*. Then, based on each industry's estimated relation between the cancelling probability (r) and the annual investment (C), we can identify the threshold value of annual investment, beyond which an R&D program can be supposed to enter the development phase. In other words, we can get the threshold value Ci^* for each industry. These boundary values for each industry between exploratory search and advanced development are shown in Table 3.3.

The mechatronics revolution occurred as a result of the technological fusion between mechanical technology and electronics technology. Thus, the minimum unit of technology fusion is the pair of two different industrial sectors. However, one-way investment might only be diversification effort and not lead to innovation.

On the other hand, if the investment is done two ways, it might lead to the creation of a new technological area, and possibly to innovation. For

Table 3.3 Identification of threshold values

Industrial sector	threshold value (Y million)
Food manufacturing	467
Textile mill products	822
Pulp and paper products	365
Printing and publishing	626
Industrial chemicals	1,834
Oil and paints	579
Drugs and medicines	300
Other chemical products	648
Petroleum and coal products	369
Rubber products	695
Ceramics	984
Iron and steel	639
Non-ferrous metals and products	1,003
Fabricated metal products	773
Ordinary machinery	656
Electrical machinery	231
Communication and electronics	355
Motor vehicles	948
Other transport equipment	650
Precision equipment	382

example, the ceramics industry had invested in product fields such as ordinary machinery, electrical machinery and electronics. However, *new ceramics* was created only after the machinery and electronics industries began to invest in ceramics.

Therefore, the essence of technological fusion is its reciprocity. It is realized only when there is two-way investment thus becoming reciprocal between two industries. We can call this investment *realized technology fusion* and formulate it as follows:

Let

$$Fijt = \begin{cases} 1 \text{ if } Rijt > Ci \text{ * and } Rjit > Ci\text{*,} \\ 0 \text{ otherwise,} \end{cases}$$

then, technological fusion is realized between the i-th and j-th industry, only of $Fijt = 1$.

After constructing a model of the realization mechanism of technological fusion, our interest is directed to analyzing the structure of technological fusion. It is best described using a graph. In the non-directed graph, each industry is represented by the vertex, and the arc is represented by the $Fijt$ so the arc exists if $Fijt = 1$.

Such a graph can be constructed for each year: some of them are shown in Figures 3.4 to 3.7 (those of 1970, 1974, 1975 and 1982).

High technology and technological fusion

Let us describe how some of the so-called high technologies such as biotechnology, mechatronics and new ceramics were developed.

First of all, through the years studied, technological fusions are clustered around three major industries—ordinary machinery, electrical machinery and industrial chemicals. The first two industries belong to the fabrication industry, while the last one belongs to the material industry. In 1970 (see Figure 3.4) there is no technological fusion realized among these three clusters.

In 1974 (Figure 3.5), the triple connection emerges among food, drugs and medicines and industrial chemicals. This can be interpreted as the emergence of *biotechnology*. The dual connection between food and drugs and medicines, which is supposed to represent fermentation technology, has appeared since 1971. By joining industrial chemicals to this connection, biotechnology was established as a high technology area.

As far as *mechatronics* is concerned, technological fusion begins to develop between the ordinary machinery industry and the electrical machinery industry after 1971. However, it is not until 1975 that the quadruple connection begins to appear persistently among ordinary

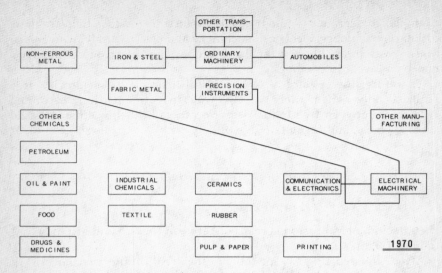

Figure 3.4   Technical fusion in Japan in 1970

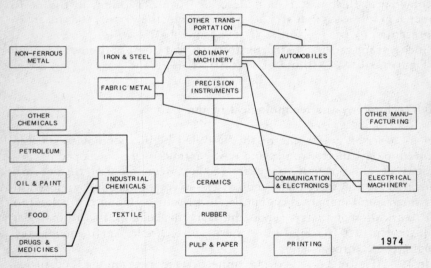

Figure 3.5   Technical fusion in Japan in 1974

machinery, precision instruments, electrical machinery and communication and electronic equipment (Figure 3.6). Therefore, we can identify the realization of the mechatronics revolution by the persistent existence of this connection.

By 1982 (Figure 3.7), the technological fusions between ceramics and ordinary machinery and between ceramics and electrical machinery were formed. This connection represents the emergence of *new ceramics*. The

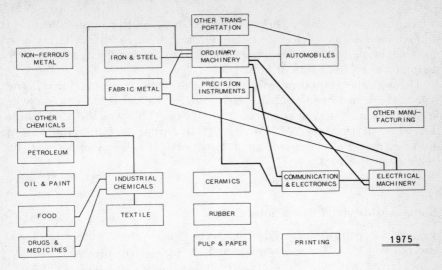

Figure 3.6 Technical fusion in Japan in 1975

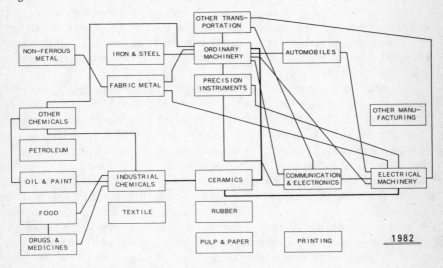

Figure 3.7 Technical fusion in Japan in 1982

connection between ceramics and ordinary machinery, which represents fine ceramics, was established in 1980. Then, the connection between ceramics and industrial chemicals, which indicates the emergence of the new material, was established in 1981.

We can make the following observation about the macro-trend of technological fusion from the 1970s to the 1980s. During the 1970s, there had been no fusion between the material industry and the fabrication one. The fusions occurred only within the fabrication industries such as mechatronics and within the material industries such as biotechnology. However, since 1980, fusions have appeared frequently between these two sets of industries.

Through this structural anlysis, we can draw the conclusion that in the 1960s there had been no major technological fusion. A first example of innovation of this type appeared in the 1970s. This was the *Mechatronics Revolution* in the mid-70s. We have found that technological fusion between material technology and fabrication technology is expected to be realized in the 1980s.

Some world-wide implications

We could identify almost all the high technologies, such as biotechnology, mechatronics and new ceramics, in terms of the technological fusion concept and method. Therefore, we can say that technological fusion will become a standard mode of innovation.

Good company-to-company relations are a condition for success in technology fusion. Still more important is R&D diversification within the same organization. If it is true, then Japan will take more responsibility as one of the world centers of innovation in the high technology area in the future.

This might be one reason why an increasing number of big foreign multinationals, including Imperial Chemical Industries, the British Chemical giant, Siemens of West Germany and Texas Instruments of the USA, are now thinking of building their own research laboratories on Japanese soil. Also, Du Pont Co has recently decided to build a research laboratory in Yokohama.

According to Du Pont, what is more important than the size and the growth potential of the Japanese market is that their products should be accepted by Japanese manufacturers, who demand very high standards of the material supplier, so that their products are proven world-wide.

The Japanese research laboratory will become one of the three focal points besides the research laboratories in Delaware and Geneva in the field of engineering plastics and be connected by an on-line information network. The technical information collected through the contacts with Japanese engineers mainly from the customer companies, are to be distributed world-wide through the on-line network.

The mechatronics revolution in Japan might have a significant impact on the developing nations. Japan has, owing to its past history, not imported any foreign labour. This has played a role in accelerating automation to enable individual business to survive. Mechatronics development played a role equal to that of foreign labour in some other countries. In other words, Japan developed a non-human work-force (such as robots) to the extent that the production plants scarcely need human labour regardless of its cost. This has created a new situation in which certain types of industry which were transplanted to developing countries have returned to developed countries.

Notes

1. Statistical Bureau, Prime Minister's Office, the Government of Japan; *Report on the Survey of Research and Development.*

References

MITI (1971), *Electronics & Machinery Industry in the Seventies*, (Tsushou-Sangyou-Chousakai.

MITI (1984), *Vision of Industrial Machinery*, Tsushou-Sangyou-Chousakai. *Newsweek* (1984), 'Can the Japanese create?', 2 July, p. 27.

Tilton, J.E. (1971), *International Diffusion of Technology*, The Brookings Institution. Washington, D.C.

Part II
Measuring Science and Technology

4 Technometrics as a missing link in science and technology indicators[1]

Hariolf Grupp

Introducing a simple input-output model

A brief look on the state of the art in science and technology (S&T) indicators from a general point of view reveals the following:

It is more difficult, both theoretically and in practice, to record the returns from research, development (R&D) and innovation than it is to cover expenditures incurred in such activities. The results of R&D as well as the possible market success of technically new products or processes cannot be measured in terms of the customary scientific understanding of 'measuring' a variable. Instead of a constitutive definition various operational ones by means of indicators are in use. The indicators must be viewed as 'representatives' for the actual variable and are not identical to R&D or innovation output or success. Validity can, therefore, only be achieved through qualitative interpretation and a synopsis of the largest possible number of different types of indicators for studying R&D and innovation dynamics.

If a systematic distinction is made in line with a chronological sequence of innovation processes between expenditure, throughput and returns (or output) indicators, then the detection of innovation processes best starts with R&D expenditure figures (*expenditure analyses*), scientific literature statistics (*bibliometrics*), *patent statistics*. In terms of market results of innovations, econometric indicators for *external trade involving research-intensive products* are especially promising, and scope for interpretation of the causes of success or failure in adequately reflecting the innovation process remains open. The role of R&D, or technical progress, in the products traded and the production methods involved can, at best, be inferred indirectly from economic figures; therefore, a *'technometric' concept* has been developed and applied since the end of 1984 as part of the activities pursued by the Fraunhofer Institute for Systems and Innovation Research. This concept permits systematic international comparison between specifications covering new products and processes. Technometric indicators are established in direct relation to the technological trade figures as well as to patent and literature statistics. Thus, it is possible to detect lines of research and innovation dynamics from the early stages and to convert them into an output-oriented description of the efficiency of S&T activities.

As the ranges of validity of these indicators are limited to certain phases or types of research, development and innovation, phase models have been introduced in West and East for the sake of analytical clarity (Freeman, 1982; Holland *et al.*, 1984; Grupp, 1987). However, the borderlines between the phases are unclear and R&D processes are neither linear nor simple (Grupp, 1990b).

Although other classifications are conceivable it is suggested to assign:

1. R&D personnel statistics to human knowledge (input indicator);
2. R&D expenditures to *formal* R&D activities (input indicator; see Dosi, 1988);
3. bibliometrics (literature statistics) to fundamental, basic, strategic and applied research (output indicator; see Grupp, 1990a);
4. patent statistics to strategic and applied research and industrial development (output indicator; for a comprehensive list see Schmoch *et al.*, 1988);
5. technometrics (technological specifications indicator) to innovation and imitation (output indicator; the basics being in Grupp *et al.*, 1987); and
6. production and trade statistics with R&D-intensive products to technological and product diffusion (output indicator).

The demarcation of R&D phases and related indicators as vague as it is raises the point whether S&T indicators—in particular patent and publication-related statistics—overlap in validity to a large extent or must be seen as supplementary pieces of information. Schneider (1983) observed the phenomenon that inventors did not cite their own patents within their scientific publications. Their oeuvre becomes visible in total only if the pieces of information were put together like a 'zip-fastener'. Le Pair (1988) concluded also that patent search and patent citation analysis provided essential additional information to normal scientific literature and that there is a 'citation gap' in R&D areas close to technological development. Schmoch *et al.* (1988) tested some 10 fields of technology and found significant correlations between R&D budget, patent, publication, technometric and trade indicators in many, but not all cases. Time-lags of up to 5 years were found, if at all, between the indicators' time series. They concluded that on the level of industry sectors or main technological fields significant regressions between S&T indicators are rare. The rudiments of correlative indicator networks are detectable preferably on the most disaggregated levels of single subfields.

Granberg (1986) also showed that microlevel patent and publication lists resemble each other in shape as in content.

Figure 4.1, in a very crude way, maps the various types of S&T indicators being in use to R&D and innovation stages which are commonly differentiated. The figure visualizes that economic figures for the results of basic research are impossible and that these results are non-patentable. To give another example, there is no chance of filing a patent by imitating existing innovations anywhere in the world (i.e., by technological diffusion activities). Therefore it is concluded that a crude structure between R&D stages and S&T indicators does exist. *With this assumption it is wise to use the various S&T indicators selectively, depending on the type of R&D to be studied.* Moreover, the stages indicate the location of R&D to a certain extent: fundamental research is performed in academia, development mostly in industry (Krupp, 1984).

The indicators mentioned may be used as *analytical tools* but hardly represent *analytical results* if standing alone. Also, combining indicator figures is rarely sufficient to assess the processes of R&D and innovation. *For meaningful applications* (some of them are mentioned in Figure 4.1) a proper interpretation of the findings based on expert opinion has to be provided (Grupp, 1990b). The advantages which result from crossing expert interviews with the formal indicators framework are briefly discussed in the final section of the chapter.

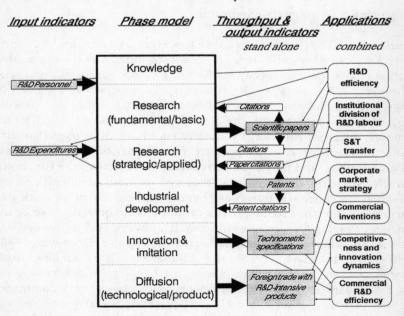

Figure 4.1 A simple input-output model for research, development and innovation stages and corresponding S&T indicators (stand alone or combined)

In the following sections of the chapter the technometric concept is passed in review (second section). Some examples in the field of laser technology are provided to elucidate the levels of aggregation that are possible. For further examples in robot technology see the contribution by Grupp *et al.* in this volume.

A quite extensive application of the technometric method is provided for enzyme technology (third section). In this comparison data from West Germany, Japan and the United States are compared to those from one of the Nordic countries (Denmark), and in the subfield of biosensors to France and East Germany.

The fourth section tries to establish a taxonomy of science, technology and innovation indicators in order to allow for easy distinctions in applicability of these indicators. As a more comprehensive synopsis of various S&T indicators including technometric figures is given elsewhere in this volume (Grupp *et al.*), in this chapter the applicability of combined S&T indicators is briefly demonstrated in the case of telecommunication R&D (fifth section). The final section (6) emphasizes the synergisms between indicators from a more general point of view.

Introducing a technometric indicator

Compared to all S&T indicators in use (see Figure 4.1), the technometric method is less well-established. Technometric indicators are aggregated figures composed of specifications in physical units (Grupp and Hohmeyer, 1986). Because the figures specify the state of the art of either a product or a process, defining distinct product and process characteristics is useful. If the product or process serves different purposes, different functional characteristics have to be used (Saviotti, 1988). Whereas process or product characteristics contain discrete physical entities, and may thus be regarded as objective, the functional characteristics or priority lists required contain deliberations on individual or collective purposes. Even renunciation of priorities or functions within the characteristics cannot ensure objectivity since the principle of exclusion continues to apply. It is always a subjective decision whether an item should be included or not (Grupp and Hohmeyer, 1988).

However, as Clark (1985) and Stankiewicz (this volume) have pointed out, as development proceeds technological diversity gives way to standardization. Particular design approaches achieve dominance and performance criteria are clearly specified. Social processes and patterns of communication between customers will influence the speed and pattern of product (or process) design and broad categorizations are broken down into related subcategories of the characteristics which are refined through experience. Therefore, it is not surprising that (industrial) experts interviewed agree on proposed characteristics and priorities.

Single technological specifications may be ranked but cannot be cardinally aggregated to form indicators. A metric system, therefore, must be introduced. It consists of a transformation of the technical characteristics into a dimensionless interval (Grupp and Hohmeyer, 1986). If countries are compared by technological specifications one by one (no aggregation), then the metric conserves the ordinal ranking of the original figures. In aggregate technometric indicators those items with considerable international disparities dominate the distinctions and indicator values. The details, including the technometric transformation formulae, are given elsewhere (Grupp and Hohmeyer, 1986).

The technological standards of the subset (e.g., country) which has made the greatest progress in terms of the specification under review, defines the international maximum value $K^* = 1$. The metric value for the other subsets is determined by the spread of the specifications within each subset and between the different subsets. When the technical standards offered to and demanded by the international market diverge a great deal—and there may be good enough economic reasons for that—lesser differences between leading firms cannot indicate a substantial technological gap. That is why the metric indicator value K^* in this case will be close to 1 for all subsets (countries).

The proposed model is linear, as are nearly all such models known from literature (see below). Dodson (1985) postulated an ellipsoidal approach, alongside several linear ones, but that has not been pursued farther because of its lack of rigour. A number of similar approaches can be found in the literature. To the author's knowledge, very few of the proposed concepts aim at a quantitative comparison of purely technological specifications at an international level. In order to indicate some major differences between the approaches made so far (without being complete) most of the recent papers may be characterized with regard to whether or not they include:

1. contemporary analysis;
2. technological analysis;
3. international comparable analysis.

A review of some 30 such models by Grupp and Hohmeyer (1988) revealed that only very few publications meet all three conditions.

Figure 4.2 represents the technometric profile of semiconductor lasers for optical communications in the year 1986 on the national level, i.e., by aggregating all single product specifications per country. A great number of product specification lists from manufacturers in the Federal Republic of Germany, the United States and Japan have been collected and processed. The corresponding company profiles are also available.

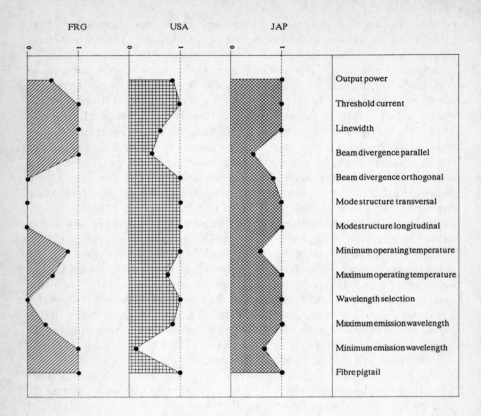

Figure 4.2 Technometric profile of semiconductor lasers for optical communication by selected countries in 1986.

Figure 4.3 displays the case of NEC as compared to all other Japanese manufacturers of semiconductor lasers (JAP- in the figure). The reasons for selecting NEC are discussed in a later section. The specifications of all Japanese producers of communication lasers including NEC are also given in Figure 4.3 (JAP+). The latter ones are the same as in Figure 4.2 for Japan. In addition to these data derived from technical data sheets and exhibition literature, a number of personal discussions with experts in development laboratories on which specifications to select have been performed. These discussions not only produced specification lists and data, but were also very important when interpreting the technometric indicators in order to learn something on R&D results embodied in the innovative products.

Figures 4.2 and 4.3 are examples for just one product group each. Approximately 10,000 technical specifications covering products and

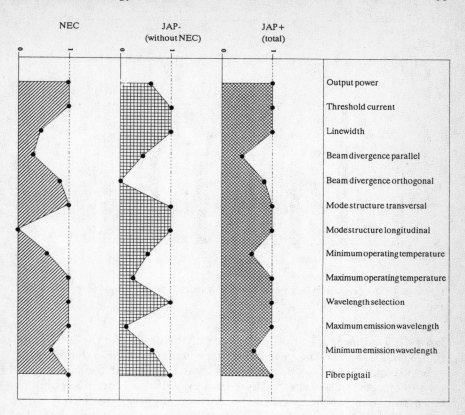

Figure 4.3 Technometric profile of semiconductor lasers for optical communication from Nippon Electric Company (NEC) and all other Japanese manufacturers (JAP-) in 1986.

processes from various industrialized countries have been stored in the Institute's computer-aided technometrics repository until now. Among them are data on other laser types, solar generators, industrial robots, sensors, immobilized enzymes, waste water treatment plants and genetically engineered drugs and diagnostics (for detailed results see Grupp *et al.*, 1987; Grupp and Hohmeyer, 1988; and Reiss *et al.*, 1989).

Figure 4.4 contains aggregate indicators for various laser types. The profiles shown in Figures 4.2 and 4.3 are parts of the diode category here. But in the diode category, semiconductor diode lasers other than those for communications shown in Figure 4.2 and 4.3 are also included. Also, the CO_2 category comprises other such lasers than power lasers (e.g., CO_2 waveguide lasers). Generally, US product specifications are best, but the technological gap towards Europe does not exist for carbon-dioxide and excimer lasers. European standards are generally higher than

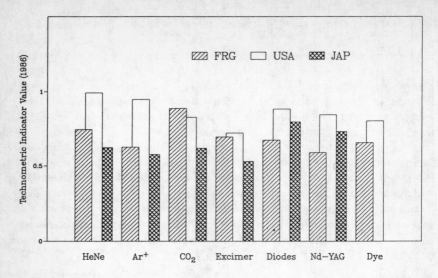

Figure 4.4 Aggregated technometric indicators for various laser types and selected countries in 1986.

Japanese standards, but not in the case of the diode and the solid-state (Nd-YAG) lasers. In the year 1986 there was no Japanese dye laser.

A systematic cross-section reveals a clear lead for the civilian market technological standards in the United States, with the Federal Republic of Germany and Japan lagging, the former slightly, the latter more noticeably, behind. It should be remembered, however, that the technometric examination contains no standardization for the size of a country, its R&D budget, or its R&D personnel. For other indicators it is customary to use appropriately weighted national data before comparing them with each other. Allowance should be made not only for the magnitude of monetary R&D investments in the different countries and for the staffing of the countries' R&D potential, but also for the different size of their domestic markets which are particularly important when new products are being introduced. At present, there is no way of relating the technometric indicators to the varying size of the countries under consideration. As the technometric indicator is available on company (microlevel), country (national level) and world level inter-national level) it is well suited when studying R&D and innovation dynamics. The technometric data may be combined with anticipated market share data in order to assess the importance of the technology factor embodied within new and successful innovations (for details see Grupp and Schwitalla, 1988).

From this type of analysis (i.e., closer inspection into many other selected fields) it is concluded that each area of applied science or technology unfolds a rich spectrum of diversity, so that the ranking of nations becomes quite complex and differentiated. Leadership in particular fields may vary significantly between countries (e.g. Japan in communication lasers, the Federal Republic of Germany in carbon-dioxide power lasers, the United States in helium-neon lasers). Further, there is a fairly consistent correlation between the ranking of nations as to the state of their civilian-market technologies, on the one hand, and their trading positions on the other. It is the technological quality of non-defence R&D-intensive products, *primarily*, which determines com-petitiveness on world markets, and to a lesser extent marketing strategies, delivery times, quality of service, monetary exchange rates and protectionistic measures. Technological quality also correlates quite well with the corresponding expenditures of national R&D input (Grupp and Hohmeyer, 1988). In more detail the correspondences of techno-metric and trade data are elaborated in the following section in the case of enzymes.

Technometric analysis of immobilized biocatalysts in six countries

Biotechnology has become a key concept in the recent discussion on technologies of the future. This field of technology has gained a great deal of popularity in view of a number of pioneering discoveries in the area of genetic engineering: these have triggered off an extensive public debate ever since the end of the 1970s about their potentialities and dangers.

In view of the great interest enjoyed by biotechnology among the public, the often exceedingly great expectations of politicians, the sometimes tempestuous progress of knowledge in certain biotechno-logical fields and the already considerable market potential of new biotechnological products, four partial areas of biotechnology were investigated by technometric methods: the economically and biologically important area of biological conversion of substances by means of biological catalysts (this section), the genetically engineered manufacture of human drugs (Grupp and Hohmeyer, 1988) and of medical diagnostics (Reiss *et al.*, 1989) and the biological treatment of waste water (Reiss *et al.*, 1989).

In order to describe the field of immobilized biocatalysts (or enzymes) adequately, both in their production and as products, as well as their use for the manufacture of other products and in biosensors, six areas have been isolated in line with the classification according to Kula (1984)—to which reference is also made for a detailed description of the process of enzyme manufacture:

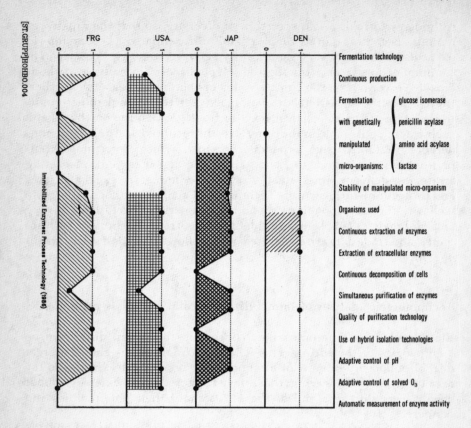

Figure 4.5 Technometric profile analysis of the manufacture of immobilized biocatalysis in the USA, Japan, West Germany and Denmark (not complete) in 1986 (from left to right: 8 characteristics for fermentation, 6 characteristics for isolation and 3 characteristics for imobilization of enzymes)

1. Biocatalyst fermentation;
2. Enzyme isolation (preparation);
3. Biocatalyst immobilization (fixation to a carrier);
4. Immobilized biocatalysts as a product;
5. Use of immobilized biocatalysts in production;
6. Use of immobilized biocatalysts in biosensors.

By way of illustration of the results, the technometric characteristics are reproduced for the three first areas. Details on the other areas may be found in a more extensive publication (Grupp *et al.*, 1987). Figure 4.5 groups together the specifications of fermentation, enzyme isolation and immobilization—i.e. process technology—in a joint profile. In the production of immobilized biocatalysts the Federal Republic of Germany seems to hold a leading place, both in fermentation technique and in isolation and immobilization. Weaknesses exist in the use of micro-organisms altered by genetic engineering for use in catalyst fermentation, with the exception of penicillin acylase. Here America and also Japan had a clear lead (in 1986) with glucose isomerase (USA) and with amino acid acylase as well as lactase (Japan). Simultaneous purification of a multitude of enzymes appears to have been mastered best in Japan in 1986, whereas the automatic measurement of catalytic activity at the various process stages seems to have advanced furthest in the USA. Data on the situation in Denmark in this subfield are so full of gaps that meaningful interpretation is impossible.

If these individual indices are aggregated according to areas and weighted according to their relative importance—in line with the judgment of the questioned experts in their scientific field—one arrives at the *overall assessment* reproduced in Figure 4.6. In Figure 4.6, the specifications of the three first areas plotted jointly in Figure 4.5 are combined to express the overall assessment for process technology. Enzyme (catalyst) product properties (area 4) and specifications for their use (area 5) are given separately as well as biosensor data (area 6).

In none of the partial areas does industry in the Federal Republic of Germany occupy either a leading or a particularly backward place, whereas Japanese industry makes a rather poor showing in process engineering, while occupying a relatively strong position in catalyst properties and catalyst application. The USA is leading in process engineering and catalyst properties, though it is doing relatively badly in catalyst application because of its poor results in lactase and in multienzyme systems. As might be expected, the relative strength of the Federal Republic of Germany lies with process engineering (downstream processing) rather than with products, whose properties are often in considerable need of improvement. If the first three areas are summed up into an *overall indicator* the countries are about equal. Allowing for the uncertainties of the data base a ranking order cannot be reliably constructed, even though the USA and Japan do seem to have certain advantages over the Federal Republic of Germany and Denmark.

Biosensors based on immobilized catalysts cannot be identified from the product groups in the foreign trade statistics. The absence of German manufacturers in this market is not detectable in the economic statistics. Technometric analysis of this field, however, reveals the state of the art (Figure 4.6) attained internationally, the situation in the principal competitor countries and the extent of the lag of West German development in this field. These reflections show clearly that opportunities for potentially vital key technologies for the future are being let slip in the Federal Republic of Germany.

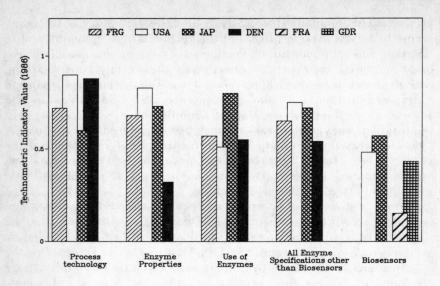

Figure 4.6 Technometric indicators (aggregated) of immobilized biocatalysts in six countries (not complete) in 1986.

Even a neat delimitation of all immobilized biocatalysts, be it for sensors or not, cannot be achieved with the breakdown provided by the *foreign trade statistics*. With the exception of calves' rennet, which is covered by a product group of its own, virtually all enzymes are included in one product group (denoted: other enzymes not listed elsewhere). Admittedly this group is likely to be dominated by free technical enzymes. Industrially used enzymes probably account for about 50 per cent of this product group. The world market for glucose isomerase in 1985 is estimated by experts questioned on this point at 100–150 million DM, that for penicillin acylase at 2–3 million DM, that for amino acid acylases at approximately 2 million DM and that for lactase at less than 1 million DM. The foreign trade turnover of the Federal Republic of Germany in the above listed product group in 1985 amounted to 156 million DM (exports) and 111 million DM (imports), representing therefore a considerably broader product range than immobilized enzymes. The world market for industrially used enzymes is at present estimated at about 1,000 million DM.

The principal suppliers of enzymes to Germany are Denmark (20.7 per cent), Japan (15.1 per cent) and the USA (12.3 per cent), i.e. the very countries considered in the technometric comparison. The enzymes from the USA and Japan have a relatively high standard price (over 150 DM/kg), whereas supplies from Denmark seem to be relatively cheap bulk enzymes. The foreign trade balance sheet with Japan and the USA closely matches the average foreign trade conditions between the Federal Republic of Germany and those countries. It is, generally speaking, a market with tough competitive conditions, one in which the Federal Republic of Germany can only hold its own in the long run if, for one thing, it becomes competitive in terms of prices for bulk enzymes and, for another, it keeps abreast of new developments in special enzymes in Japan, the USA and probably also Switzerland.

In spite of the incompleteness of the data base for technometric evaluation, it is clear that it is capable of complementing the economic analysis in two respects. First, economic statistics in the field of immobilized biocatalysts are not sufficiently differentiated to allow for this field to be analysed separately. Foreign trade in free enzymes here masks some interesting developments in immobilized catalysts and prevents some important trends from being perceived without a lot of additional information. On the other hand, the technometric method makes it possible to identify the emerging outlines of new developments at a much earlier stage and to assess their technical relevance.

If one now combines the findings of an economic analysis of the overall field with the technometric assessment of the narrower field under investigation, of the national state of the art and of emerging international trends, one arrives at a much more solid assessment of a future competitive position than would have been possible with economic analysis alone. On the other hand, the economic analysis of the present situation, as shown by the example of enzymes with relatively low standard prices (Denmark), can result in a relativization of the assessment of technological competitiveness. Especially in the case of Denmark, with its relatively poor technometric showing for immobilized biocatalysts, the trade position suggests that problems of cost and of the product range on offer have a decisive influence on an actually attained internationally competitive position. This calls for appropriate allowance in a comprehensive study, especially one that is oriented to the state of technical development.

Taxonomy of science, technology and innovation indicators

With the technometric indicator being added to bibliometric, econometric and patent indicators the question arises how and to what extent the various types of indicators which are valid for various stages of the R&D and innovation processes may be interconnected. First, a simple taxonomy of indicators is needed.

Most of the established R&D indicators are of reporting type (i.e., they are precise but isolated) and may not be used for a consistent *evaluation of S&T output*. Of course, there is the need for statistical offices to have precise definitions and clear-cut compilation procedures. Without 'keeping it simple' the response rate of questionnaires would be low. There is no criticism of using *reporting type S&T indicators* for accounting purposes. For analytical purposes, however, a comparative type of S&T indicators is needed (Kodama, 1987; Schmoch *et al.*, 1988).

For the construction of *comparative indicators* structural networks are required, the coverage of the indicators to be compared must be similar, and, therefore, correspondences between the classification systems are needed. In order to connect indicators, sometimes mutual cuts in delimitations of subfields to be studied are inevitable. In the case of enzymes (section 3), for example, data for the market shares are not available for immobilized enzymes alone, and complete technometric data for all four major countries to be compared are missing. This means that a formal cross-section analysis between technometric and trade data is impossible. It is needless to say that time series—if available as in the case of trade data—must always be of comparable type, the delimination of subfields has to be constant for the various years and the coverage of the data banks used must be stable.

If various comparative indicators are combined, then an *evaluative type of indicator* seems to be possible. For evaluation purposes integrated networks of data have to be constructed and causal or statistical relationships have to be verified. Evaluative networks of S&T indicators have to be complete. Such networks based on correlations seem to be desirable, but are difficult.

Exploring the usefulness of such a network of evaluative indicators an extensive analysis of time series and cross-sections of technometric, bibliometric, econometric and patent indicators has been performed (Schmoch *et al.*, 1988). What turned out to be required was mutual support in delimiting corresponding subfields for research, technology and innovation indicators. When using only one classification system one might not be aware of the problems inherent in the words and terms used. If two or more such classification systems have to be used, different 'languages' of science and engineering communities, or even their slangs which are included by tradition, may be recognized and, thus, the awareness of different 'terminology cultures' arises. Therefore, until further notice, the personal expertise of scientists and technologists is an essential addition to any S&T indicators to bridge the inconsistencies and the lack of adaption of the classification systems to modern innovative products. Industrial R&D people know and name new technological trends first, it is true. The technometric concept consequently played a central role for the sequential patent search strategy, the bibliometric and the econometric analyses embodied in the cross-indicators study mentioned.

Some of the problems inherent in patent and bibliometric indicators, and the usefulness of comparative technometric data, are briefly touched on in the next section on telecommunications (see also Grupp, 1990a). As most fixed classification systems are not flexible enough to allow for the required disaggregation (compare, e.g., the problem of trade data for immobilized enzymes in section 3), *on-line searches* and the *inclusion of keyword analyses* in data banks are necessities, if the data bank does offer these possibilities. Trade data pools do not, of course. Often, the traditional classification systems do not follow quickly enough the new decisive trends in technology development. The researchers themselves always use the most up-to-date keywords in describing their inventions or when publishing the results; therefore, it is advisable to include regularly a thorough keyword analysis together with the use of classification systems even if the latter are finely broken down.

The case of telecommunications

With the help of advanced on-line techniques, the field of tele-communications was broken down into 11 subfields (see caption to Figure 4.7). For each of the subfields, and for the major R&D performing institutions in eleven countries including Sweden, Japan and West Germany, profiles of telecommunication activities have been derived on national and microlevel. Figure 4.7 represents patent and publication data for Nippon Electric Company (NEC) in Japan. Patent applications at the European and German Patent Offices combined (no double counting), US patents and internationally published papers by this company (registered within the INSPEC data bank) are compared (methological details in Grupp, 1990a).

This particular company was selected for the paradigmatic purpose pursued in this section as it is one of the four leading manufacturers of telecommunication equipment in Japan (together with Hitachi, Oki and Fujitsu). The industry structure and the competitive challenge in Japan are completely different from, say, Sweden and West Germany with a leading company in each country (Ericsson and Siemens respectively). Thus the study of activity shares per subfield of telecommunications by NEC as compared to the other large domestic competitors was *a priori* more interesting than the (large) national shares of any leading concern.

Figure 4.7 does not show much correlation between publications and patents (insignificant and negative), whereas the two patent profiles are quite similar (positive on a 1 per cent level of significance). There are no patents in the telecommunication subfields of theory and software, because the correspondent research or development results are hardly patentable. NEC's shares per subfield differ much from each other denoting indeed strong technology competition between the leading concerns (manufacturers and carriers). The strong technology position

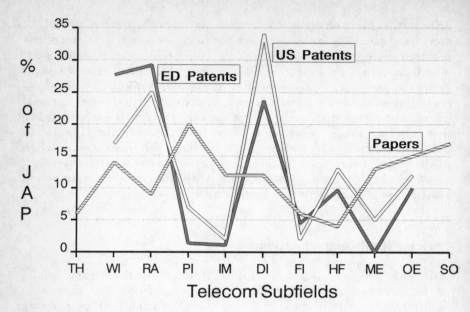

TH—Theory and Artificial Intelligence; WI—Wired Telecommunications; RA—Radio; PI—Picture Transmission; IM—Image Communications (Facsimile); DI—Digital Technology; FI—Fibre Optics; HF—Radar; ME—Telemetry; OE—Other telecommunications equipment not mentioned elsewhere; SO—Software, Services.

Figure 4.7 Telecommunication R&D activities by Nippon Electric Company, 1984–86, as a percentage of all Japanese activities.

of NEC in the radio field is obviously not based on much activity in research, whereas the R&D activities of this company in the subfield of picture transmission is more of a research type. Here, legal protection of patentable R&D results—if there are any—abroad (i.e., in Europe and the USA) is obviously not of primary concern. The dominance of NEC's technology within Japan is strongest in the field of general and digital technology, the key technology for the digital telecommunication networks of the future.

Further, the deviation in patent shares between the target markets in Europe and the United States is most marked in the field of wired communications—a more or less protected technology. Interviews with industry representatives revealed that the European markets are regarded as harder to penetrate than the US market. Therefore, quite a number of smaller Japanese companies do not aim at patent protection in Europe and are, therefore, absent from foreign applications in Europe. This means that the share of NEC within Japan is much higher in European patents than in US patents.

The *differences in papers and patents profiles do not invalidate one of the indicators* but represent and reflect different aspects of NEC's and the other Japanese actors' R&D activities. The obvious discrepancies in patent shares with respect to wired telecommunications are not related primarily to NEC's strengths in this technological field but rather are influenced by the industrial structure of the Japanese competitors to NEC. In terms of R&D competition, as distinct from product competition, not only are the above mentioned manufacturers of telecommunication equipment competing with NEC but also the carriers NTT and KDD (see Grupp and Schnoering, 1990). The marked differences in the science or technology positions between the eleven subfields of technology indicate that aggregation towards an overall position in telecommunications (or even electronics) would hide many interesting facts.

In the case of telecommunications no systematic technometric assessment has been undertaken so far. Only data on semiconductor lasers for optical communication compiled within the survey on lasers are available (see section 2). Figure 4.2 represents the technometric profile of semiconductor lasers for optical communications in the year 1986 and Figure 4.3 displays the data for NEC and the other Japanese producers.

Figures 4.2 and 4.3 are examples for just one product group with relevance for optical telecommunications. Conclusions with validity for the overall subfield must not be derived from them. It is the purpose of this section to demonstrate that in addition to patent and bibliometric indicators other information on the technical state of the art may be helpful. The overall low activity share of NEC in optical communications (see Figure 4.5) in terms of patents and papers within Japan does not necessarily correspond to low technological performance levels of its related products. For the laser light sources NEC is obviously among the technology leaders within Japan. If one aggregates the technometric data from Figure 4.3 (equal weights per specification) NEC's technometric index would be 0.752, that of all other manufacturers combined 0.661.

Technometric and bibliometric statistics are always of world-wide character. Patent applications, however, are legal documents with impact only in one country (or, as for example in the case of the European Patent Office, in a region of the world). If protection is looked for internationally the domestic priority application has to be repeated (so-called foreign applications) with possible modifications according to national legislations. The selection of data from only one patent office, therefore, is not always representative for the world's output of inventions (Schmoch and Grupp, 1989).

Synergisms between indicators

The case of lasers, the case of enzymes and the case of telecommunications are each single cases. *On the way towards a correlated system of science, technology and innovation indicators many more of those case studies have to be performed.* Therefore it should not be assumed that the various indicator relationships always result in highly significant positive correlations. Why should they? The phase model (Figure 4.1) suggests that the indicators are not equally valid for a study of the various R&D and innovation phases and the various R&D-performing groups of institutions. In many cases, however, with allowance for time-lags between the indicators, a highly significant positive correlation may be found (Schmoch *et al.*, 1988). In these cases, one of the indicators being compared seems to be obsolete but until a deeper understanding of indicator networks is reached many of them should still be used in parallel. Additionally, most sets of indicators are far from being complete. Therefore, until further notice, peer evaluation and personal expertise are an essential addition to science and technology indicators to bridge the inconsistencies and the lack of adaptation within the indicator systems. As the technometric approach is largely based on interviews with experts, the technometric indicator plays a central role in any science and technology indicator network. Synergisms between indicators do exist and should be explored (see Schmoch *et al.*, 1988).

First, there is mutual support in delimiting corresponding subfields for research, technology and innovation indicators. Synergisms from similarities of indicator values give more credibility to each of the indicators used. Distinctions between indicator values are also of synergetic quality, because they guide the way to qualitative interpretations or at least indicate that additional clues are needed. For the identification of striking versus normal facts and events the location of an issue in quite different indicator systems is very helpful, raises validity and prevents one from drawing obviously erroneous conclusions.

The synoptic use of various indicators allows for comparisons between different R&D phases and different R&D-performing institutions, and for comparisons between input and output measures, and thus opens the door for efficiency deliberations. The integration of expert opinion and statistics of whatever type is a great advantage for comprehensive evaluation of research programs.

Notes

1. This paper partly draws upon a jointly-authored writing with Beatrix Schwitalla on 'Technometrics, bibliometrics, econometrics, and patent analysis: towards a correlated system of science, technology, and innovation indicators' in A.F.J. van Raan, A.J. Nederhof, H.F. Mold (eds) (1989), *Science*

Indicators: *Their Use in Science Policy and Their Role in Science Studies,* D.S.W.O. Press, Leiden.

References

Clark, K.B. (1985), 'The interaction of design hierarchies and market concepts in technological evolution', *Research Policy*, vol. 14, pp. 235–51.

Dodson, E.N. (1985), 'Measurement of state of the art and technological advance', *Tech. Forecast. Soc. Change*, vol. 27, pp. 129–46.

Dosi, O. (1988), 'Sources, procedures, and microeconomic effects of innovation', *Journal of Economic Literature*, XXVI, pp. 1120–71.

Freeman, C. (1982), *The Economics of Industrial Innovation*, 2nd edn, Frances Pinter, London.

Granberg, A. (1986), *A Bibliometric Survey of Laser Research in Sweden, West Germany, and Japan*, Research Policy Studies Discussion Paper 172, Research Policy Institute, Lund.

Grupp, H. (ed.) (1987), *Problems of Measuring Technological Change*, TÜV Rheinland, Köln.

Grupp, H. (1990a), 'On the supplementary functions of science and technology indicators—the case of West German telecommunication R&D'. *Scientometrics* (in print).

Grupp, H. (1990b), 'The measurement of technical performance in the framework of R&D intensity, patent, and trade indicators' (forthcoming).

Grupp, H. and Hohmeyer, O. (1986), 'A technometric model for the assessment of technological standards and their application to selected technology-intensive products', *Techn. Forecast Soc. Change*, 30, pp. 123–37.

Grupp, H. and Hohmeyer, O. (1988), 'Technological standards for research-intensive product groups' in A.F.J. van Raan (ed.). *Handbook of Quantitative Studies of Science and Technology*, Elsevier, Amsterdam, pp. 611–73.

Grupp, H., Hohmeyer, O. Kollert, R. and Legler H. (1987), *Technometrie-Die Bemessung des technisch-wirtschaftlichen Leistungsstands*, TÜV Rheinland, Köln.

Grupp, H. and Schnoering, T. (1990), 'International comparison of research and development in the telecommunications field' (forthcoming).

Grupp, H. and Schwitalla, B. (1988), 'Innovationsdynamik der fuehrenden Marktwirtschaften im technometrischen Vergleich' in P.J.J. Welfens and L. Balcerowicz (eds.), *Innovationdynamik im Systemvergleich*, Physica-Verlag, Heidelberg, pp. 323–41.

Holland, D., Albrecht, E. and Paetzold G., (1984), 'Innovationsprozesse aus der Sicht des Zyklus Wissenschaft-Technik-Produktion', *Wissenschaftswissenschaftliche Beitrage* der Sektion Wissenschaftstheorie und -organisation der Humboldt-Universität 31, pp. 29–63.

Kodama, F. (1987), 'A system approach to science indicator' in H. Grupp (ed.), *Problems of Measuring Technological Change*, TÜV Rheinland, Köln, pp. 65–87.

Krupp, H. (1984), 'Basic research in German research institutions', *Proceedings of the Japan-Germany Science Seminar*, Japan Society for the Promotion of Science, Tokyo, pp. 73–109.

Kula, M.-R. (1984), 'Enzyme' in *Handbuch der Biotechnologie*, 2nd edn., Oldenbourg, Munich, pp. 379–411.

Le Pair, C. (1988), 'The citation gap of applicable science' in A.F.J. van Raan (ed.), *Handbook of Quantitative Studies of Science and Technology*, Elsevier, Amsterdam, pp. 537–53.

Reiss, T. Hohmeyer, O. Grupp, H. (1989), *Bemessung des technischwirtschaftlichen Leistungsstandes der Bundesrepublik Deutschland, der Vereinigten Staaten und Japans in Teilbereichen der Biotechnologie*, FhG-ISI, Karlsruhe.

Schmoch, U. and Grupp, H. (1989), 'Patents between corporate strategy and technology output: an approach to the synoptic evaluation of US, European, and German patent data (1989)' in A.F.J. van Raan, A.J. Nederhof and H.F. Moed (eds), *Science Indicators: Their Use in Science Policy and Their Role in Science Studies*, D.S.W.O. Press, Leiden.

Schmoch, U., Grupp, H., Mannsbart, W. and Schwitalla, B. (1988), *Technik-prognosen mit Patentindikatoren*, TÜV Rheinland, Köln.

Schneider, M. (1983), 'Zur Patentanalyse als Prognosemethode', *Wissenschaft-swissenschaftliche Beitrage* der Sektion Wissenschaftstheorie und -organisation der Humboldt-Universität 27, pp. 143–53.

Saviotti, P. (1988), 'The measurement of changes in technological output' in A.F.J. van Raan (ed.), *Handbook of Quantitative Studies of Science and Technology*, Elsevier, Amsterdam, pp. 555–610.

van Raan, A.F.J. (ed.) (1988), *Handbook of Quantitative Studies of Science and Technology*, Elsevier, Amsterdam.

Welfens, P.J.J. and Balcerowicz, L. (eds) (1988), *Innovationsdynamik im System-vergleich*, Physica-Verlag, Heidelberg.

5 Laser research in Sweden, West Germany and Japan

Anders Granberg

Introduction

The main task addressed by the Research Policy Institute (RPI) in the Three-Country Project has been that of exploring the differential involvement of the three national R&D systems in the development of new strategic fields of technology. More specifically, the work undertaken at the RPI has been guided by two major objectives. The substantive aim has been to elucidate and compare the overall dynamics and institutional structure of the national R&D efforts in particular science-based fields of technology. The methodological aim has been to assess the possibilities and limitations of bibliometric methods, complemented by patent analyses, in the mapping of developmental patterns and institutional actors. Toward these ends, cross-national bibliometric surveys and patent scans of selected technologies have been carried out.

The study presented in the following provides a comparative outline, based on output data, of the development efforts of Sweden, West Germany and Japan in the field of laser technology. Two types of output indicators are used: journal articles and US patents. Depending on the indicator, the period covered extends from the early or mid-1970s to the early or mid-1980s. Information regarding output volumes and institutional sources has been collected from commercially accessible databases. The material has been compiled and analysed in an attempt to estimate (i) the relative magnitude and overall dynamics of the national R&D efforts in laser technology; (ii) the relative involvement, in these efforts, of different sectors of the national R&D systems; and (iii) the relative prominence of individual institutional actors as contributors to the national output. Apart from its substantive aim, the study also has the methodological objective mentioned above.

The reader will find in this chapter, first, a background sketch of laser technology, followed by a presentation of the output-centered approach, including the files and search procedures used and the kinds of data assembled.[1] The results obtained will then be presented—verbally and in a series of charts and tables—and commented upon.

The technology

What is meant here by 'laser technology'? How should the field be delimited for the purposes of our survey? What are the relevant structural and developmental features of the technology? These are the questions that will be considered in this section.

The delimitation of the field

Like fiber optics or genetic engineering—which are among the fields investigated in the larger project—laser technology is an example of what may be termed a basic technology or, more specifically, a basic technology of a generic character (the nature and significance of basic technologies are analyzed in the contribution by R. Stankiewicz in this volume, i.e. it is a technology which is based on the exploitation of certain natural processes (phenomena or effects) in the performance of various functions, and which is defined by reference to that 'process base' rather than to some application or set of applications.[2] Laser technology may, accordingly, be characterized as a technology which utilizes the fundamental processes of stimulated emission and the generation of highly coherent light for the achievement of various practical ends. Note that as the technology is kept open on the applications side, the discovery of a new use does not call for a redefinition of the field.

We may think broadly—and more concretely—of laser technology as an evolving body of knowledge that can be structured by reference to a physical systems hierarchy extending from materials (or lasing media) and basic components at the bottom, through the laser device itself, to lasers-cum-accessories and larger application systems at the top. For the purposes of our survey two major subfields have been distinguished:

1. *Laser I:*   This is the core technology; it is centered on lasing processes and laser devices (covering, e.g., lasing action in solids, liquids and gases, and the design and the mode of functioning of the various types of lasers).
2. *Laser II:*   This is the subfield of applied laser technology, comprising the various uses of the laser that have been identified and explored to date (from measurement and material processing to isotope separation and plasma generation) and the anatomy and physiology of the required systems.

It stands to reason that the boundaries between these subfields will not always be sharp and unambiguous. Some overlap seems inevitable.

Military and civilian applications

Military interests have always, from the very beginning to the present day, exerted a strong influence on the evolution of laser technology. An early, 1967, review of the field calls attention to this aspect with the following words:

Like few other major scientific or technological discoveries made during periods of relative world tranquility, the laser is linked inseparably to military interests. Indeed, in large measure the origins of the laser, the rapidity of its early development, and the excitement it sparked in government and industrial circles all can be traced to an underlying belief in its ultimate applicability to military or weapon systems. Today, nearly seven years after coherent light was first generated, it is apparent that were it not for the military motivation, the laser would hardly be more than a promising albeit exciting scientific invention. (Fishlock, 1967)

This is not to deny the fact that a variety of potential applications of a civilian nature were identified early on. A great many of these have now been realized. It is important to bear in mind, however, when considering the paper-count figures for a given country, that the production of scientific and technological articles for the open literature (which is entered into the data base) may not—depending on the extent and nature

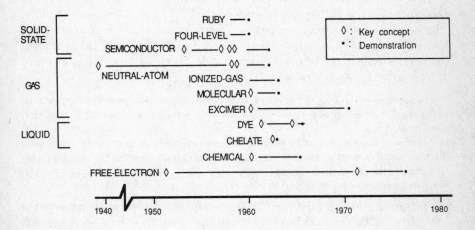

Figure 5.1 The development of major laser types (Main source: Bertolotti, 1983)

of the military involvement in the development of the technology—provide a reliable indicator of the *overall* national R&D effort in the laser field. One must expect the patent material to be similarly limited. In other words, what the facts and figures presented in the following *do* indicate is the relative prominence of a country or institution in the production of public or unclassified scientific and technological information in the field. Military applications may, of course, be included, but they are likely to be heavily underrepresented.

The time perspective

The conceptual innovations which directly underlie the laser occurred in 1957/8. The first operating laser, a device using ruby as the active medium, was demonstrated in 1960. The first gaseous laser (CO_2) appeared in 1961, and the first semiconductor laser (GaAs) in 1962. Over the next few years there followed, in the words of one observer, 'a tremendous explosion of publications on laser transitions in hundreds of different materials and on the properties of laser devices' (Dummer, 1977). During the 1960s, the basic laser types (within the general classes of solid-state, gas, and liquid-media devices) that are of practical interest were established, the major exceptions being the excimer lasers and the special category of free-electron lasers which were first operated in the 1970s (see Figure 5.1). The decade of the 1960s also saw the identification of a broad spectrum of potential laser applications, including measurement and control, surgery, material processing, communications and navigation.

The continued evolution of laser technology from about 1970 on—through the still open phase described by a historian of the field as 'the second-generation laser period' (Bertolotti, 1983)—is characterized by a growing emphasis on the development and refinement of those laser properties which are relevant to particular applications. Thus, a recent state-of-the-field review notes that:

lasers are now providing the solution to numerous practical problems in material processing, communications, medicine, remote sensing, and research, and that continuing laser research and development are now commonly end-use motivated; examples include work on 'long-wavelength' (i.e. 1– to 1.5– μm) laser diodes for fiberoptic transmitters, on blue-green lasers for underwater communication, on high-energy lasers for laser fusion, and on ultraviolet-emitting excimers for material processing (Levitt and Holmes, 1985).

The implications for our survey are twofold: (i) With a starting-point in the early 1970s the data base scan will cover only the period of second-generation laser development. In other words, the initial reactions of the three countries to the emerging technology (driven by pioneering efforts in the USA, USSR and, to some extent, France) and their participation in further first-generation developments lie outside the scope of the survey. (ii) The search through the subfield of Laser I, or the core technology, is likely to yield a significant number of items that are in some sense applications-oriented or practically motivated. Again it is clear that the distinction between Laser I and Laser II is more a matter of differential emphasis than of a strict separation into non-applied and applied.

The methodology

In this section, the main features of the output-centered approach followed in the RPI surveys will be presented. Its general objectives and requirements will be considered together with the particular procedures and practical problems of the laser field scan. (For an overview and assessment of output-based measures within the broader context of S&T indicators, see the contribution by H. Grupp in this volume.

The uses of literature and patent data

Output-based studies of scientific and technological research activities may be undertaken for a variety of purposes. A major, well-known and somewhat controversial, use of bibliometrics is in the evaluation of research performance. Thus, publication counts, citation frequencies and other kinds of quantitative, output-based measures are often employed in assessments of the strengths and weaknesses of research groups, organizations and larger R&D systems. Such methods can, of course, also serve as tools of description and analysis in studies where performance evaluation is not a prime objective. Instead, the aim may be, for example, to elucidate the cognitive structure of a discipline, to map the evolving networks of research cooperation and communication, or to explore the geographical distribution of R&D activities.

The three-country technology surveys carried out at the RPI fall within the broad confines of the second category. A common objective of these studies is to explore the possibilities of using easily accessible output data—preferably data which can be readily retrieved from existing data bases—in a first approach to the mapping of the national R&D landscapes in a given field of technology. The main assumption underlying these investigations is that such data may provide useful quantitative indicators and qualitative descriptions of the kinds of organizational actors and institutional settings involved, as well as the relative scale and overall dynamics of the national development efforts in the field in question. The collected data, whether they pertain to papers or patents, must of course be complemented by, and checked against, other types of information on the inputs, outputs and organization of R&D.

The survey material has been retrieved from two data base sources, containing literature and patent references, respectively.

The literature file

As in the fiber optics study, the data source used in the literature survey is the INSPEC (Information Services for the Physics and Engineering Communities) on-line data base. The INSPEC file is one of the largest in the physico-technical domain. In the mid-1980s, i.e. at the end of our search period, it had an annual growth rate of more than 200,000 abstracts and had reached a total volume of some 2.5 million references. As the earliest entry year is 1969, the time period that can now be scanned is 20 years at most. Depending on the technology to be studied, this may or may not be a serious drawback. Its implications for the laser study have just been indicated. A further limitation inherent in the data base is that 'Lasers' was introduced as an index term at a later stage, in January 1973, which makes analysis of developments prior to that date less reliable.

The subject profile of the INSPEC data base—with an emphasis on physics, electronics, electrical engineering, control, computing and information technology—is such that satisfactory coverage of Laser I may be assumed. It is likely, however, that some laser applications outside the areas of measurement, control, communications and information technology will be underrepresented in the search material.

The INSPEC data base, like most bibliographic data files, is fed by processes of information selection. When such a file is used for the purposes of a cross-country survey, the question of built-in biases inevitably arises. Specifically, one would like to know whether the comparative picture of national conditions and developments that emerges from the search data is likely to be, in some ways, distorted by the very construction and mode of expansion of the data base. The choice of journals representing different language communities and the relative emphasis placed on various subject areas are major potential sources of bias. However, the size of the INSPEC file and the mid-1980s scanning figure of more than 3,000 journals suggest a low degree of selectivity and thus a limited scope for such factors to be influential. Still, our knowledge of these matters is not entirely satisfactory. For instance, INSPEC's coverage of Japanese journals has reportedly been expanded in the later years of our scanning period, but the magnitude and timing of that expansion have not been specified. What we do have, in this case, is a piece of qualitative information that should be taken into consideration when examining the time series generated by the search.

The patent file

Information on Swedish, West German and Japanese invented laser patents in the US patent system has been drawn from the Patent Citation Files of CHI Research/Computer Horizons, Inc. The search covers *all* US patents issued between 1975 and 1983; accordingly, questions of data base selectivity and bias do not arise here.

In turning to so-called third-country patenting (the 'third country' being, in this case, the United States), we are adopting the approach which is generally taken when, in the context of international comparisons, patent volumes are to serve as indicators of technological development efforts or innovative activities. The use of measures based on third-country patenting has several important advantages. Thus, in a methodological review by Keith Pavitt (1985), it is pointed out that such measures eliminate, for a given country, domestic patenting based on foreign innovative activities and equalize the costs of patenting from whatever national sources; that innovative organizations are more discriminating and selective in their patenting in foreign countries; and that there is a strong statistical relationship between international differences in the volume of industrial R&D and the volume of third-country patenting. It is advisable, however, not to choose a third country which has uncommonly close trade relations or other economic links of a special nature with one of the countries to be compared (e.g. USA/Canada). Generally speaking, the

U.S. patenting data are particularly useful, given their degree of detail and accessibility, and that Western European countries are now moving towards a Europe-wide patent system of application and grant, which may change the propensity of innovators to atent through the national patent systems of European countries. However, one shortcoming of using the U.S. patenting database is that it precludes valid comparisons including patents of U.S. origin. (Pavitt, 1985)

Search procedures

The on-line search of the INSPEC file was set up so as to cover the journal articles produced by Sweden, West Germany and Japan in the laser field from 1973 through to 1984. Note that only journal articles were sought; books, conference reports and other kinds of published documents were not included. The target sets of Laser I and Laser II were defined by means of the controlled term 'laser-' in conjunction with the appropriate classification codes. The latter include, in the case of Laser I, the codes of the basic lasing processes and the various types of laser devices, and, in the case of Laser II, the codes of the various application areas or uses. From the resultant sets, LI and LII, the subsets of Swedish, German and Japanese items were drawn on the basis of corporate-source data, more specifically, the national identity of the organization with which the (first) author is affiliated.

On the patent side, the search procedure applied to the CHI Research/Computer Horizons file was as follows. First, all patents with at least one inventor from (i.e. residing in) one of the three countries were selected from the US Patent Office Class entitled 'Coherent Light Generators'. In the same way, Swedish, West German and Japanese patents were then selected from the set containing all patents with 'laser-' (word root) in the patent title, and from the set containing all patents with 'laser-' or 'coherent light' as abstract keywords. Duplications and triplications due to overlapping sets were eliminated.[3] As in the paper search, an attempt was made to distinguish between the core technology, Laser I, and the technology of laser applications, Laser II. In this case, the boundary was drawn on the basis of the information provided by titles and abstracts, using the following definitions: Laser I includes making lasers, making anything used in making a laser and ways of improving the performance of a laser. Laser II includes any use of the laser radiation, anything that makes the laser beam available for use and anything that alters the characteristics of the laser beam. Again, it is obvious that the boundary between the two subfields can be rather arbitrary.

The data

In the INSPEC search, information was collected which tells us, for each country, the number of laser articles produced in each subfield and the distribution of that output over various institutional sources or actors. Similarly, the information retrieved from the patent files gives us the volume and distribution of laser patents by subfield, country and (within each country) assignee, or patent-holding organization. In addition, certain types of citation data—based on examiner's references—have been developed, including: (i) for each subfield, country and the period as a whole, lists of citing/cited assignees with the number of citing/cited patents for each assignee; and (ii) for the three countries jointly and for each year from 1975 to 1980, lists of the twenty most highly cited patents (and ties) within the laser field as a whole. The latter lists also specify, for each patent, its subfield and the number of cities received.

THE TIME DIMENSION

The journal-article data have been compiled and examined on the basis of three-year periods, i.e. 1973–5, 1976–8, 1979–81, 1982–4. The main reason is the practical consideration of facilitating the time-consuming task of institutional-source checking. There is also the consideration, which pertains chiefly to Sweden, of avoiding the excessively small numbers and blanks that may appear in a series of annual output counts. The patent material, on the other hand, which is drawn from a pre-cleaned file, is presented on a year-to-year basis, from 1975 to 1983 or, in the case of the highly cited patents, from 1975 to 1980.

THE IDENTIFICATION OF SOURCES

For the purposes of our study, it is, of course, imperative that the sources of the paper and patent outputs are correctly identified. This is the very basis of the cleaning process described below. It may also, as our experience suggests, be the most laborious part of a data base survey. A detailed knowledge of the R&D systems involved, including companies and industrial laboratories, is obviously a key asset. When personal knowledge is insufficient or is not on tap, directories of R&D institutions and firms will have to be consulted. In the present survey, the handling of the Swedish material was, understandably, wholly unproblematic. The examination of the West German lists was greatly facilitated by recourse to a comprehensive STU guide to the R&D system of the Federal Republic (STU, 1984). In the case of Japan, some minor problems did arise due to the incomplete coverage provided by the available directories.

THE CLEANING PROCESS

The INSPEC search yields a number of print-out lists, one for each country/nationality, subfield and three-year period, stating the number of papers produced by particular organizations. These lists must first be 'cleaned', a process which involves the following: (i) Sources which have been erroneously included, or which cannot be properly identified (because of an incomplete or garbled description, say), or which lack a clear national identity (e.g. a joint Franco-German research institute) must be eliminated; in the present survey, their number proved to be very small. (ii) The INSPEC file provides only a set of all-German lists, which means that East German sources must be identified and excluded; it turns out that such screening reduces the all-German production by some 18 per cent. (iii) When paper counts are made for individual sources care must be taken to include all variant designations, subunits, branches etc. that may appear on the lists. It should be pointed out here that the degree to which the sources appearing on the INSPEC lists are specified varies considerably. The range extends, in the academic sector, from project groups within departments (which is rare), to departments and faculties, or (which is common) entire universities, and, in the case of companies, from laboratories and divisions to firms and enterprise groups.

THE CLASSIFICATION OF SOURCES

When the number of sources is large, classes of institutional actors will have to be distinguished and used in the processing and presentation of the data. In this survey, as in other output-based studies within the project, the sources involved have been divided into three broad categories. In principle, the classification is applicable to patent sources as well as to paper sources; one may reasonably assume, however, that the vast majority of the patent assignees will fall into one of the three categories delineated below, viz. that of companies.

1. *Academic institutions*, comprising universities, institutes of technology, colleges and other institutions of higher education and learning, including academic-sector institutes, laboratories, centers etc. As might be expected, the number of laser-paper sources of this type is very large indeed. Production figures for each individual source can, of course, be generated, though the required 'cleaning' would make it rather time-consuming. In the present survey, this has been done only in the case of Sweden.
2. *'Institutes'*. This is the designation given those R&D establishments— institutes, laboratories, centers etc.—which lie outside the academic sector and are not part of individual companies or enterprise groups. Paper counts have been made for all sources in this category. In the case of West Germany, where the number and variety of such sources are considerable, the following subcategories have been distinguished (in accordance with the previously mentioned STU guide); (a) Federal Research Institutes (*Bundesforschungsanstalten*); (b) Max-Planck Institutes; (c) National Research Centers (*Grossforschungseinrichtungen*); (d) Institutes of the Fraunhofer Society; (e) Institutes of the industrial research associations; (f) so-called Blue-list institutes; and (g) Battelle.
3. *Companies*, including all business enterprises—private or public, in manufacturing or services—and their laboratories. Output figures have been generated for all sources in this category.

Findings

The material retrieved from the paper and patent files will now be presented and commented upon. The thematic emphasis and the overall structure of the presentation are the same as in the fiber optics report. Thus, a general picture of the involvement of the three countries in the development of the laser field will be sketched, focusing on the relative scale and the institutional settings of their R&D efforts. The main quantitative dimensions and qualitative features of the picture are displayed in a series of charts and tables inserted into the text.

National shares: static and dynamic perspectives

Let us first consider the proportions in which Sweden, West Germany and Japan contribute to the accumulated three-country outputs of papers and patents in the laser field as a whole (LI and II). It should be pointed out that the figures obtained by adding the output volumes of LI and LII are somewhat inflated by areas of overlap. A closer examination of the problem leads to the conclusion that these areas are small and that there is no reason to believe that they would favor one country over the others.[4]

The general picture shown by Table 5.1—the dominant role of Japan, the modest contributions of Sweden and the intermediate position of West Germany—may or may not be a cause of surprise, depending on one's prior knowledge of the actual laser efforts of these countries. To put the national output figures in a proper perspective, it would, of course, be desirable to relate them to a closely matched set of input data, such as the total R&D expenditures of each country in the laser field over the period in question. In the absence of such data, the table below presents the ratios formed by the national output shares and the national shares of the three-country GERD (Gross Domestic Expenditure on R&D) for the year 1979, chosen as an approximate midpoint of the search periods. The

Table 5.1 National shares of the three-country production of papers and patents in LI&LII, 1973–84 and 1975–83, respectively, and ratios of these shares to the national shares of the three-country GERD for 1979

	papers No.	papers %	patents No.	patents %	pap./ GERD	pat./ GERD
SWE	103	2.65	27	3.55	0.56	0.75
FRG	1194	30.76	277	36.40	0.79	0.94
JPN	2584	66.58	457	60.05	1.18	1.06

Source (GERD): OECD Science and Technology Indicators—Resources Devoted to R&D; OECD, Paris 1984

hypothesis which may, with due qualifications, be derived from these ratios is that the R&D effort undertaken by Japan in the laser field is larger, not only in absolute but also in relative terms, than those of West Germany and Sweden, in that order. It is also worth noting that the Japanese dominance is most marked in the production of papers, somewhat less so in the production of patents.

The question of national shares will now be addressed to the two subfields of laser technology, LI and LII. The distinction yields the percentages shown in Table 5.2. What strikes the eye, first and foremost, is the clear emphasis in the Swedish output—both in papers and patents—on applied technology, or LII. The West German and Japanese outputs are more balanced, although there is a discernible bias, in the German production, towards LII and, in the Japanese production, towards the core technology LI.

It may be of interest to consider also the relationship between the patent volumes and the paper volumes produced by each country. Table 5.3 presents the patent-to-paper ratios for the field as a whole and for the two subfields. We can see, first, that the ratios obtained for each subfield are remarkably similar across the countries. Second, one finds that the ratios for LII are much higher than those for LI. This seems reasonable, considering that the paper outputs of LI are likely to contain a substantial portion of basic-science or 'non-device-oriented' items.

Finally, if we look upon the paper outputs as indicators of a broader spectrum of laser-related activities, extending from fundamental studies to product development, the figures suggest that the (relative) 'patent yield' of the overall, LI&II, effort is somewhat greater for Sweden than for West Germany and Japan, in that order. Clearly, the interpretation of the data is hazardous and the table is best used a source of tentative hypotheses or conjectures.

The subject of national shares has so far been explored in a static perspective, focusing on the aggregate outputs of the search periods. Let us now briefly examine the dynamic side of the picture. The changes over time that are shown in the following line chart must be treated with caution, bearing in mind, in particular, the expansion of the INSPEC file and the successive introduction into that data base of new classifications

Table 5.2 National shares of three-country production of papers and patents in LI and LII, 1973–84/1975–83

Country	Papers		Patents	
	LI	LII	LI	LII
SWE	1.72	4.61	1.82	4.25
FRG	29.36	33.70	30.91	38.63
JPN	68.93	61.69	67.27	57.12

Table 5.3 Ratio of patent volume to paper volume by country and subfield, 1973–84/1975–83

Country	LI	LII	LI&II
SWE	0.09	0.40	0.26
FRG	0.09	0.49	0.23
JPN	0.08	0.40	0.18

and terms. Thus, one possibility which has already been mentioned is that of a data base-induced inflation of the Japanese output figures towards the end of the period. Nevertheless, the general trends behind the paper production curves of Figure 5.2 seem clear enough. What stands out, when looking at the laser field as a whole, is the steeply inclined Japanese curve and the moderately rising curves of West Germany and Sweden.

In terms of relative output volumes, one finds that the Japanese share is expanding continuously over the entire 12-year period, that the German share is diminishing and that the Swedish share remains fairly constant. A closer inspection of the underlying data, separated into LI and LII, reveals that the picture is by and large the same in the two subfields—with some deviations in the 1982–4 figures for LII.

The patent data of Figure 5.3, which cannot be called into question on the grounds of a selective data base, are broadly supportive of the above

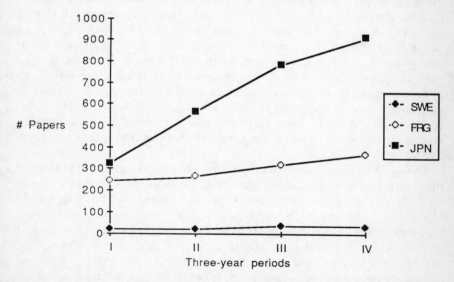

Figure 5.2   Paper production by country and three-year period, 1973–84

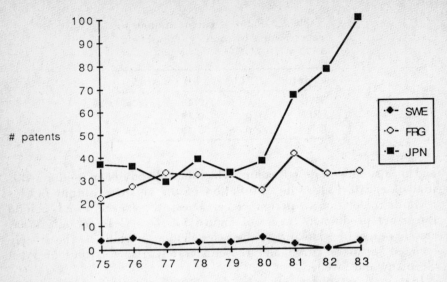

Figure 5.3   Patent production by country and year, 1975–83

paper findings. Again, we can see that the Japanese share is increasing—in this case rather dramatically. It should be noted, however, (i) that there is little growth in the patent production of any country over the first six years of the period; (ii) that the trend lines of Sweden and West Germany are horizontal, or nearly so, over the entire period; and (iii) that the marked post-1980 upturn of the Japanese curve is due largely to an expansion in the subfield of applied laser technology. (It may be added that the production of core-technology patents appears to be somewhat more stable over time than the production of applications patents.) The orientation of the Japanese laser R&D efforts towards different types of devices has been examined in the patent studies of H. Grupp *et al.* A comparison of the patenting activities (1973–84) of that country with those of West Germany and the United States revealed a strong and growing Japanese emphasis on semiconductor lasers (Grupp, 1988).

The general impression, based on the quantitative material presented here, of a strong and escalating Japanese development effort in the laser field is amplified by the citation data supplied by CHI Research/ Computer Horizons. The analysis of citation frequencies adds a qualitative dimension to our study since it enables us to estimate the 'importance' attributed to a patent or set of patents. More precisely, citation data may be used to measure, in a rough fashion, the perceived technical relevance of a patented invention to the ideas of other patentees. The measures used in the following are based on (i) the

Table 5.4 Highly cited patents: percentage of
HC patents of all patents in respective cell,
1975–80

Country	LI	LII	LI&II
SWE	33.33	31.58	31.82
FRG	38.46	32.58	33.92
JPN	44.87	39.55	41.51
SWE+FRG+JPN	42.50	35.79	37.78

identification, for each year 1975–80, of the 20 most highly cited patents
(including ties) in the three-country output; (ii) the citation frequency, or
the number of cites received, of each highly cited (HC) patent; (iii) the
subfield of each HC patent; and (iv) the total number of patents produced
by each country in the years 1975–80.

Table 5.4 gives the percentage of HC patents of all patents within a
given table cell in the relevant period. For example, the figure in the top
left cell tells us that 33.33 per cent of the Swedish patents in LI are HC
patents. The chief message conveyed by this table is that, in every field,
Japan is credited with a higher HC proportion than West Germany and
Sweden, in that order. Furthermore, it suggests that—in every
country—core-technology patents are more likely to belong to the HC
category than are applications patents.

Within the HC category, citation frequencies may vary considerably,
from a top score of 40 to a minimum of 2. Table 5.5 shows the average
number of cites received by the HC patents in a given cell. Two features
are easily discernible:

i. The above-mentioned national rank order repeats itself here, i.e. the
    Japanese patent sets are consistent top scorers, the German patents
    are second and the Swedish third.
ii. The previously noted tendency of the applications patents to be
    underrepresented in the HC category is counterbalanced by their
    consistently higher citation averages.

The two basic citation measures presented in Tables 5.4 (HC
percentages) and 5.5 (average citation frequencies of HC patents) have

Table 5.5 Highly cited patents: average number
of citations received per HC patent, 1975–80

Country	LI	LII	LI&II
SWE	3.00	4.00	3.86
FRG	4.13	5.53	5.17
JPN	5.49	6.83	6.30
SWE+FRG+JPN	5.04	6.12	5.76

Table 5.6 Citation indices, accumulated patent output, 1975–80

Country	LI	LII	LI&II
SWE	0.47	0.58	0.56
FRG	0.74	0.82	0.81
JPN	1.15	1.23	1.20

been combined into a 'National Citation Index'.[5] The index has been constructed so as to vary from 0 to approximately 2, with the value 1 corresponding to the joint three-country average. A country may, for instance, obtain an index score of 1 either by being above average in terms of its share of HC patents and below average in terms of citation frequencies, or vice versa, or—of course—by being average in both respects. Table 5.6 gives the citation indices for the accumulated 1975–80 patent production of the three countries. Not surprisingly, the rank order of the countries is preserved: Japan first, West Germany second, Sweden third. As a complement to the total-period indices of Table 5.6, annual indices for the laser field as a whole have been generated. The figures obtained (not shown here) indicate a stable ranking of the countries over time.

Sector-level patterns

The remainder of the paper will consider the institutional aspects of the Swedish, West German and Japanese production of laser papers and laser patents. In the present section, the role of the three major institutional categories or sectors defined earlier will be examined, i.e. 'Academic Institutions', 'Institutes', and 'Companies'. The distribution of outputs by these categories is a question which pertains mainly to the production of papers, since national patent outputs tend to be too strongly tied to a single institutional sector. An inspection of our patent assignee lists reveals, unsurprisingly, that 93 per cent of the assigned patents are held by company-sector organizations. The only non-company assignee of some national significance is the Max-Planck Society of Germany. We shall return to the subject of patents and patent assignees in a later section, when exploring the composition of the institutional sectors and the positions held by individual sources.

Figure 5.4 shows the proportions in which the three sectors contribute to the national outputs of laser articles (LI&LII) accumulated over the period. As a frame of reference, the corresponding sector shares found in the fields of fiber optics and VLSI have been included in the diagram.

Let us first examine the laser columns. The patterns which are discernible in that part of the chart can be described as follows:

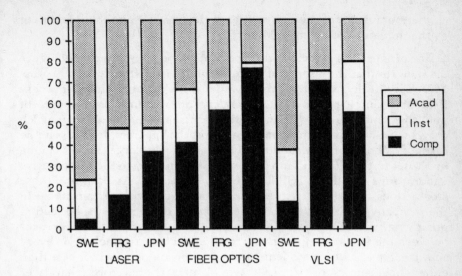

Figure 5.4   Institutional-sector shares, by country, of the accumulated, 1973–84, paper outputs in the fields of fiber optics, laser technology (LI & LII) and VLSI

1. The academic sector is clearly, in every country, the dominant source, accounting for at least half of the total national output. Sweden, however, sets itself apart from the others by virtue of its very heavy dependence on that sector:Swedish academic institutions account for more than 75 per cent of the country's total as compared with shares slightly above 50 per cent for West Germany and Japan.
2. It is in West Germany that the institute sector, as a rather heterogeneous category of sources, plays its by far most prominent role with some 32 per cent of the total; Sweden follows at 19 per cent, trailed by Japan at 12 per cent. At this point, an important piece of information must be added regarding the classification of a major Japanese source, namely Nippon Telegraph & Telephone(NTT), the public corporation in charge of domestic telecommunications services which has since been privatized. In this study, as in the fiber optics and VLSI surveys, NTT has been placed in the company sector. The classification may, admittedly, be disputed; thus, some might find it more appropriate to let NTT, or at least the laboratories of that corporation, be included in the institute sector.
3. The rank order changes but the positions remain well separated as we turn to the contributors of the company sector. In Japan, these sources account for 36 per cent of the national output; in West Germany, the corresponding figure is 16 per cent and in Sweden (beware of the small numbers!) a mere 4 per cent. It appears, in short, that Sweden and Japan are placed at opposite ends of the scale, as it were, considering

the prominence of the universities in the one case and the strength of the industry sector in the other.

The proportions shown by the fiber optics and VLSI columns of Figure 5.4 indicate that the laser field is not unique in its institutional make-up. More specifically, we can see that Sweden is the country which—in every field of technology—is most dependent on academia as a source of published contributions. Japan, on the other hand, is the country which draws most heavily on the company sector, the apparent deviation in the case of VLSI notwithstanding. (The relatively large share of the institutes in the VLSI column of Japan is due entirely to the Cooperative Laboratories of the VLSI Technology Research Association; these laboratories are, of course, very closely affiliated with certain actors in the company sector.) West Germany may, in these respects, be seen as occupying an intermediate position. As to the institutional differences between the fields, it is interesting to note that laser technology, in every country, has a stronger academic and a weaker company-sector base than either fiber optics or VLSI. It would appear, therefore, that laser technology is still—in spite of its having entered the stage of 'second-generation developments'—a research field of considerable attraction to the academic scientist or technologist. However, one must add to this picture the qualification that the bibliometric survey makes no pretense of covering the domain of military R&D.

The variations in the output share of the institute sector, across countries and technological fields, are not immediately suggestive of some general pattern or underlying regularity. A proper interpretation of the survey data must await a closer examination, at lower levels of aggregation, of the national development efforts, including the behavior of individual actors. Nevertheless, a conjecture concerning the West Germany situation may be advanced. The comparatively large laser-field share held by the institutes of that country has been remarked upon. Figure 5.4 also shows the corresponding shares in fiber optics and VLSI to be fairly small. Going across the fields, from VLSI through fiber optics to laser technology, one finds that the relative contribution of the institutes grows with an expanding academic (and a shrinking company) share. This pattern may be partly explained by the fact that the R&D system of the Federal Republic—unlike those of Sweden and Japan— includes a very significant group of institutes which are chiefly concerned with basic research, including research on the foundations of technology, and which are distinctly publications-oriented in their activities, namely the institutes of the Max-Planck Society.

It would not be unreasonable to expect companies to generate a larger share of the literature in the applications-oriented subfield, LII, than in the core technology, LI, and that the opposite should be true of the academic sector and its published output. However, this expectation is

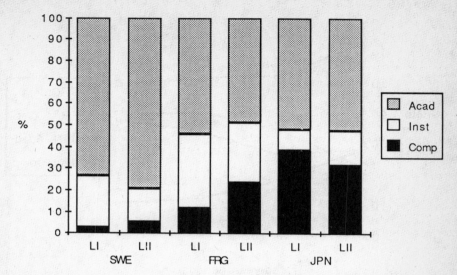

Figure 5.5 Institutional-sector shares of accumulated, 1973–84, paper outputs, by country and subfield

not borne out by the INSPEC data displayed in the column chart of Figure 5.5. To be more precise, the hypothesis does receive some support from West Germany but not from Sweden or Japan. What stands out is the fact that the institutional patterns that were found within the general field are observable also in the subfields: the relatively large share of (i) the academic sector in the case of Sweden, (ii) the company sector in the case of Japan, and (iii) the institute sector in the case of West Germany.

The institutional patterns outlined above have not changed dramatically over the twelve-year period. However, certain broad trends are discernible. Figure 5.6 provides a selective view of these changes (the exclusion of Sweden from the chart is due to the small-number problems posed by the time series of that country). We may note that the portion of the West German output accounted for by the company sector has undergone a steady decline, accompanied by a rise on the part of the institutes. In Japan, by contrast, the company-sector share has grown continuously while that of the academic sector has diminished. These patterns of change are stated here merely as a guidepost for further inquiry and a source of conjectures about the national development efforts. Again, it is clear that questions regarding the significance and determining factors of the patterns cannot be answered on the basis of the search data alone.

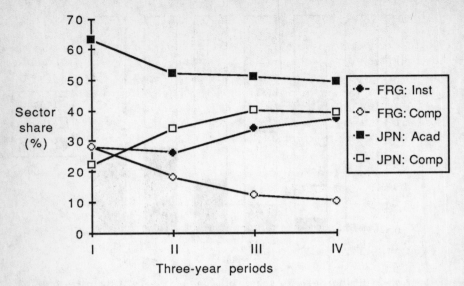

Figure 5.6 Institutional-sector shares of paper production, by country and three-year period, 1973–84

Actor-level patterns

The composition of the three sectors in terms of contributing organizations will now be examined. Patent data will be used chiefly in the analysis of the company sector.

ACADEMIC INSTITUTIONS

As was pointed out earlier, paper counts have not (with the exception of Sweden, where little additional effort was required) been carried out for individual sources within this category. Nevertheless, some well-supported impressions have been gained that are worth stating. In every country one finds—as might be expected—that some sources figure more prominently on the lists than others; in Japan, for instance, this is true of the Tokyo Institute of Technology, the University of Tokyo and Osaka University with its Institute of Laser Engineering. What is more noteworthy, however, is the fact that, in both West Germany and Japan, contributions to the laser literature are broadly dispersed over a large number of universities and other academic institutions. The most salient feature of the Swedish situation, on the other hand, is the marked concentration (by nearly 60 per cent) of the academic output to a single source, namely the Chalmers Institute of Technology—most notably the CTH Department of Electrical Measurements.

INSTITUTES

The institute-sector sources of three countries are listed, in the order of the paper quantities contributed, in Tables 5.7–5.9. The results can be summarized as follows:

In Sweden, the sector production is strongly concentrated, with two institutes accounting for 85 per cent of the total, the Microwave Research Institute (IM; later renamed Institute of Microelectronics) and the Defense Research Establishment. Our data corroborate the

Table 5.7 Swedish sources in the institute sector, with number of papers produced

Sources	Nos. of papers
Instituet för mikrovågsteknik (IM)	9
Försvarets forskningsanstalt (FOA)	8
Flygtekniska försöksanstalten	1
Statens bakteriol. laboratorium	1
Stiftelsen för metallurgisk forskning	1

Table 5.8 West German sources (categories) in the institute sector, with number of papers produced

Sources	Nos. of papers
Max-Planck-Gesellschaft	181
Grossforschungseinrichtungen	95
Bundesanstalten	68
Battelle	15
'Blaue Liste'	10
Fraunhofer-Gesellschaft	10
Einrichtungen d. ind. Gemeinschaftsforschung	2

Table 5.9 Japanese sources in the institute sector, with number of papers produced

Sources	Nos. of papers
Electrotechnical Laboratories	108
Inst. Phys. Chem. Res., Saitama	51
Nat. Res. Lab. Metrology	49
J. Defense Agency Establishments	43
Min. of Post & Telecom./Radio Res. Lab	16
Gov't Ind. Res. Inst., Osaka	4
Prof. societies	7
Others (var. small, mostly single-item, sources)	26

impression conveyed by the fiber optics and VLSI surveys of IM as a national center for electronics and optoelectronics R&D.

In West Germany, the number and variety of institutes involved are considerable. However, a few categories are credited with a large majority share of the overall sector output. These are, first, the Max-Planck Institutes with some 48 per cent (the following sources are clearly dominant: the MPI für biophysikalische Chemie with its laser research unit, the MPI für Quantenoptik and the MPI für Plasmaphysik; the latter, however, is classified as a national center); second, the Grossforschungseinrichtungen, or national research centers, at 25 per cent (again, certain large producers stand out, such as the DFVLR (Deutsche Forschungs-und Versuchsanstalt für Luft- und Raumfahrt) and the Kernforschungsanlage Jülich); and, third, the Bundesanstalten, or federal research institutes, at 18 per cent. The remaining categories are minor contributors, the smallest being the institutes of the industrial research associations. A comparison with the institute lists obtained in the fiber optics and VLSI surveys underscores the strong positions held by the Max-Planck institutes and the national research centers in the laser field (some MPIs, but no national centers, are present in fiber optics; neither category is represented in VLSI). This, of course, accords with the view of laser technology as a relatively research-intensive field.

What stands out in the Japanese list is the dominant role of the national or governmental R&D establishments. Nearly 90 per cent of the sector production is attributable to sources of this type. As in the case of fiber optics, the list is headed by the Electrotechnical Laboratory of the Agency of Industrial Science and Technology.

COMPANIES

The institutional actors presented in the following include both paper and patent producers. It has already been pointed out that an overwhelming majority of the laser patent assignees are indeed to be found in this sector. What has not been considered is the fact that not all patents are institutionally assigned; there are also 'inventor's patents', or patents which are held exclusively by individuals. A brief remark on the composition, in this respect, of the US patent material is in order. An examination of the national outputs reveals that the proportion of inventor's patents varies widely, from Sweden's 26 per cent, to West Germany's 13 per cent, down to Japan's 2 per cent. How are these differences to be accounted for? The available data only permit us to speculate on the underlying conditions. For instance, the differential shares may seem reasonable given the INSPEC-based findings regarding the relative weight of the academic sector in the three countries, and given the assumption that academics are an important category in the generation of inventor's patents in the laser field. The fact that the Japanese universities, unlike those of Sweden and West Germany, may and do engage in patenting is also relevant as it would tend to reduce the volume of unassigned patents; however, it would not, in this case, be sufficient to account for the exceedingly small percentage shown by Japan.

Tables 5.10 and 5.11 give the rankings by output of the company-sector sources of journal articles and patents in the laser field. When examining the patent columns, the reader should bear in mind that

Table 5.10 Company-sector sources of papers (1973–84) and US patents (1975–83), ranked by number of items produced

Country	Papers	Patents
SWEDEN (all sources)	LM Ericsson (2) Volvo (1) Focus Laserteknik (1)	Bofors (8) Saab-Scania (4) AB ID-Kort (1) AB Nike Hydraulik (1) AB Samefa (1) -Asea (1) Micronic AB (1) Siemens (1)
WEST GERMANY (top 10)	Siemens (60) AEG Telefunken (43) Philips GmbH (11) Zeiss (Oberk.) (9) Standard Elektrik Lorenz (7) MBB (6) Lambda Physik GmbH (4) Bosch (4) Messer Griesheim (3) Disa Elektronik (2) (Note: there are six additional sources at the two-paper level; one of them, Kraftwerk Union, is also among the top ten on the pat. list.)	Siemens (45) MBB (18) Krautkramer-Bransoner (14) Bayer (10) Erwin Sick GmbH (8) Kraftwerk Union (8) Licentia Patentverw. GmbH (8) Hauni-Werke Korber & Co. (7) Hoechst (7) U.S. Philips Corp. (5)
JAPAN (top 10)	NTT (378) Hitachi (111) NEC (109) Fujitsu (97) Mitsubishi El. (51) Matsushita El. (41) NHK (26) Kokusai Denshin Denwa (24) Toshiba (22) Sharp (13)	Hitachi (64) NEC (44) Fuji Photo Film (41) Matsushita El. (37) Canon (28) Toshiba (27) Fujitsu (15) Mitsubishi El. (14) Olympus Optical (13) NTT (378)

nationality has been determined on the basis of the inventor's country of residence, which need not be the same as the assignee's country of registration. A few discrepancies of this kind do appear in the tables.

Table 5.10 provides a parallel listing, for each country and in the order of output volumes, of the company-sector producers of papers and patents, respectively. Let us first consider the paper-source column, beginning with a quick glance at the Swedish situation. Sweden, as noted earlier, is something of an extreme case in view of the very limited contribution of the company sector to the laser literature. We can now see that the modest sector output of four items has been generated by three sources, including one small, specialized laser-technology firm.

The complete West German and Japanese paper-source lists—only the top portions are shown in the table—are of respectable length, the total number of contributing companies amounting to 44 and 32, respectively. In both countries, certain high-volume producers stand out: on the German side, Siemens and AEG, with a joint share of the country's company-sector output of 54 per cent; on the Japanese side, most strikingly, NTT, with a national sector share of 41 per cent (the reader should be reminded here of the somewhat unclear sector affiliation of NTT). A difference which may be noted is that the West German list shows a very rapid decline from the leading duo to the long string of small contributors, while the Japanese list contains a group of relatively large contributors which separates the leader from the 'tail'.

Now to the patent column of Table 5.10. On the background of the paper-source lists, the following picture presents itself:

1. What stands out in the case of Sweden is the fact that the list is dominated by certain defense-oriented assignees. The German assignees, and even more so the Japanese, are predominantly civilian. We may also note, in the case of Sweden, that there is no overlap between the paper and patent lists, even though the lists are exhaustive. It is possible that the extremely meager paper contribution of the Swedish company sector is, at least in part, due to publication constraints imposed on military R&D.
2. The West Germany patent lists, like the paper list, is headed by Siemens. Also, the hierarchy is similarly shaped, with a steep decline from the leader to the large group of small producers. Furthermore, we can see that there is some overlap between the lists, however limited. A notable imbalance is the weak patent position (held by the subsidiary Licentia) of paper co-leader AEG. The reason for this is not clear.
3. The Japanese patent lists resembles the paper list in shape as well as in content. Thus, the hierarchy is again relatively broad at the top, with several large contributors in close attendance of the leader. The overlap between the lists is, in this case, very considerable: seven of

the top ten patent assignees appear on the INSPEC list, and Hitachi and NEC are among the first three on both lists. What may seem puzzling here is the spectacular drop of NTT from first to last position as we move from papers to patents. It is important to know that NTT—whose R&D activities in the laser field are known to be sharply focused on semiconductor devices—is not itself a manufacturer of telecommunications equipment. Instead, it has established close relations with certain large domestic suppliers, primarily NEC, Hitachi and Fujitsu. These three companies are all to be found on the patent list, two of them in the topmost ranks. This raises the question as to how the technical knowledge generated by the NTT laboratories is transferred to the equipment makers. Our data suggest that mechanisms other than patenting and licensing are used—assuming that reliance on domestic patenting alone would not be satisfactory to NTT.

Table 5.11, finally, is shown as a complement to the patent column of Table 5.10. It identifies, for each country, the assignees holding two or more highly cited (HC) patents. With due reservations about the small numbers involved, a comparison of the HC lists with the overall lists brings to light the following, now familiar, patterns: on the West German side, once again, agreement between the lists is limited essentially to the fact that both have Siemens as a clear-cut leader, separated by a substantial gap from the nearest rivals. A majority of the German HC assignees are too small in terms of total output to be included in the overall list; or, to put it differently, there are several high-ranking overall contributors who are weak in terms of HC patents. On the

Table 5.11 Patent assignees credited with at least two highly cited patents (1975–80)

Sweden	West Germany	Japan
Saab-Scania (3)	Siemens (17)	Hitachi (12)
	Jenaer Glasw.Schott (3)	Fuji Photo Film (11)
	F:a Dr. Joh. Heidenheim (3)	NEC (11)
	Krautkramer-Branson (3)	Matsushita El. (9)
	Licentia. Pat.verw. GmbH (3)	Canon (7)
	Gebr. Eickhoff M.u.E. (2)	Toshiba (5)
	Richard Wolf GmbH (2)	Mitsubishi El. (4)
	TED Bildplatten AG (2)	Sony (4)
	Winkler & Dunnebier (2)	Hoya Glass Works (3)
		Hagiwara (2)
		Nippon Kagaku (2)
		Nippon Selfoc (2)
		NTT (12)

Japanese side, by contrast, a high degree of correspondence obtains between the two lists.

Concluding remarks

It seems appropriate now to round off the presentation of laser-field findings by briefly reviewing the major observations in a broader technological context, and by offering a summary appraisal of the on-line scanning experience.

The major patterns observed

To what extent are the patterns found in the laser field shaped by the requirements of that particular technology and by the specific, laser-related conditions obtaining in the different countries? A brief glance at the other fields surveyed at the Research Policy Institute—i.e. genetic engineering, fiber optics, VLSI and robotics—may yield at least a partial answer.

The most salient result of such a comparison is that the laser case confirms many of the general observations made in the other surveys. The following features are particularly noteworthy:

1. An aggregate national-share pattern suggesting that the Japanese R&D efforts are stronger not only in absolute, but also in relative (GERD-share) terms.
2. An overall growth pattern indicating rapidly expanding activities in Japan, in contrast with the more moderate or near-horizontal growth trends of West Germany and Sweden.
3. An intra-field pattern showing a tendency for Swedish efforts to be more narrowly applications or development-oriented than those of West Germany and Japan (in the cases of VLSI and fiber optics, this is combined with a late field entry or delayed activity upswing on the part of Sweden).
4. A sector-level pattern which places Sweden and Japan at opposite ends of the institutional spectrum, as it were, by virtue of the prominent role of the academic sector in the first, and the corporate sector in the latter case; West Germany, with a large and diversified institute sector, can be seen as occupying an intermediate position.
5. An actor-level pattern which, above all, underscores the inherent constraints and possibilities of small versus large national R&D systems; witness the tendency for Sweden to be represented, in any given field and sector, by a small number of actors and for one or two of these to be clearly dominant in the national effort. An interesting

difference between West Germany and Japan appears in the company sector where the contributor hierarchies of the former tend to far more pronounced (typically with Siemens as the undisputed top producer) than those of the latter country.

What, then are the distinguishing features of the laser field when compared with the others? The question is not easily answered in general terms, without going into the descriptive details of the matter. However, one overarching, cross-national trait is readily discernible, namely the breadth of the field in terms of the types of activities and institutions involved. Thus, in our studies, laser technology presents itself as a field which still, despite its age, poses a considerable challenge to the academic research community, which attracts contributions from a large variety of institutes, and which—as a generic technology—offers commercial opportunities to an equally diverse collectivity of companies.

The functions of output data scanning

The study presented in this paper shows how output data of a basic and readily accessible kind may be used in the comparative investigation of the development efforts undertaken by a group of countries in a particular field of technology. It is suggested, in conclusion, that the strength of the output-centered approach illustrated here lies primarily in the performance of two closely interrelated functions.

The first function is that of a scanning device, or a tool for the development of an initial sketch map of the evolving R&D landscape, focusing on the overall dynamics and the major institutional character-istics of the national efforts. A confrontation of the empirical results obtained in the five surveys with our more detailed, qualitative knowledge of the underlying activities and conditions (especially, of course, as regards Sweden) suggests that the on-line scanning approach is indeed useful and broadly valid as a means of capturing significant features of the R&D scene. It stands to reason, however, that the patterns obtained cannot be accepted entirely at face value. As no mapping method can be wholly distortion free, the output-based picture must properly interpreted and qualified for reliable conclusions to be drawn about the actual objects of study.

The second function, which follows from the tentative nature of the descriptive results, is that of a question generator. The data base survey, that is, provides us with a set of questions and hypotheses, general and specific, that will guide further inquiry. Seen as the first step towards a more comprehensive, detailed and reliable charting of the field, the survey performs this 'quizzical' function in two days. First, the weaknesses and uncertainties of the data base material and the exclusive reliance on output indicators inevitably give rise to question of validity and significance that must be dealt with. Second, granted the tenability of the descriptive findings, questions of interpretation and explanation will present themselves that can only be partially or conjecturably answered on the basis of the available output data; such questions and hypotheses, too, will impart structure and direction to subsequent studies. Both forms of question generation are illustrated, explicitly and implicitly, in this chapter.

Notes

1. The methodological portions of this report are, in parts, identical with those of the previously published survey of fiber optics (Granberg, 1985). Data from the fields of fiber optics and VLSI are used at some points in this study for the purpose of comparison.
2. For a presentation and discussion of the concept of a generic technology, see Granberg and Stankiewicz, 1981.
3. The first step in the search procedure (US Pat. Office Class 'Coherent Light Generators') resulted in 215 candidate patents. The second step ('Laser-' in title) produced 317 patents, 166 of which were also in the step-one set. The third step ('Laser-' or 'Coherent Light' as abstract keywords) yielded 731 patents, 336 of which had already been found in the earlier searches. The final set thus included 761 patents, with 27 having Swedish inventors, 277 having German inventors and 457 having Japanese inventors. It is interesting to note that none of these patents has inventors from two of the three countries in question. There are several patents with inventors from more than one country. Seven of the Japanese patents also have a US inventor, 6 of the German patents also have a US inventor and 7 of the German patents have an inventor from a country other than the US.
4. This has been checked for Sweden and Japan by means of a paper count for LI and LII (as opposed to LI and LII separately). The overlaps that were found amounted to 6% and 5%, respectively.
5. The citation index has been constructed as follows:
   [(%HC patents of all patents for a given country): (%HC patents of all patents for the three countries jointly)] x [(average number of cites received per HC patent for the country in question): (average number of cites received per HC patent for the three countries jointly)]

   Example: Sweden obtains an index value for its LI patents = (33.33 : 42.50) x (3.00 : 5.04) = 0.47.

References

Bertolotti, M. (1983), *Masers and Lasers—An Historical Approach*, Adam Hilger Ltd, Bristol, p. 6.

Dummer, G.W. A. (1977), *Electronic Inventions 1745–1976*, Pergamon Press, Oxford, p. 122.

Fishlock, D. (ed.) (1967), *A Guide to the Laser*, London, p. 68.

Granberg, A. (1985), *A Bibliometric survey of Fiber-Optics Research in Sweden, West Germany, and Japan*, Research Policy Institute, Lund.

Granberg, A. and Stankiewicz, R. (1981), *The Development of 'Generic Technologies'— The Cognitive Aspects*, Research Policy Institute, Lund.

Grupp, H. (ed.) (1988). *Technikprognosen mit Patentindikatoren*, Verlag TÜV Rheinland GmbH, Köln, pp. 167ff.

Levitt, M. and Holmes, L. (eds) (1985), *Frontiers of Laser Technology*, Tulsa, p. 1.

Pavitt, P. (1985), 'Patent Statistics as Indicators of Innovative Activities: Possibilities and Problems', *Scientometrics*, vol. 7, nos. 1–2.

STU (1984), *FoU-landskapet i Förbundsrepubliken Tyskland*, STU-information nr 405-1984, Stockholm.

6 Developing industrial robot technology in Sweden, West Germany, Japan and the USA

Hariolf Grupp, Ulrich Schmoch, Beatrix Schwitalla and Anders Granberg

Introduction, demarcation and overview

As a result of three basic technologies:

1. Servomechanics, developed in the 1940s at the Argonne nuclear research centre;
2. Digital computer and data processing technology, developed in the early 1950s for, among other things, the control of numerically controlled machine tools; and
3. Semiconductor electronics, also developed in the 1950s.

the industrial robot represents an advanced technological development which basically involves the integration of mechanics and electronics; this is sometimes described by the term 'mechatronics'. Robot technology comprises the following individual technological areas: kinematics, drive technology, control technology, electronic data processing and sensor technology. Data processing and sensor technology, in particular, are not always located 'on the equipment' but may go far beyond it. This raises the problem of delimiting the robot from its peripherals. In this contribution the mechanics (the 'equipment') and the controls, as well as the interfaces with superordinated computers and sensors are regarded as belonging to the industrial robot, though not the computers or sensors themselves (Grupp and Hohmeyer, 1988, p. 643).

Robots are nearly always classified as belonging to handling machines and hence unambinguously to mechanics. In the field of mechanics the specific characteristic of the robot is its free programmability, i.e. robots are seen primarily as mechanical equipment furnished with flexible control. Within the concept of mechatronics it would also be conceivable to classify the robot, more especially the intelligent robot, as falling within the category of information technology, its specific feature being the translation of processed information into *mechanical actions* (computer with attached motion actuators). Comparison of the European definition of the robot with the Japanese definition shows that the latter puts greater emphasis on the control, programming and intelligence functions of the equipment (*combination of motion functions* with the functions of judgment, recognition, adaption or learning).

There is a further difference between the Japanese and the Western definitions of a robot, one which has resulted in misunderstandings, especially in the past, in connection with the interpretation of the very high Japanese robot employment figures: the Japanese definition expressly includes automatic handling systems which are *not* flexible, or flexible only on the basis of *mechanical intervention*, i.e. systems which lack free, flexible programmability. In Western Europe and the USA, such permanently or mechanically programmed motion systems are *not* regarded as robots. In technical parlance they are known as pick-and-place equipment. More recently, in adaptation to the Western definition of a robot, the term 'high technology robot' has come to be used in Japan (Yano, 1985); this corresponds to Western understanding of a robot and does not include pick-and-place equipment (these demarcation aspects follow Grupp and Hohmeyer, 1988, p. 643).

The vast and complex field of robotics can be subdivided according to technical types (e.g. according to kinematics, types of drive, or nominal load). In this contribution, however, the classification will be according to application. For a closer investigation of the state of technology four areas of application—spot welding, arc welding, painting and assembly—are chosen. In terms of installed equipment and turnover, these four areas are the most important both in Japan and in the USA, and indeed also in the Federal Republic of Germany. This is likely to continue to be the case into the next decade (Smith and Heytler, 1985).

Spot welding is the oldest and most widespread application of tool-handling robots. In the USA spot welding is still the largest application area. The first spot welding robots were installed at General Motors, USA, in 1969 (26 Unimate robots). In the Federal Republic of Germany the first spot welding robots were used at Daimler Benz in 1971. In the spot welding field saturation of the market has been achieved also in Japan (Yano, 1985) and is impending in the Federal Republic (Schraft, 1985). The major technical demands are rapid acceleration, flexibility (six axes), high nominal load and resistance to wear and tear. Spot welding robots make relatively small demands on control and sensor technology. Employment of robots for spot welding is largely confined to the motor industry, although in the Federal Republic of Germany a few of them are at present being employed in the production of domestic appliances (refrigerator chassis etc.).

Spray painting, until about 1980, was the second most important area of application in the Federal Republic of Germany, after spot welding, but since that date it has decreased in importance. In Germany painting robots are employed principally in the ceramics industry, the electrical appliances industry and in the automobile ancillary industry. In the motor industry, because of its stringent demands (especially in the application of finishing coats), painting robots are still only at the initial stage of their utilization. In this field of application, more than in any other, the early use of multipurpose industrial robots was not a success. The principal technical requirements are a high degree of flexibility (more than six axes), easy programmability, great speed, protection against explosion (flammable solvent vapours), adequate work space, good track holding, sufficient load-bearing and a low corner error. A low corner error is important for the spraying behaviour at the reversal points (good overlap of spray path; Schiele, 1984).

Application in *arc welding* is much more widespread in Japan than in the Federal Republic of Germany or in the USA. In Japan it is now the biggest market for industrial robots (Yano, 1985). Because of the great number of manufacturers the prices there have generally collapsed. In Europe a great future is being promised for this area of application (Schraft, 1985). Technological requirements are, in particular, great track accuracy and stringent control.

About 60 to 70 per cent of the production costs of an average industrial product are incurred in *assembly*. This is therefore the field where the biggest growth rates are generally being predicted. Employment of assembly robots is strikingly underdeveloped in Europe compared with Japan or with the USA, even though the Japanese figures probably include simple pick-and-place machines. The demands on technology are particularly great in assembly; here the industrial robot is directly competing with human skills (especially in the three-dimensional fitting of component parts). Specific technological requirements are, most notably, a high degree of repetitive accuracy and a high track speed. At present 80 per cent of all assembly robots in Japan are used for the installation of printed circuits (two-dimensional assembly). Some additional features of the four main fields of application are considered elsewhere (Grupp *et al.*, 1987).

The main purpose of this contribution is to explore the range of applicability of science and technology indicators in the field of industrial robots. From this viewpoint the case of robots is just a paradigmatic case study. So far this chapter follows the guidelines described elsewhere in this book (see Grupp's chapter in this volume). However, as will be shown in the following, the combination of various science and technology indicators leads—if correctly interpreted—to a valid and most helpful representation of trends in robot research and technology; thus, the reader will be provided with a considerable amount of information on this field of research and technology in the United States of America, Japan, West Germany and Sweden.

This contribution, by its nature, does not allow for a microlevel analysis of R&D activities as provided in the previous chapter by

Granberg on lasers. The discussions which follow are focused on conditions and developments on the national level. Only some parts of the patent and literature statistics are broken down to the institutional level. For technometric indicators such disaggregation is made difficult by the fact that some technical information on robots is considered as confidential by the manufacturers and may not be displayed here. As regards international trade data, analysis at the microlevel is generally not feasible (see also Grupp's chapter in this volume).

The next section presents the data sources used and considers the problem of source heterogeneity. The third and fourth sections then discuss the assessments that can be made on the basis of patent statistics and literature data (bibliometrics), respectively. The fifth section centres around technometric properties of industrial robots. The following deals with international trade in robot-related product groups. The fifth and sixth sections are essentially a revised reprint of parts of a prior publication (Grupp and Hohmeyer, 1988, pp. 643–51). The seventh section tries to combine the various data and information sources and explores the correlations between the indicator sets. The last section provides an outlook on the time regime between research, development, innovation and commercialization in the robot field.

Data sources

The data used in this contribution stem from various sources. Their compilation was *not* performed in a concerted effort although it was agreed already at the beginning of the three countries' study in 1984 that robotics is a technology of major interest to all parties (see also Kondo in Chapter 7 of this volume).

Early in 1987 patent data was compiled on-line by FgG-ISI from the then operating—but now extinct—data base PATSEARCH (Host: PERGAMON). This is the source of our US patent data. European (EPO; European Patent Office) and German (DPA; Deutsches Patentamt) patent applications were extracted from PATDPA (Host: STN; Scientific and Technical Information Network) by excluding double counting. A combination of keywords and classification symbols of USPOC (US Patent Office Classification) and IPC (International Patent Classification) was used; the details are given elsewhere (Schmoch *et al.*, 1988, pp. 110). For the importance of combined patent searches, see Chapter 4 in this book. The patents were assigned to countries of origin by residence of the inventors. This means for example, that an invention by a citizen living in West Germany, the laboratory being located in that country, was regarded as German even if the patentee is a US corporation. The data base properties are extensively discussed elsewhere (see Schmoch *et al.*, 1988) and not repeated here. The construction of the new patent indicators applied is also discussed by Schmoch and Grupp (1989).

The bibliometric data was compiled on-line from INSPEC by RPI (Research Policy Institute) and STU (Swedish Board for Technical Development) in 1986. They do not include data on the USA. The search was set up so as to cover, first of all, the 'focal field' of industrial robotics (defined by the index term 'industrial robots'). Within that field, two sub-areas were distinguished: one hardware–oriented (CS200: control equipment and instrumentation) and one software–oriented (index term 'programming' or C6140: programming languages). In addition, three 'background fields' relevant to the development of industrial robots were also scanned on-line, namely (1) control theory and automata theory (C1300 or C4220); (2) artificial intelligence (C1230); and (3) pattern recognition and image processing (C1250 or A4230S or A4230V). As regards publication type, only journal articles were retrieved. For further details of the bibliometric approach see also Granberg's chapter in this book.

The technometric approach is outlined in several publications (Grupp *et al.*, 1987; Grupp and Hohmeyer, 1988; for a summary, see Chapter 4 in this volume). Specifications and data for industrial robots were compiled in 1986. To this end 25 interviews were conducted in Germany, 8 in the USA, 14 in Japan, and 3 in Sweden. The data collection also included information requested in writing from a large number of manufacturers (prospectuses, specification sheets, technical data, etc.) and exhibition materials.

Bilateral trade data from the West German foreign trade statistics (WA; Warenverzeichnis für die Aussenhandelsstatistik) were extracted. This is because international data compilations (SITC; Standard International Trade Classification) do not specify for industrial robots. However, a detailed examination of the West German foreign trade balance sheet with regard to industrial robots still comes up against the problem that even at the lowest possible breakdown level the product list for the foreign trade statistics contains no product group which includes industrial robots exclusively. Instead robots are always listed among other equipment, so that an accurate extraction of economic indicators is impossible. However, in interpreting the figures about to be discussed it is helpful to remember that industrial robots within the product groups under examination always represent the product with the highest standard prices, so that at least a rough estimate is possible on whether robots predominate or are insignificant within the product groups examined.

Spot welding robots are included under fully automatic welding equipment with resistance welding (WA 8511 340), painting robots under automatic machines and equipment for surface treatment (WA 8459 832), arc welding robots under arc equipment for fully-automatic welding (WA 8511 320) and assembly robots under 'other machines' for lifting, loading, unloading or conveying (WA 8422 879). In addition to the above-mentioned difficulty of locating industrial robots within more broadly defined product groups, there is the additional fact that welding robots are occasionally listed not under mechanical but under electrical engineering products. These difficulties of delimination should not be lost sight of in the considerations which follow, even though more reliable data than those obtainable from the product list are not available.

Industrial development

Table 6.1 compares the countries' specialization trends in US patents and European or German patent applications. For the differences in the legal patent systems see Schmoch *et al.* (1988). According to the phase model (see Chapter 4), patent statistics reflect industrial development trends (as opposed to basic research trends) primarily. The specialization index (Revealed Patent Advantage—RPA) is sometimes referred to as an 'activity index' (see Schmoch and Grupp, 1989), a term which is somewhat misleading as the denominator of that indicator contains all patents of the country in question and all countries' patents in the particular field of technology. Therefore a high level of activity might result in a low 'activity' value if there is strong activity in other fields or if other countries have little activity in fields other than that under consideration.

Bearing this in mind, the specialization trend in US robot development is not significant: the country was not particularly strong in this field over the total period considered. This applies both to domestic and foreign (EPO/DPA) property rights. As the patent examination period at the USPTO (US Patent and Trademark Office) is about 2–3 years, the 1983–5 patent dates correspond roughly to the 1981–2 priority dates. Since the overall US patenting activity decreased during the period recorded in Table 6 (but not so in the robotics field), the below average specialization in robotics now seems to be improving. Japan has always

Table 6.1 Specialization index RPA in US patents (by patent date) and EPO/DPA applications (by priority date) in the field of industrial robots

Country	USPTO			EPO/DPA	
	1975–78	1979–82	1983–85	1981–82	1983–84
USA	−31	−4	−14	−20	−29
JAP	101	33	36	98	57
FRG	−4	−46	−48	−65	10
SWE	185	114	109	135	125

been strongly specialized in robot development, more so in Europe than in the United States. Exactly the same applies to Sweden. The below average specialization of West Germany was terminated in the first years of the 1980s and the country is now placed at about world average in robot-related developments.

Inventors, applicants and patent attorneys, by and large, have a preference for domestic patenting. For hobby inventors this is the cheapest way to gain the honour of receiving a patent grant. The relevant inventor laws in various countries force corporations, for the sake of their employees, to apply for patents—but not abroad. Thus, it is critical that activities should be observed at more than one patent office (Schmoch and Grupp, 1989).

It is suggested that patent indicators be based mainly on foreign applications—because of the international importance of such applications—when comparing invention activities between countries or corporations. Therefore, every *patent position indicator* should be derived from the nominal numbers of patents applied for at more than one patent office.

Unlike specialization trends, patent position indicators should also contain corrections for the preference of patent applicants for their country of residence and the technology specific strategic preference to apply for patents in countries considered to be relevant market-places. With these corrections a so-called *International Technological Performance (ITP)* was defined. The formulae are explained at length elsewhere (Schmoch *et al.*, 1988, p. 54) and are not reported here. Finally, the *Revealed Technological Performance (RTP)* combines the output indicator ITP with the market preferences in order to indicate the bandwidth of output uncertainty in patent statistics due to corporate strategies. The different RTP indicator values define a bandwidth of technological positions. The bandwidth takes into account the uncertainty factors due to different strategic patenting policies of the corporations or countries compared in the robotics field (per year and per region or market). The patent positions in the particular markets compared are given by the edges of the RTP band and thus reflect technology output *and* regional corporate preference factors.

Figure 6.1 indicates that in the 1970s the three large countries under examination were essentially on the same patenting level. In the case of the USA, we observe a more or less steady increase for 1977 up to the invention year 1973, followed by a decline. The same is found for West German robot technology, with a late take-off in 1982 and a similar decline in 1984. The take-off in the case of Japan is more dramatic, but the levelling trend starts one year earlier (in 1982). Swedish data are not included in Figure 6.1 due to lower absolute numbers and hence stronger fluctuations (see Figure 6.2).

From Figure 6.1 it is to be concluded that, despite the fact that regional

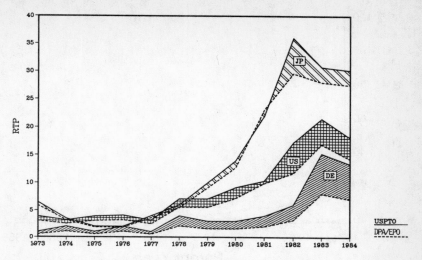

Figure 6.1 Revealed technological position (RTP indicator) for industrial robots by year of invention (priority year) for three selected countries

corporate strategies do exist, a clear ranking in terms of technology output is possible: Japanese companies lead the world in the 1980s. West German technology must be considered quite strong since the country is much smaller than the United States and the patent positions are close to each other. In the three countries under consideration, patent application activity has now ceased to grow. But this should not be interpreted in terms of a decline of technological position (which, unfortunately, is often done by other authors) since a considerable number of new inventions are still produced every year (at least in Japan), adding up to an ever increasing stock of existing patents. In terms of differential calculus the correct interpretation of the findings is that the second time differential coefficient is zero. This means that the rate of growth of increase (the acceleration) in the existing patent stock vanishes. It should be mentioned that innovation theories do claim that the pool of possible inventions in a certain field of technology is not infinitely large but that there is a point in time when this pool is completely exploited by industrial property rights. As early as 1935 Gilfillan mentioned the 'cumulative aspect of inventions' (Gilfillan, 1935). A recent review of this aspect may be found elsewhere (Schmoch *et al.*, 1988, p. 53). The exploitation of robot technology has far progressed; our data suggest that the point of inflection (of an assumed S shape growth curve) was passed around 1982 (see Figure 6.1).

Figure 6.2, by contrast, is based only on US patents by patent (grant) date. Here the large number of domestic US patents with no international relevance is striking. Because the pending period in some

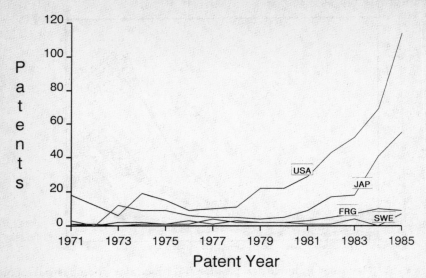

Figure 6.2   US patents for industrial robots by patent year (grant date) for four selected countries

modern fields of technology is up to 3 years or even more, the leveling off is not yet visible in the 1985 grants.

Figure 6.2 provides a picture of the relative positions of Japan, West Germany and Sweden in the US patent system, all of them being foreign patentees. It can be seen that the Swedish and German patent positions were at the same level in the seventies. This indicates a very strong position of the Swedish development laboratories in robotics. In the eighties West German activities grew considerably (this is also indicated by Figure 6.1) whereas Swedish activities stagnated. Due to the small Swedish numbers, fluctuations for example in the patent year 1985 should be interpreted with caution.

The keyword search strategy is suited, above all, to ensuring early detection of the spread of a new technology to other technical and economic areas (the process of *technology diffusion*). If the preliminaries of the patent application prior to commercialization are considered, the diffusion-oriented actions adopted by competing companies and entire national economies can be detected at an early stage (Schmoch and Grupp, 1989).

If one applies the *entropy indicator* (First derived by Kodama (1987) from information theory for the analysis of research and development expenditures; see Grupp (1988) for details of its use in scientometrics) to technology diffusion—with the aim of obtaining a measure for the equality of involvement of industry branches affected by the spread of technology—one finds, in the case of robotics, that after a phase of diffusion up to 1982 a phase of concentration has begun (see Figure 6.3).

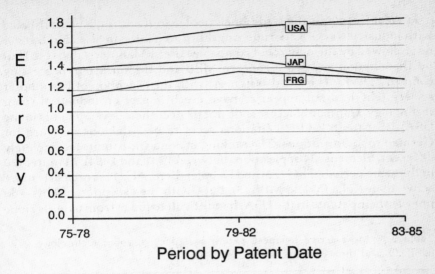

Figure 6.3 Subfield entropy (diffusion) of industrial robots in selected countries between 1975 and 1985 based on patent data (by patent date at the USPTO)

Some interested branches obviously found, at least in Japan and West Germany, that robot technology is not suitable or not competitive enough for them. If one bears in mind the decline of robot patent applications after 1982, it becomes clear from Figure 6.3 that some competitor branches went out of the field, but that nothing happened to the core of robot technology. This particular key technology entered the consolidation phase in an economic sense. The entropy indicator for US robot patents lacks comparability (see Grupp, 1989) as it is based on domestic patents which are less well related to corporate strategies.

The most important actors in industrial robot development as identified by US patents are given in Tables 6.2 to 6.4 per country. Also given is the number of citations in other US patents from 1975 to 1985. As in the case of the USA, this includes domestic patents with no external application; only the countries foreign to the US market are compared.

In Japan (Table 6.2) most of the patents are held by Fujitsu-Fanuc or by Hitachi. The government laboratories' inventions are filed by MITI's Agency of Industrial Science and Technology which ranks in a middle position together with Tokico and Mitsubishi. A long list of other companies, including medium-sized ones, follows (not included in the Table). The numbers of citations, in other US patents, to the patents of the listed institutions are not much different; however, the government labs do not seem to have an equally large impact on robot technology as the leading companies. Also Hitachi's patented robot technology is more visible in US patent examinations than Fanuc's, taking into consideration the difference in patent output.

In West Germany, the traditional robot manufacturer, Kuka, affiliated with Industriewerke Karlsruhe Augsburg AG, is the field leader. But it is not followed by the new robot companies (Reis, Manutec, Cloos etc.) but by the aviation and space concern MBB and the nuclear reprocessing company DWK. The listed assignees, with the exception of Fraunhofer society (FhG) do not appear to have much impact on industrial robot technology. Car manufacturers do not protect their developments in the USA. US patents and US citations seem to be a dubious measure for German robot inventions. The ranking in domestic patents is completely different: Siemens (34 applications between 1981 and 1984), Manutec (30 in the same period), FhG (13) and Daimler-Benz AG (11) are clearly more active than Kuka (8) and MBB (5), but—with the exception of FhG—do not file their patents in the USA. It is difficult to judge from patents alone

Table 6.2 Most active Japanese patent assignees in robot technology (USPTO) and their citation impact, 1975–85

No. of US patents	No. of citations received	Assignee
44	38	Fujitsu Fanuc Group
21	33	Hitachi
10	7	AIST (MITI)
9	21	Tokico Ltd.
9	9	Mitsubishi K.K.
7	8	Toyoda K.K.

Table 6.3 Most active West German patent assignees in robot technology (USPTO) and their citation impact, 1975–85

No. of US patents	No. of citations received	Assignee
5	1	Kuka GmbH
3	1	MBB
3	0	DWK
2	6	FhG
2	2	Industriewerke Karlsruhe Augsburg AG
2	3	Pfaff GmbH

Table 6.4 Most active Swedish patent assignees in robot technology (USPTO) and their citation impact, 1975–85

No. of US patents	No. of citations received	Assignee
10	24	ASEA AB
2	0	AB Carbox
2	6	ESAB AB
2	3	AB Gustavsbergs

whether their robot technology is lacking an international viability or whether the corporations do not aim at legal protection in America (compare the section on technometric judgments entitled: Technological state of the art).

In Swedish robot development ASEA is clearly leading both in number of patents and in citation impact. All other actors, not listed in Table 6.4, took out only one US patent in the 11-year period covered (as is also the case in Table 6.3 for Germany). Swedish corporations, most notably Asea, seem to attach greater importance to US patent rights other than do their German counterparts.

The patent indicators do cover the robot field well but regional corporate strategies play a role indeed and invalidate US patent statistics to a certain extent. Therefore, the combination of data from more than one patent office, as done in this section, is clearly desirable when development output is going to be measured by patent documents.

Research activities

In this section, the USA is not included as the allotted space does not permit an adequate treatment of her large and varied research activities. Publication figures from the INSPEC data bank have been generated for the focal field of industrial robots and for the three background fields (see the section on data sources).

The focal field publication set (Figure 6.4), surprisingly, does not contain many papers in the 1970s. This may be a problem of the data bank which is strong in controls and electronics but less complete in robot mechanics. In the 1980s, Japanese and German research activities took off steeply from the ground level, with Japan gaining the lead over West Germany only in the mid-1980s. On a lower level Swedish activities become visible.

A completely different internation distribution of research activities is obtain in the background fields of robotics: artificial intelligence, pattern recognition and so forth (see section entitled: Data sources). As shown in figure 6.5 (which includes the focal field as well as the background fields, but which is heavily dominated by the far more voluminous output of the latter), Japanese activities were on a very high level already in 1973 with comparably little increase since then (as compared with the focal field of robot technology). The increase in both Japanese and German publications is more or less linear, with Swedish activities staying on a constant level. The Japanese publication output was—in the period covered in Figure 6.5—three times larger than of the Federal Republic, with little change over time. Interpreting these observations one must bear in mind (see section 1) that the intelligence functions of robots have always been of major concern in Japan, more so than in Europe. Many

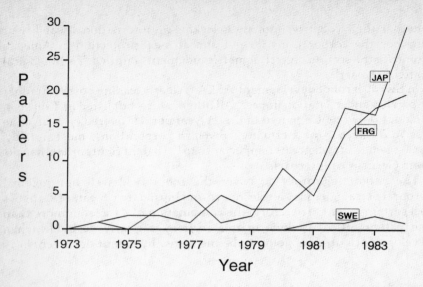

Figure 6.4 Publications in robotics (focal field) by publication year for the three selected countries

academic researchers were attracted by the challenges and possibilities of these research fields and, thus, a greater share of the university-sector efforts was probably dedicated to the intelligence functions of robots than to the classical core research fields (drives, mechanics etc.).

But is it really true that academic research does play a role in the robot field? Who are the main actors in this field according to publication statistics?

For the sake of topicality, only the 1984 set of background-field publications is displayed in Figure 6.6 (focal field and background fields; note, again that the latter are strongly dominant). It turns out that, in all of the countries studied, universities do play a major role in this field. Hence it may *not* be concluded that publication output is strongly related to industrial applications. The institutes (government laboratories, national research centres, private non-profit organizations, and the like) hold their own in this field of research only in Japan and West Germany. Some of them are not aiming at industrial applications but rather at specialized robot solutions in space, nuclear plants, defence and below sea level.

The most active organizations in industrial robot development in terms of publication output in the national context are Hitachi, Mitsubishi, Siemens and ASEA. Because of the acquisition of BBC (by ASEA) which has now taken place, BBC's and ASEA's publications have been combined and are denoted as 'ABB', even though the company did not exist in the time period studied.

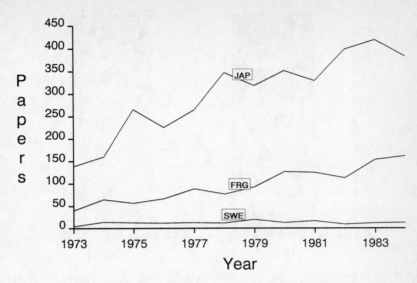

Figure 6.5 Publications in robotics and related fields (background set) by publication year for the three selected countries

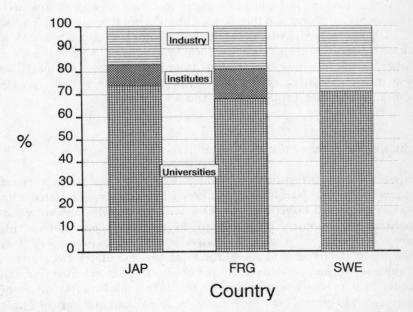

Figure 6.6 Publications in robotics and related fields by sector of origin in 1984 in percentage

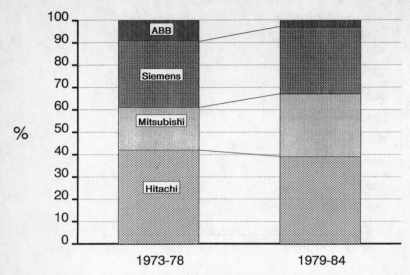

Figure 6.7 Publications in robotics and related fields by four concerns in the 1970s and 1980s in percentage

Figure 6.7 clearly indicates the strong position of Hitachi. The company's share, as well as Siemens', remained nearly unchanged over the 12-year period. Mitsubishi's output in terms of applied research results increased more than their competitors' whereas that of ASEA and BBC (ABB) decreased. Unfortunately the bibliometric figures are too low to allow for structural studies of the focal field alone or of the subfields of robotics. It is interesting to note that the four companies compared do play a major role in patenting, but not necessarily in the foreign US patent statistics (see Tables 6.2, 6.3 and 6.4).

Technological state of the art

Figure 6.8 shows the technometric profile of *assembly robots*. As far as speed is concerned, a clear lead is held by a new US device which is fitted with integral articulated direct electric drive with anti-explosion protection (brushless DC motor). With regard to the listed parameters this superiority is also reflected quantitatively in its transverse speed. It is employed in electronic and computer assembly, for motor car electrics and engineering and occasionally in the chemical industry. Two German bending arm robots are superior to the other machines it terms of maximum and nominal load. However, a nominal load in excess of 5 kg is not required for bending arm robots in most present-day uses. On the other hand, such capability in horizontal bending arm machines is highly

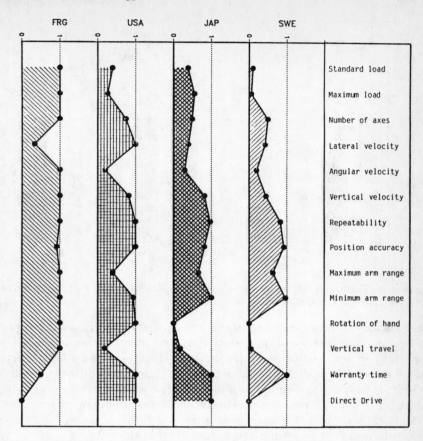

Figure 6.8 Technometric profile at assembly robots (horizontal bending arm types only) in selected countries (1986)

desirable for future assembly tasks (engines, domestic appliances, lorry parts, etc.). The German machines for the medium-load range are thus thrusting into a future market (one manufacturer is a potential large-scale user of assembly robots in the domestic appliances field). In terms of reach the West German machines have a slight lead, and the Japanese machines on offer are at a slight disadvantage with regard to claimed accuracy.

In Figure 6.9, technometric indicator values for robot mechanics, aggregated by technology profiles, are compared. What stands out is the very good position of West German *mechanical industrial robot technology*. The advantage enjoyed by German machines is thought to be due to solid mechanical engineering know-how. This is particularly true of *one* German robot manufacturer. German robots are superior in terms of precision, rigidity, robustness, readiness for operation, wear and tear,

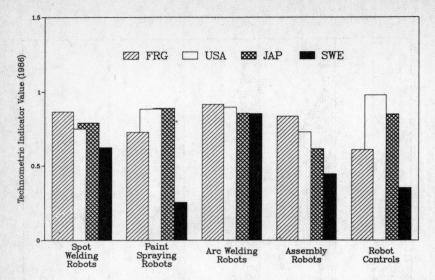

Figure 6.9 Technometric indicator values for industrial robots by application in selected countries (1986)

gear backlash and ease of maintenance. American machines are often rather poor in terms of precision characteristics, a fact conceded—especially in comparison with Japanese products—even by US experts (see e.g. Nevins *et al.*, 1985, pp. 3–52). The judgement of international experts is fully confirmed by the indicators: the parameters for precision, aggregated over all robot applications, show the following characteristics: 0.97 for West German machines, 0.87 for Japanese, 0.79 for Swedish, and 0.71 for American industrial robots.

West German specifications are lagging behind in robot controls. The slight Japanese lag is due to the fact that, for many years, Japanese manufacturers imitated American pioneer achievements—which they are doing to this day with regard to control equipment—instead of showing initiative and an innovative spirit, as they are not increasingly doing. Swedish robot standards are very high considering that the breadth and quality of the development efforts are not being fully conveyed by our indicator values because of the extremely limited number of robot manufacturers (about three, depending on classification).[1]

Foreign trade and competitiveness

The market for industrial robots has been expanding over the past few years; figures for their use, in relation to individual countries, individual years and specific application ranges have, in some cases, increased by over 100 per cent (e.g. in the Federal Republic of Germany for assembly robots in 1986). The world market for robots today has an annual turnover of approximately 5,000 million DM, although this figure includes some Japanese handling equipment which is still, contrary to the customary definition, described as robots. The Federal Republic of Germany is likely to account for 10 per cent of the mid-1980s world market turnover. This means, according to different estimates, between 3,000 and 3,600 robots in 1986. By the end of 1986 well over 12,000 industrial robots were installed in the Federal Republic of Germany. A little more than one-third of the world market is transacted in Japan and about one-fifth in the United States.

As an illustration some detailed economic data are given for arc welding robots only (the other robot categories are summarized in the next section). The average unit value of trade category WA 8511 320 (see the section on Data sources) lies a good deal below the estimated unit value of arc welding robots. For some industrialized countries, however, it falls into the correct order of magnitude; hence one may assume that the arc-welding robots—i.e. the most complex and expensive arc welding equipment—contribute very significantly to the volume of that product group. West Germany's foreign trade figure for the product group is close to the average value for all manufactured industrial goods, i.e. it is neither particularly good nor particularly bad. Foreign trade, if anything, declined at the beginning of the 1980s: good balances were achieved, almost without exception, in relation to Britain, in 1983 and 1984, and also in relation to Japan, but there was very little export to the United States or to Sweden. Annual fluctuations in this product group were considerable, and the export volume is not very great; consequently a few major orders may greatly affect annual results.

A useful indicator of competitiveness is the so-called Revealed Comparative Advantage (RCA). The RCA values indicate the extent to which export surpluses in the product group under consideration deviate from the average for manufactured industrial products (Grupp and Legler, 1987). Light and shade assume clearer outlines for arc welding robots if the RCA indicator is used as a yardstick. In 1985, given the average result of West Germany *vis-à-vis* all countries, the USA and Sweden had a positive showing, and Japan, if anything, the most negative compared to West Germany. Only bilateral data from the West German balance sheet are available since the international trade classification does not allow for a specification of arc welding robots (see the section on Data sources above).

Combining the pieces of partial information on industrial robot R&D

What conclusions are there to be drawn from the conspectus of science, technical and economic indicators for the selected areas of robot application? The slight technological lead of West German manufacturers (Figure 6.9) in *spot welding robots*, based as it is on a high standard of mechanical engineering, would seem to be exploitable, especially with regard to Japan and other countries, but less so with regard to the United States. In spite of overall slightly below-average export results, the German position was clearly enhanced *vis-à-vis* the USA and Japan. This trend can surely be consolidated or continued only if a high standard is maintained for spot welding robots and if the innovations predicted world-wide are embarked upon at an early date.

With regard to *spray painting robots* the West German machines are technologically somewhat behind those from their main competitors (Figure 6.9). Even though the international market result is, on the whole, very positive , it is below average with regard to the United States. It may therefore be assumed that technologically improved painting robots will find sectors of the world market that can be captured. Investment in more efficient technology would probably be repaid by marketing results. In the field of *arc welding robots* there is technological parity at a high level: all the countries under review, including Sweden, have equally good and similarly high specifications (Figure 6.9). Sweden's strength emerges clearly from its foreign trade figures: it is only in the product group comprising arc welding robots that Sweden has been able to achieve, in 1985 and on average over the past few years, an above-average export-import balance *vis-à-vis* the Federal Republic of Germany (see section 6). The overall international competitive position with regard to arc welding robots is undecided: bilateral strengths and weaknesses alternate from country to country. This is one more reason why the West German and the Swedish economy must strive to remain the world lead for arc welding robots; failure to do so would almost certainly result in inroads into the countries' foreign trade. The United States and Japan are not dependent on exports in this particular product group and it is therefore unlikely that a less advanced technology would have a significant influence on international trade sheets.

For *assembly robots* the question of the appropriate foreign trade category is more problematic than for other applications. Although the West German economy dominates all bilateral trade relations in this field, this is probably due chiefly to trade in ordinary fully automatic handling machines rather than in assembly robots. However, the technologically favourable position in the assembly robot field, especially in the medium-load range, would seem to be a guarantee of continued international marketing success in the future. After all, the country's dominant economic position is a fairly recent achievement: against the two major competitors, that position has been held only since the beginning of the eighties.

It is clear from our examination of foreign trade that available statistical data do not ensure the necessary degree of breakdown. It is encouraging to note, however, that industrial robots for different applications are classified in different product groups, and that these product groups—even though they contain other fully automatic equipment—correspond fairly well to the applications chosen in this study. Overall, a fairly positive foreign trade balance emerges for the West German economy with regard to those product groups which include industrial robots. The technical indicator—except for robot control—also shows similarly good values by comparison with the principal competitor countries. The West German economy does not lag behind its main competitors technologically—certainly not in the area of robot mechanics—nor has it adopted a defensive stance in world trade. From both the technological and the mercantile point of view it is holding its own, especially against Japan and the United States.

A similar conjunction of technological and competitiveness assessment may also be performed for other countries provided their respective national trade classification allows for a satisfactory product-group definition of industrial robots.

The patent data cannot be sorted by robot type. In Figure 6.10, therefore, the average technometric indices and the patent ITP indices (see the section on Industrial development) are displayed by country. There is a good correspondence between the two—at least in ranking—with one notable exception: Japanese patents seem to be overvalued and do not correspond to the relevant product specification achievements. The reasons for this kind of strategic foreign patenting must be seen—as interviews in the Japanese Patent office have shown—in the visionary emphasis this country put on places on the notion of 'artificial man', a notion actively promoted by government agencies around 1980 with the very aim of building a strong international patent position in this field. Today the Japanese Patent Office tries to convince applicant companies to take a more realistic stance towards market-oriented patents in robotics. A detailed analysis of these patents has revealed that the team size of Japanese-origin foreign patents (as measured by the number of inventors per patent) is considerably smaller than in other Japanese key technologies (Schmoch *et al.*, 1988, p. 285), which is an indication of the lower R&D staffing cost of the Japanese robot patents and, hence, of the assumption of their lower value.

Patent and publication numbers correlate strongly: time series regression analysis leads to highly significant results both for the focal-field and the background-field papers (level of significance below 1 per cent). This is true for the Japanese as well as for the German data (because of the territorial limits of patent protection, the ITP indicator was used instead of national patent data). The relatively limited Swedish data set shows considerable fluctuations; in this case, time series regressions are not statistically meaningful.

Finally, the bilateral competitiveness indicator RCA as well as FRG

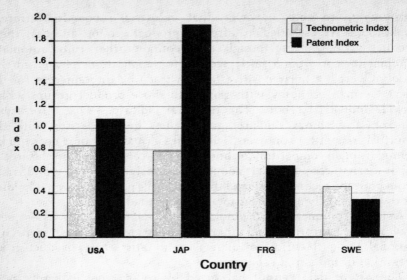

Figure 6.10   Synopsis of technometric and patent indicators for industrial robots in selected countries

production figures for robots were tested for correlations with patent data (ITP and specialization indicators RPA respectively). Various time-lags between the indicators (up to four years, with patents ahead) were allowed for. The best results of the multiple regressions are given in Table 6.5. The Table shows clearly that only some regressions are significant, even if analysis is limited to patents which relate to mechanical parts and not to controls. (The product categories do not always include controls). International trade is obviously—and more so than domestic production—influenced by many non-technological factors which disturb some of the correlations on this high level of disaggregation. However, patent rights and international market success with industrial robots are not completely unrelated despite the fact that:

1. many important characteristics of modern robot technology are not, or only to a limited extent, patentable (software); and
2. many important characteristics in robot mechanics are free of patent protection because the relevant patents have expired.

In conclusion, it may be said that the network of indicators provides interesting additional clues and supports the framing of appropriate interpretations. The case of industrial robots thus illustrates some of the points made in more general terms in Chapter 4 of this volume.

Table 6.5 Levels of significance for time series regressions of selected bilateral economic and patent data (n.a. = not available)

Variables (independent, dependent)	All Robot patents (%)	Robot mechanical patents (%)
ITP (FRG), Production (FRG)	< 10	< 5
RPA (FRG), RCA (FRG, world)	n.a.	< 12
ITP (FRG/USA), RCA (FRG/USA)	< 5	< 1
ITP (FRG/JAP), RCA (FRG/JAP)	uncorrelated	uncorrelated

Outlook on the innovation time regime in robotics

Some comments on the basic role of synoptic applications of various science and technology indicators are given in Chapter 4. A view towards a correlated and consistent set of quantitative data for the evaluation of a given field of science and technology is also provided there.

By way of concluding this case study on industrial robots, it is interesting to analyze the time regime between research, development and commercialization, bearing in mind that we are dealing with a key technology of vital importance for the countries compared. Table 6.6 does not give an unequivocal answer: depending on the indicators selected the best fit time-lag varies. But it is obviously not wrong to argue that robotics R&D tends to lead to early commercialization. Robotics is *not* a field of basic research. It has a time horizon of some one or two years from the date of invention to marketable results. It is extremely interesting to note that in a field like robotics, where patents do play a role, scientific publications in related (applied) research do not appear earlier but rather later (at least in Germany). The novelty of a patent application is questioned by most patent offices if the invention has already been disclosed in a paper or conference contribution. As the

Table 6.6 Time-lag between science and technology indicators in industrial robotics

Variables (independent, dependent)	All Robot patents (years)	Robot mechanical patents (years)
ITP (FRG), Production (FRG)	1–4	1–4
RPLA (FRG), RCA (FRG, world)	n.a.	2
ITP (FRG/USA), RCA (FRG/USA)	1	1
ITP (FRG/JAP), RCA (FRG/JAP)	–	–
ITP (JAP), Publications (JAP)	2	n.a.
ITP (FRG), Publications (FRG)	0–2	n.a.

submission dates of publications are not accessible on-line one may assume that they precede the publication dates (which are known) by one year on average. The fact that there is generally no time-lag between patent priority year (which is usually the same as the year of invention) and paper submission year makes clear why relevant papers (if any) are typically published after priority claims: they are written at about the priority date.

For the future study of the robotics field two major conclusions may be drawn:

1. If one wants to arrive at plausible *predictions* of structural and innovation trends, S&T indicators have to be very up-to-date as the commercialization process is rather short; and
2. The patent literature is as important as scientific papers and conference proceedings in providing access to the latest R&D results.

Robotics R&D may thus be characterized as a highly complex field, which holds many pitfalls but which is none the less amenable to analysis by quantitative methods.

Note

1. For more details of the technometric assessment of robots, see Grupp *et al.* (1987). An abridged version has also been published by Grupp and Hohmeyer (1988).

References

Gilfillan, S.C. (1970), *The Sociology of Invention*, Cambridge/London, 1935; quoted from the paperback edition of 1970.

Grupp, H. (1989), 'The concept of entropy in scientometrics and innovation research—an indicator for institutional involvement in scientific and technological developments', *Scientometrics*, 17, pp. 471–89.

Grupp, H. and Hohmeyer, O. (1988), 'Technological standards for research-intensive product groups and international competitiveness', in A.F.J. van Raan (ed.), *Handbook of Quantitative Studies of Science and Technology*, Elsevier, Amsterdam, pp. 611–73.

Grupp, H. and Legler, H. (1987), *Spitzentechnik, Gebrauchstechnik, Innovationspotential und Preise: Trends, Positionen und Spezialisierung der westdeutschen Wirtschaft im internationlen Wettbewerb*, TÜV Rheinland, Köln.

Grupp, H., Hohmeyer, O., Kollert, R. and Legler, H. (1987), *Technometrie—Die Bemessung des technisch-wirtschaftlichen Leistungsstands*, TÜV Rheinland, Köln.

Kodama, F. (1987), *Dynamics of National R&D Program, Research on Socio-Economic Aspects of Energy Systems*, Mombusho, Tokyo.

Nevins, J., Albus, J., Binford, T., Brady, M. and Caplan, N. (1985), JTECH Panel

Report on Mechatronics in Japan, La Jolla.

Schiele, G. (1984), 'Kenngroessen zum Vergleich von Industrierobotern in der Oberblaechentechnik', *Maschinenmarkt*, 90, pp. 86–9.

Schmoch, U. and Grupp, H. (1989), 'Patents between corporate strategy and technology output: an approach to the synoptic evaluation of US, European, and German patent data', in A.F.J. van Raan, A.J. Nederhof and H.F. Moed (eds), *Science Indicators: Their Use in Science Policy and Their Role in Science Studies*, D.S.W.O. Press, Leiden.

Schmoch, U., Grupp, H., Mannsbart, W. and Schwitalla, B. (1988), *Technikprognosen*, TÜV Rheinland, Köln.

Schraft, R.D. (1987), 'Robots boost production economy', *Transfer*, 2 (1985) pp. 40–52. Reprint in H. Grupp (ed.), *Problems of Measuring Technological Change*, TÜV Rheinland, Köln.

Smith, D.N. and Heytler, P. (1985), *Industrial Robots, Forecast and Trends*, Dearborn.

Yano Research Institute (1985), *The High-Technology Robot Market in Japan*, Yano, Tokyo.

7 Japanese R&D in robotics and genetic engineering[1]

Masayuki Kondo

Introduction

This chapter is primarily intended to indicate some characteristics of the Japanese R&D system—both internally and in comparison with a global system. The methodological approach has been inspired by the attempts in recent years to use various data bases for an analysis of R&D activities and R&D policies, at the level of national or industrial sectors, or even smaller agglomerations such as emerging technological fields. It is realized that the method, although containing many pitfalls, provides a quick and illuminating way of screening a technological landscape which is discussed in some detail in Granberg's chapter. Brief methodological comments are introduced towards the end of this chapter to illuminate for the reader some of the inherent problems in this kind of analysis.

In the following I will analyze and discuss five different aspects of measuring technological change by using quantitative data for patent and publication activity in robotics and genetic engineering: (i) the changing levels of R&D activities in Japan and in the rest of the world; (ii) the relation between R&D activities and information diffusion in Japan, and in other countries; (iii) the time-lag between research results and application; (iv) the Japanese patenting pattern in Japan and abroad; and (v) the relation between the date of publication for journal articles and patents.

Japan and the world

R&D activities

Original scientific papers are one indicator of R&D results. Thus, the level of R&D activity can be studied by analyzing the trend of original paper publication. The Japanese trend and the world trend of original papers in the field of robotics showed a synchronized movement implied from the fact that the correlation coefficient was the highest when there was no time-lag. This was the same in the fields of robots and industrial robots, which are subfields of robotics. In particular, the correlation between the trend of original paper publication in Japan and that in the world with no time-lag was highest, that is, 0.9934 (see Table 7.1). These facts indicate that Japan is one of the leading countries in the world in the field of robotics research. See also Chapter 6 by Grupp *et al.* in this volume.

In the field of genetic engineering, with regard to original papers, the correlation coefficient was the highest when Japan's lag was one year, though the coefficient did not decrease very much with the change of time-lag reflecting the fact that both Japan and the world showed a steady increase. In other words, Japan lagged behind the world by one year with regard to the trend of original paper publication which reflects R&D activities in the field of genetic engineering. This suggested that Japan was a late comer in this field and is struggling to catch up with the outside world.

Table 7.1 shows the correlation coefficients adjusted for degrees of freedom with or without time difference between the Japanese trend and the world trend. The correlation coefficient is the highest when two trends are similar. Then, it can be determined quantitatively whether one trend is lagging behind, or synchronized with, or is going ahead of the other trend by examining the values of correlation coefficients.[2]

Figure 7.1 shows the Japanese trend and the world trend of original papers in the fields of robotics and genetic engineering. Japan and the world show similar trends in the field of robotics, while Japan in the field of genetic engineering shows a more rapid but later expansion than the world in 1980s.

Information diffusion activities

The character of information diffusion activities in Japan and abroad is another important factor affecting the development of a scientific or technological field. This parameter can be analyzed by observing changes in the publication of general articles in journals since those explain new technology or a current technology trend. Their publication can thus be considered as an information diffusion activity in a written form.

The Japanese trend and the world trend of general articles in the fields of robotics and genetic engineering are shown in Figure 7.1. Japan and the world show quite similar and simultaneous movement in the field of genetic engineering. On the other hand, Japan showed a sharper increase in the early 1980s than the world in the field of robotics.

Table 7.1 Correlation analysis of time-lags for original papers and general articles on robotics and genetic engineering (Japan and the world)

(1) Robotics
(a) Original papers

Japan's lag (years)	-3	-2	-1	R 0	1	2
Robotics	—	0.7986	0.9191	0.9883*	0.9566†	0.9092
Robots	0.4752	0.8465†	0.8130	0.9934*	0.8280	0.8105
Industrial robots	—	0.7793	0.8625	0.9758*	0.9042†	0.8708

(b) General articles

Japan's lag (years)	-2	-1	R 0	1	2
Robotics	0.7134	0.8879	0.9841*	0.9446†	0.8095
Robots	0.5029	0.7997	0.9227*	0.8234†	0.6243
Industrial robots	0.7370	0.8949	0.9854*	0.9551†	0.8237

(2) Genetic engineering

Japan's lag (years)	-2	-1	0	R 1	2	3
Original papers	—	0.9213	0.9560	0.9882*	0.9668†	0.9468
General articles	0.8273	0.9267†	0.9986*	0.9244	0.8087	—

Note: *shows the highest coefficient and †shows the second highest one in each row.

The results of correlation analysis for the time difference with regard to general articles were as follows. The correlation coefficient was the highest when there was no time-lag between Japan and the world in the field of robotics see Table 7.1. This was the same in the field of robots and industrial robots, which are subfields of robotics. This means that the Japanese trend of information diffusion activities was in the same phase as the world trend in the field of robotics. Therefore, it could be said that, in the field of robotics, Japan and the world show the same trend with hardly any time lag in either R&D activities or information diffusion activities.

In the field of genetic engineering, the correlation coefficient was the highest when there was no time-lag between Japan and the world with regard to the trend of general article publication, which was also the case for robotics. This means that information diffusion activities in the field of genetic engineering in Japan show the same trend, with no time-lag as to the rest of the world. If taking the second highest correlation

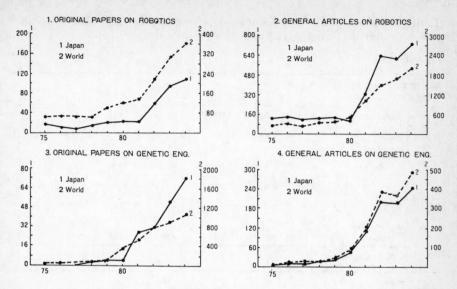

Figure 7.1 Comparison of time-lags for original papers and general articles on robotics and genetic engineering (Japan and the world)

coefficient into account, the Japanese trend was a little ahead of the world trend, which reflects the Japanese enthusiasm in the field of genetic engineering or biotechnology.

The results of original paper analysis suggest that Japan was a little behind the world in R&D activities in genetic engineering. However, Japan showed great interest in genetic engineering and her information diffusion activities were carried out vigorously or a little over enthusiastically.

R&D and information diffusion

The relation between R&D activities and information diffusion activities, in Japan and in the world, has been analyzed. The actual analysis was done by studying the relation between the number of original papers, which represent R&D activities, and the number of general articles, which represent information diffusion activities, in the field of robotics and genetic engineering.

The following points could be observed. In the field of robotics, it seemed that the number of original papers began to increase sharply in 1981 both in Japan and in the world, while the number of general articles began to increase sharply in 1980, both in Japan and in the world, though the tendency was more pronounced in Japan than in the world. This suggests that information diffusion activities began to increase one year

Table 7.2 Correlation analysis of time-lags for general articles against original papers on robotics and genetic engineering (Japan and the world)

(1) Robotics

Lag of general articles (years)		-3	-2	-1	R 0	1	2	3
Japan	Robotics	0.5477	0.8285	0.9777*	0.9252†	0.7826	—	—
	Robots	—	0.6315	0.6617	0.9208*	0.7048	0.7769†	0.4141
	Industrial robots	0.4939	0.8393	0.9931*	0.8920†	0.7209	—	—
World	Robotics	0.8473	0.9389	0.9923*	0.9715†	0.9246	—	—
	Robots	—	0.7622	0.9271	0.9479*	0.9383†	0.7005	—
	Industrial robots	0.8518	0.9480	0.9901*	0.9584†	0.9161	—	—

(2) Genetic engineering

Lag of general articles (years)	-3	-2	-1	R 0	1	2
Japan	0.8972	0.9375	0.9501*	0.9449†	0.9261	—
World	—	0.8396	0.9387	0.9880*	0.9708†	0.9262

Note: *shows the highest coefficient and †shows the second highest one in each row.

earlier than R&D activities in the field of robotics both in Japan and in the world.

In the field of genetic engineering, the number of original papers in the world began to increase in 1979 and the number of general articles began to increase gradually around 1980 and then decreasing in 1983. In Japan, the number of original papers in this field began to increase in 1980 while the number of general articles began to increase gradually around 1980 and decreased in 1983. The results of correlation analysis with time difference are shown in Table 7.2

The trend in time-lag in the field of robotics between general article publication and original paper publication in Japan was the same as that in the world. In the field of industrial robots, the trend of original paper publication lagged behind the trend of general article publication by one year, both in Japan and in the world. This relation in the field of industrial robots reappeared in the field of robotics, which is the union of the field of robots and that of industrial robots, since articles on industrial robots dominated those on robots in number.

In other words, original paper publication was done at the same time as general article publication or a little earlier, if considering the second highest correlation coefficient in the field of robots, while original paper publication was done one year or less later than general article publication in the field of industrial robots. Information diffusion activities were thus carried out at the same time or a little later than R&D activities in a research-oriented field like robots, and information diffusion activities were done a little earlier than R&D activities in an application-oriented field like industrial robots, both in Japan and in the world.

This implies that information diffusion activities begin after R&D activities are accumulated in a research-oriented field. On the other hand, information diffusion activities boost R&D activities to some extent in an application-oriented field. There is a policy implication here that information diffusion activities have an important role to guide R&D activities in an industrial application field.

In the field of genetic engineering, the situation in Japan differed fron the situation in the world. There was no time-lag between the trend of publishing original papers and that of publishing general articles in the world, whereas in Japan, the trend of original paper publication lagged behind that of general article publication by one year. This result reflects the former result that the Japanese trend of original paper publication lagged behind the world trend by one year while the Japanese trend of general article publication synchronized with the world trend in the field of genetic engineering. Information diffusion in the field of genetic engineering in the world was thus done steadily as in a research-oriented field like robots, while the information diffusion in the field of genetic engineering in Japan was done in a more passionate way as in an application-oriented field like industrial robots.

Research-oriented fields versus application-oriented fields

A time-lag was observed between a research-oriented field and its related application-related field, that is, between the field of robots and the field of industrial robots. The results of the correlation analysis, with time differences, are shown in Table 7.3.

In Japan, the trend for industrial robots lagged behind the trend for robots by one year with regard to original paper publication, which represents R&D activities, whereas the trend of industrial robots and the trend of robots were synchronized with regard to general article publication, which represents information diffusion activities. Since the number of general articles outnumbered that of original papers in the field of both robots and industrial robots, the relations between two fields which appeared in all journal articles were the same as those which appeared in general articles. It could be said that a research-oriented field had a time lead against an application-oriented field in R&D activities but that information diffusion activities were done in the same phase in both fields in Japan concerning robotics.

Table 7.3 Comparison of time-lags between research-oriented fields and application-oriented fields—robots and industrial robots

(1) Japan

Lag of industrial robots (years)	-2	-1	0	R 1	2		
All journal articles	0.7186	0.8527†	0.9453*	0.7862	0.5251		
Original papers	0.8492	0.8523	0.8948†	0.9532*	0.6708		
General articles	0.6573	0.8110†	0.9337*	0.7213	0.4240		

(2) World

Lag of industrial robots (years)	-4	-3	-2	R -1	0	1	2
All journal articles	—	0.8459	0.9147	0.9794*	0.9788†	0.8915	0.7224
Original papers	0.6301	0.9578†	0.9613*	0.9378	0.9373	0.9430	0.7569
General articles	—	0.7851	0.8906	0.9744*	0.9698†	0.8697	0.6906

Note: *shows the highest coefficient and †shows the second highest one in each row.

The relation is quite different when comparing the rest of the world with Japan. With regard to general article publication which represents information diffusion activities, the trend for industrial robots had one year time lead against the trend for robots. With regard to original paper publication which represents R&D activities, the trend of industrial robots had a two-year time lead against the trend of robots. It could be said that the interest in robots, a research-oriented field, was, in the world, much influenced by the interest in industrial robots, an application-oriented field.

Thus it could be argued, for robotics, that in Japan a research-oriented field influenced activities in an application-oriented field. Some reasons why Japanese researchers started R&D in robotics before the industrial applications were clearly identified and discussed in the author's paper.[3]

Domestic patents and foreign patents

Two topics were analyzed: (1) the relation between patents applied for in Japan by Japanese and those applied for overseas and; (2) the relation between patents applied for in Japan by Japanese and those applied for in Japan by foreigners.

It is generally thought that patents applied for overseas must be leading ones since costs are high for overseas applications. The patents applied for by foreigners tend to have an earlier phase than the domestic

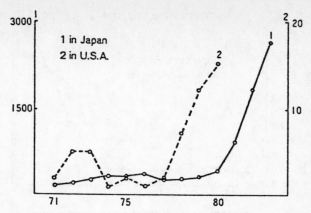

Figure 7.2 Patents by Japanese on robotics, in Japan and in the USA

patents which include various quality of patents. The relation between the trend for robotics patents, applied for by Japanese in Japan, and the trend for original application for patents acquired by Japanese in the United States is shown in Figure 7.2. See also Table 7.4(1). It should be noted that patents acquired in the United States were analyzed according to the date of original application in Japan.

The analysis offers the following observations. First, the trend for patents on robotics applied for by Japanese in Japan shows a horizontal movement followed by a sharp increase from 1980 and onwards. Second, the trend for robotics patents acquired by Japanese in the United States shows more changes before a sharp increase from 1977 onwards. It could be inferred that the time-lag between the two trends might be around three years. The correlation analysis for time differences is shown in Table 7.4(1) which indicates that the trend of original application at the

Table 7.4 Comparison of time-lags for domestic patents and foreign patents

(1) Japanese patents in Japan and in USA

Lag of domestic patents (years)	0	1	2	3	4			
			R					
Robotics	0.1964	0.7719	0.8795†	0.9488*	0.8409			

(2) Japanese patents and foreigners' patents

Japan's Lag (years)	−3	−2	−1	0	1	2	3	4
				R				
Robotics	0.5206	0.7303	0.8610	0.9546†	0.9798*	0.9014	0.7693	0.4220
Genetic engineering	0.9368	0.9621	0.9850	0.9892	0.9923*	0.9903†	0.9850	0.9429

Note: *shows the highest coefficient and †shows the second highest one in each row.

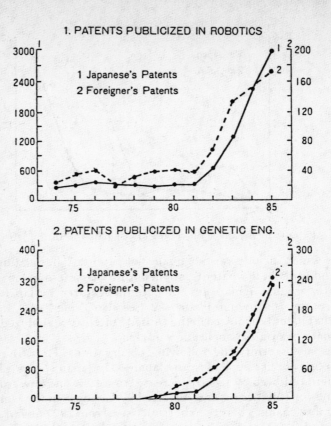

Figure 7.3 Patents by Japanese and foreigners in Japan

home of the patents applied for overseas had a three year or less time lead against the application trend of domestic patents. A similar fact was found in the relation between the trend of research papers published overseas and the trend of research papers published at home.[4]

The trend of the publicization of patents applied for in Japan by Japanese and the trend of the publicization of patents applied for in Japan by foreigners in the field of robotics and genetic engineering was also analysed (see Figure 7.3).

The trend of the publicization of patents in Japan, applied for by Japanese, lagged behind the trend of the publicization of patents applied for by foreigners in the field of robotics by one year or less (see Table 7.4(2). Even taking into account the fact that it takes two or three months longer for patents applied for in Japan by foreigners to be publicized in Japan after their original application at home, the trend of patent application in Japan by Japanese lagged behind the trend of original application at home of the foreigners' patents reapplied for in Japan by around one year in the field of robotics.

Suppose that the relation between the trend of application of domestic patents and the trend of original application at home of patents applied for overseas in foreign countries was the same as in Japan. Then the lag between the two trends was also three years or less in foreign countries from the analysis of Japanese robotics patents applied for in Japan and in the United States above. Then it could be said that the trend of Japanese patent application had about a two-year time lead against the trend of patent application of foreign countries in the field of robotics. This suggests that Japan was one of the leading countries in the world, for patent application in robotics.

In the field of genetic engineering, the correlation coefficient was highest when Japan's lag was one year and was second highest when the lag was two years. However, the correlation coefficient did not decrease very much with the change of time-lag reflecting the fact that both trends showed a steady increase and resembled each other. Thus, it could be argued that the trend of publication in Japan of patents, *applied for by Japanese*, lagged behind the trend of publicization in Japan of patents, *applied for by foreigners*, by one year or more. Japan's lag was a little longer in the field of genetic engineering than in the field of robotics. If it is assumed that the relation of the domestic patent application and the trend of original application at home of patents applied for overseas in the field of genetic engineering was the the same as in the field of robotics, then, it could be argued that the Japanese trend of patent application had a time lead against the trend of patent application of foreign countries in the field of genetic engineering despite the fact that the Japanese trend of original paper publication lagged behind the world trend in the field of genetic engineering.

Publication of articles and the publicization of patents

Finally, the time-lag between publication of journal articles and publicization of patent in Japan will also be discussed. In the field of robotics, the trend of patent publicization lagged behind the trend of publication of original papers by one year or more, and lagged behind the trend of publication of general articles by two years or less (see Table 7.5). Patents are publicized eighteen months after application in Japan and original papers were published after patents were applied for. Taking into account the editing time of original papers, it may be assumed that original paper writing and patent application took place almost at the same time. On the other hand, general article publication took place a little earlier than patent application in the field of industrial robots.

In the field of genetic engineering, the trend of patent publicization lagged behind the trend of publication of original papers by three years or more. Thus, original paper publication took place a little earlier than

Table 7.5 Correlation of time-lags for original/general articles and patents (robotics and genetic engineering)

(1) Robotics
(a) Original papers and publicized patents

Lag of patents (years)	R				
	-1	0	1	2	3
Robotics	0.8155	0.9238	0.9825*	0.9564†	0.8567
Robots	0.7887	0.8924	0.9394*	0.9243†	0.8347
Industrial robots	0.7986	0.9063	0.9693*	0.9173†	0.8599

(b) General articles and publicized patents

Lag of patents (years)	R					
	-1	0	1	2	3	4
Robotics	0.6718	0.8060	0.9177†	0.9646*	0.8950	0.6549
Robots	0.6625	0.7931	0.8681*	0.8353†	0.7315	—
Industrial robots	0.6658	0.7996	0.9171†	0.9721*	0.9104	0.7059

(2) Genetic engineering

Lag of patents (years)	R				
	0	1	2	3	4
Original papers	0.7937	0.9765†	0.9801*	0.9374	0.8924
General articles	0.7584	0.9037	0.9335	0.9882*	0.9684†

Note: *shows the highest coefficient and †shows the second highest one in each row.

patent application and general article publication took place much earlier than patent application in the field of genetic engineering.

From the analysis above, it could be argued that information diffusion activities had, in the past, an earlier phase than patent application. This is more noticeable in the field of genetic engineering. It also could be said that R&D activities were more closely related to patent application in the field of robotics since original paper writing and patent application took place almost at the same time. On the other hand, R&D activities in the field of genetic engineering had less relation with patent application since original paper publication had an earlier phase than patent application.

Methodological comments

Use of bibliometric data

The JICST (Japan Information Center for Science and Technology) data base was used to count the number of specified articles. The data period was from 1975 to 1984. The following retrieval items of the JICST data base were used for this analysis:

a. keywords: robots, industrial robots, genetic engineering, DNA recombinant, cell fusion, etc.;

b. kind of articles: books, original papers (original academic papers), general articles (explanatory articles), patent articles, etc.; and

c. languages: Japanese, English, etc.

The advantage of using JICST is that the JICST data base categorizes articles into 'original papers (academic papers)', 'books', 'general articles (explanatory articles)', 'patent articles', and so on. Another advantage is that keywords for retrieval are given to every article. The disadvantage is that the nationality of the author is not specified.

There are a number of pitfalls when using bibliometric data for the kind of analysis which is presented in this chapter. In order to clarify for the reader the assumptions and restrictions, some methodological comments are given below. These include comments on the data bases themselves as well as different ways of interpreting the data.

Sampling some articles on robotics and reading their summaries showed that articles with the keywords 'robots' are research-oriented and that articles with the keyword 'industrial robots' are industrial application-oriented. However, some articles have both the keyword 'robots' and 'industrial robots'. Therefore, the articles on robots, which is a research-oriented field, are defined to be articles which have the keyword 'robots' but do not have the keyword 'industrial robots'. The articles on industrial robots, which is an application-oriented field, are defined to be any articles which have the keyword 'industrial robots'. Then, the articles on robotics, the field of which is the union of the field of robotics and that of industrial robots, are articles on robots or articles on industrial robots. The articles on genetic engineering are defined as articles which have the keyword 'genetic engineering', the keyword DNA 'recombinant', or the keyword 'cell fusion'.

The Japanese articles are defined to be articles written in Japanese, since the nationality of authors is not a retrieval item in the JICST data base.[5] The ratio of Japanese articles on robotics did not change much over time. Thus, it is assumed that the coverage of foreign articles did not significantly change much.

The correlation between the articles written in Japanese and those written in foreign languages was calculated in order to check the analysis, since the portion of the articles written in Japanese was fairly large. The tendency for the results of time-lag relation was almost the same. The difference was that the correlation coefficients were slightly smaller and in some cases the second largest coefficient appeared in different places.

Use of patent data

The JAPIO (Japan Patent Information Organization) data base was used to count the number of specified patents. The period was from 1974 to 1985 —based on publicization date. Since patents are publicized approximately one year and a half after application in Japan, the data period was from 1972 to 1983 based on application date. The advantage of using the JAPIO is that keywords are given to every patent.

The patents on robotics are defined as patents which have the keyword 'robots' or the keyword 'industrial robots'. The patents on genetic engineering are defined as patents which are classified as C12N15, A01H1/06 or A01H1/08 according to the International Patent Code. Moreover, the nationality of applicants was used to determine the nationality of a patent.

Another kind of patent data was also used. The US patent data was used for patents on robotics applied for by Japanese. Patents on robotics are defined as patents which have the word *robot* in the abstract, although patents on toy robots were excluded by checking the content of abstracts. Patents applied for by Japanese were searched by checking the nationality of applicants.[6] These patents have two kinds of application date. One is the date of original (first) application in Japan and another is the date of application in the United States. The original application date in Japan was used in this paper. This data was supplied by the University of Lund in Sweden through private correspondence.

Other data considerations

The number of articles or patents of each category described in the preceding two sections were counted year by year. Then, several kinds of time-series data were obtained. Using these time-series data, correlation coefficients were calculated. As the time difference becomes greater, the number of data periods, available to calculate correlation coefficients, becomes smaller. Therefore, freedom-adjusted correlation coefficients were calculated instead of ordinary correlation coefficients in order to compensate for the variation of data periods available.

Some articles have both the keyword 'robot' and the keyword 'industrial robots'. Some have only one of these keywords. The articles which have the keyword 'robots' only seemed to be academic-oriented. It should be noted that 'robots' or 'industrial robots' may include toy robots. It depends on who gives the keywords to each article or patent. However, as far as the patents granted in the United States are concerned, toy robots are excluded by checking the content of each patent.

Concluding remarks

This paper provides a quantitative analysis of the dynamics of Japanese R&D in the two fields of robotics and genetic engineering, using bibliometric data, i.e., publication data and patent data. This paper clarifies the dynamic relation between Japanese activities and world activities, with regard to R&D in research-oriented fields, and R&D activities and information diffusion activities, the relation between R&D in research-oriented fields and R&D in application-oriented fields, the relation between domestic patents and foreign patents, and the relation between R&D activities and patent application activities, by calculating correlation coefficients with the time difference.

The trend of Japanese activities shows the same phase as the world trend with regard to both R&D activities and information diffusion activities in the field of robotics. However, the situation is different in the field of genetic engineering. The trend of Japanese R&D activities in the past lagged behind the trend of world R&D activities while the trend of Japanese information diffusion activities shows the same phase as the world trend. This would indicate that Japan has a good ability for information diffusion in promising research areas.

It was generally thought that information diffusion occurred after R&D activities were well executed. However, the trend of information diffusion activities show an earlier phase than the trend of R&D activities or they are in phase with R&D activities.

In the field of robotics, the field of *robots* was thought to be a research-oriented field and the field of *industrial robots* was thought to be an application-oriented field. When looking at the trend of original paper publication in Japan, i.e. the trend of R&D activities in Japan, the application-oriented field shows a lag against the research-oriented field, as expected. However, the R&D trend in the research-oriented field shows a time-lag against the trend in the application-oriented field in the world. This suggests that, in the field of robotics, R&D started from basic research in Japan and applied research followed, while applied research stimulated basic research in the world.

With regard to patent applications, it is clear that patents applied for in the United States by Japanese show an earlier increasing trend than patents applied for in Japan by Japanese in the field of robotics. It is also clear in the field of robotics and genetic engineering, that the trend of publicization of patents applied for in Japan by Japanese show a little time-lag against the trend of publicization of patents applied for in Japan by foreigners. It could be inferred, based on a certain hypothesis, that the Japanese patent application trend has an earlier phase than the world trend in both fields.

Some characteristics are evident about the relation between publication of papers and application of patents. Original papers on robotics were published after patents were applied for. This suggests a very close relation between R&D and patent application, in the field of robotics. On the other hand, original papers on genetic engineering were published before patents were applied for. This suggests that R&D in the field of genetic engineering had a more academic orientation. Finally, information diffusion preceded patent application.

Notes

1. This work was done while the author served as an associate professor at Saitama University and this chapter is a revision of the author's earlier paper (1988), Quantitative analyses of the dynamics of Japanese R&D on robotics and genetic engineering using publication and patent data', *J of Science Policy Research Management*, vol. 3, no. 2, pp. 172–81, Japan.
2. The ratio of Japanese articles on robotics did not change much over time. Therefore, it seemed that the coverage of foreign articles did not change much either.
3. Kondon, M., 'Japanese R&D developments in robotics' in Grupp, H. (ed.) (1986), *Problems of Measuring Technological Change*, Verlag TUV Rheinland GmbH, Koln, pp. 250–295, 1986.
4. Tsukahara, S. and Yamada, K. (1982) 'A note on the time lag between the life cycle of discipline and resource allocation in Japan', *Research Policy*, 11, pp. 133–40.
5. It appears that the coverage of foreign language journal articles in the JICST is limited. The number of articles written in Japanese was about one-third of all articles on robotics. In the proceedings of one international conference on robotics held in Tokyo, which I attended, the papers written by Japanese authors did not occupy so large a ratio. As far as the absolute number is concerned, the coverage of foreign articles of the JICST is not small. The number of articles on robotics in 1984 written in foreign languages in JICST was about 1,700 and the number of articles on robotics in the world in 1984 in INSPEC was about 1,100.
6. Some articles have both the keyword 'robot' and the keyword 'industrial robots'. Some have only one of these keywords. The articles which have the keyword 'robots' only seemed to be academic-oriented. It should be noted that 'robots' or 'industrial robots' may include toy robots. It depends on who gives the keywords to each article or patent. However, as far as the patents granted in the United States are concerned, toy robots are excluded. Keywords are not given to those patents which were picked up because there is a word 'robot' in the abstract.

References

Kondo, M. (1986); Japanese R&D developments in robotics in Grupp (ed.). *Problems of Measuring Technological Change*, Verlag TÜV Rheinland GmbH, Köln, 250–295.

Kondo, M. (1988); Quantitative Analyses of the Dynamics of Japanese R&D in Robotics and Genetic Engineering Using Publication and Patent Data, *J of Science Policy and Research Management*, **Vol. 3, 2,** 172–181.

Tsukahara, S. and Yamada, K. (1982); A note on the time lag between the life cycle of discipline and resource allocation in Japan, Research Policy II, 133–140.

8 Technological entropy dynamics: towards a taxonomy of national R&D efforts[1]

Fumio Kodama

Abstract

Certain national R&D efforts are common in most industrialized countries. Large amounts of public funds are spent on, for example, R&D programs directed toward space development, information technology and environmental protection. In terms of the interaction between national R&D programs and industrial development, these national R&D efforts can be formulated as a learning process centering upon which industrial technologies are relevant and which ones are irrelevant.

Japanese R&D statistics provide us with industry's intramural expenditures through selected R&D objectives such as Nuclear Energy Development, Space Development, Ocean Development, Information Technology and Environmental Protection. Furthermore, industry's intramural expenditures for these objectives are disaggregated into 22 manufacturing sectors. By calculating the share of each industrial sector's R&D expense in the total expenditure for each objective, the concept of 'entropy' can be applied to measure the dynamics of each national R&D effort.

Since entropy is the measurement of 'uncertainty', the time-series entropy value tells us how search spaces are progressively narrowed down as uncertainty decreases or how they are enlarged as uncertainty increases as the national efforts progress. Thus, these 'entropy dynamics' reflect the learning process of national R&D efforts.

On the basis of this measurement of entropy dynamics, a new scheme for the taxonomy of national R&D programs is derived. We find three general patterns. In a national program referred to as the 'mission' type, such as environmental protection, the entropy dynamics follows a pattern of decreasing entropy, because its task is to solve the problems as efficiently as possible. On the other hand, in a program referred to as the 'generic' type, such as information technology, it follows the pattern of increasing entropy, because its task is to explore the relevant industrial technologies as widely as possible.

However, in several national programs which are both generic and mission type, the entropy pattern follows a cyclic behavior. In a program of new science, such as nuclear development, the cyclic behaviour is generated by changes in the supply side of the program, such as the occurrence of unexpected incidents, while it is generated by the demand side of the program, such as enhancement of its targets, in a program of new frontier, such as space and ocean development.

Thus this new way of understanding national R&D efforts produces several policy implications in terms of policy formulation, policy management and international relations. A new scheme of international cooperation, 'option-sharing', is proposed, based on the findings derived from this analysis.

Introduction

Aside from security considerations, there seem to be two major justifications for spending public funds on national R&D efforts. One of the justifications is that the government is a major customer of these system developments. The government is responsible for missions such as securing energy supplies, establishing communication networks and protecting the environment. Therefore, the government has to share the cost for technology development because it is one of the major beneficiaries of the technology.

However, the privatization of many of these government activities is also common in most industrialized countries. It is no longer taken for granted that the government is the sole agent in fulfilling these missions. Thus some skepticism arises as to whether or not the government should spend so much public money on R&D in these areas.

The other justification is the 'spill-over' effect of the large national technology development programs which deal with basic technologies, whether they be materials, devices, or systems development. These technologies can be used by industries for their own product developments.

However, observers of innovation are coming to a consensus that the spill-over effect of national programs is not as great as expected (Rosenberg, 1988). One reason for this is that systems are becoming so sophisticated that the requirements by government procurement increasingly depart from that of the ordinary consumer and industrial market. In addition, large portions of the budgets for national R&D programs are allocated to testing and evaluation of the system, with only a small portion allocated for R&D.[2]

All these facts indicate the need for a new way to look at these national R&D efforts. In this chapter, first, a new formulation for national R&D efforts is presented. Second, the data base and the methodology which accommodate this new formulation are described. Third, the results of the measurement of several national R&D efforts and their interpretation are presented. Fourth, on the basis of these measurements, a new taxonomy of national R&D efforts is derived. Finally, conclusions and policy implications are offered.

New formulation of the national R&D effort

W. Abernathy studied patterns of industrial innovation and found that there exist two distinct patterns: one is the 'fluid' pattern in the early stage of innovation; and the other is the 'specific' pattern which arises in the later stage of innovation (Abernathy, 1978). He states:

One pattern of technological innovation can be seen in the important changes that occur in established high-volume product lines, such as incandescent light bulbs, rolled steel, refined gasoline, and auto engines ... The markets for such goods are well defined; the product characteristics are *specific* and often standardized.

However, major new products do not seem to be consistent with the first pattern of incremental change. A more *fluid* pattern of product change is associated with the identification of an emerging need or a new way to meet an existing need; it is an entrepreneurial act.

When a major product innovation first appears, performance criteria are typically vague and little understood ... In this second pattern of innovation, the diversity and *uncertainty* of performance dimensions for major new products might be expected to require a more flexible organization and technical approach and a greater degree of external communication than in the first pattern.

These patterns are not independent of one another, however. It is apparent in several industries that products currently represented by the specific pattern were much more like the fluid one at the time of their origin.

As described above, in the early stage everything is fluid both in the performance dimensions and in the technology dimensions. Therefore, the major task at this stage is to reduce the fluidity in identifying both the performance criteria and the technical approach to meet these criteria.

As far as the government policy implications of these fluid characteristics are concerned, R. Nelson studied the supersonic transport (SST) program of the 1960s, and the liquid metal fast breeder reactor (LMFBR) of the Atomic Energy Commission (AEC) during the same period, and came to the conclusion that it is not just that the particular proposals were not cost effective but also that the form of the proposed subsidy was generally an unwise form (Nelson, 1977). He argues:

The organizational model for these proposals was that of the Manhattan Project. The style involves a willingness to make large early bets on particular *technical options* and force these through at very high cost. Furthermore, although the early batting average has been dismal, there had been a tendency to stick with the game plan despite mounting evidence that it is not a good one.

As far as what happened to the two programs are concerned, the heart of the programs was *early commitment of governmental funds to a particular design*. In the case of the supersonic transport, it is highly unlikely that Boeing would have persisted so long in pushing its swingwing SST design *had the bulk of the funds been its own, and had it the ability to make that decision on its own*. Similarly, the AEC was persisting in R&D on a design long after evidence had accumulated that the route was not an attractive one. The AEC has also been very sticky about *initiating work on new concepts*.

One of the pitfalls in a government's aggressive support of technological projects is the 'early commitment of governmental funds to a particular design', in the stage where both the performance criteria and the technological approach are still very fluid. Therefore, the policy problem for the government is how to avoid this kind of pitfall (Oshima and Kodama, 1988).

In this context, therefore, the best way to formulate national R&D efforts is to do so as a process of reducing the uncertainty inherent in the fluid stage of innovation, in terms of performance criteria, and as the process of identifying the best technological option through a trial-and-error process. In other words, we can formulate it as a learning process: a search for a correct solution, where 'search spaces' are progressively narrowed down as certainty increases about which solution is the right one.

Only by this formulation of national efforts can we focus on the R&D programs themselves, exclusive of the spill-over effects. In other words, we can justify national R&D programs without the questionable concept of spill-over effects. This formulation can also provide a clear-cut conceptualization of the division of labor between government and private industry. Thus, governmental R&D programs can survive despite the privatization of these R&D activities.

Data base for analysis

Japanese R&D statistics collected by the Prime Minister's Office provide us with industry's intramural expenditures by selected R&D objective, together with the total Japanese expenditures, as shown in Table 8.1. In the table, industry's intramural R&D expenditures are divided into five objectives: nuclear energy development; space development; ocean development; information technology; and environmental protection.[3]

Industry's share of the total expenditure varies from one objective to

Table 8.1 R&D expenditure for five objectives and industry's shares (1987)

Objectives	Total R&D expenditure (A)	Industry's expenditure (B)	Ratio (B/A) (%)	5-year average (%)
Nuclear development	421.3	67.5	16.0	17.9
Space development	171.1	38.9	22.7	21.9
Ocean development	61.4	17.8	29.0	28.4
Information technology	608.5	554.5	91.1	88.0
Environmental protection	156.4	105.1	67.2	70.4

(unit: billion yen)

another: its share is as high as 88 per cent in information technology; and it is as low as 18 per cent in nuclear development. However small industry's share is, it reflects the industry's spontaneous response to these national R&D efforts. In other words, it reflects the decision made by the industry on its own.

Furthermore, industry's intramural expenditures for these five objectives are disaggregated into twenty-six industrial sectors as is shown in Table 8.2. In this table, the number of companies involved is also shown, in order to show how widely the industry's interests are diffused in industrial sector. This data base has been available every year since 1970, and the number of industrial sectors has been fixed through all the years.

As described before, national R&D efforts are formulated as a process of reducing the fluidity both in performance and technology dimensions. The fluidity can be interpreted as the uncertainty in identifying which industrial sector has the capacity to develop a new technical approach which might satisfy the emerging performance criteria. Therefore, this disaggregation of R&D expenditures of each objective, into these different industrial sectors, is an absolute necessity for the formulation of the national R&D effort.

A more detailed investigation about how companies are compiling data for the survey by the Prime Minister's Office reveals the following. Sometimes, companies report government contracts as part of their intramural R&D expenditure. But, they include only research and related contracts. They do not include procurement contracts. On the other hand, in governmental sector, the R&D expenditure includes procurement costs. In the case of NASDA (the National Space Development Agency of Japan), all the governmental budget for this institution is categorized as R&D expenditure, because this institution was established as an R&D organization in the field of space development. However, the organization is engaged in launching satellites into orbit. Therefore, expenditures such as satellites and rockets procurement are categorized as R&D expenditures in the governmental budget. This also includes

Table 8.2 Number of companies performing selected objective R&D (in FY 1987)

Name of industrial sector	(A)	(B)	(C)	(D)	(E)
Agriculture, forestry and fisheries	—	—	1	—	—
Mining	3	—	3	1	3
Construction	12	1	24	36	34
Manufacturing Industries:					
Food manufacturing	2	—	4	2	8
Textiles manufacturing	—	—	1	3	—
Pulp and paper manufacturing	—	—	—	—	1
Printing and publishing	—	—	—	6	—
Industrial chemicals/chemical fibres	5	3	4	9	8
Oils and paints	2	1	1	5	8
Drugs and medicines	4	—	—	—	2
Other chemical products	1	1	—	1	7
Petroleum and coal products	1	—	—	—	—
Plastic products manufacturing	—	—	1	1	2
Rubber products manufacturing	—	1	1	3	—
Ceramics	1	1	1	3	4
Iron and steel manufacturing	9	4	6	5	4
Non-ferrous metals and products	5	1	4	4	3
Fabricated metal products manufacturing	1	—	—	8	4
General machinery manufacturing	11	1	8	41	20
Electrical machinery/equipment/supplies	4	4	—	20	5
Communication and electronics equipment	4	5	3	60	4
Motor vehicles	—	3	—	4	5
Other transportation equipment	4	5	7	7	6
Precision instruments manufacturing	3	—	—	10	1
Other manufacturing	—	—	1	3	—
Transport/Communication/Public Utilities	7	2	9	20	16
Total	79	33	79	252	145

(A): Nuclear development (FY1976)
(B): Space development
(C): Ocean development
(D): Information technology
(E): Environmental protection

expenditures for the procurement and purchase of services concerning rocket launching.

On the basis of this investigation, we can resonably assume that industry's intramural expenditures reflects industry's decisions which would have been made had the funds been its own, even if the industry's intramural expenditure includes government money. However, the portion of governmental funding which is included in the companies' R&D expenditure is related to long-term research contracts. And in fact, government has a tendency to issue contracts to the companies in those R&D efforts which might initiate new work on new concepts.

Therefore, the industry's intramural expenditure in this data base is assumed to reflect the intrinsic change of the nature of national R&D efforts. In other words, by excluding the portion of R&D expenditures by the governmental sector, which corresponds to procurement contracts, we can eliminate the bias brought about by government's early commitment to a particular design and by its tendency to stick with the original plan despite mounting evidence that it is not a good one.

However, those portions of governmental funding which correspond to initiating work on new concepts are included in industry's intramural R&D expenditure. Therefore, we can conclude that this data base of the industry's intramural expenditures for selected objective R&D can fully accomodate our formulation of national R&D efforts described in the preceding section.

Methodology for measurement

As described before, we formulate national R&D efforts as the process of reducing the fluidity both in performance dimensions and in technology dimensions. And fluidity can be measured by estimating the degree of uncertainty in identifying which industrial sector has the capacity to develop a new technical approach which might satisfy emerging and newly-formulated performance criteria.

We can then employ the concept of *entropy* developed in the field of information sciences (Kodama, 1986). In order to use this concept, the definition of the technical approach should be specific (Kline, 1985). It is widely recognized that the technical approach is usually industry-specific or firm-specific (Kodama *et al.*, 1986; Pavitt, 1984; Pavitt *et al.*, 1989). Therefore, we can safely assume that a one-to-one correspondence exists between the technical approach and the industrial sector, i.e., we can equate technology with each industrial sector.

In order to accommodate this equation, we confined our anlysis to a fixed set of twenty-two industrial sectors within the manufacturing industries, because we assume that those technologies which really solve the problems confronted by national R&D programs are owned and developed by the manufacturing industries. Another reason is that the classification scheme for manufacturing industries is better organized than for the other industries. For example, the category termed as 'transport, communication and public utilities' obviously includes several sectors such as communication service companies, railroad companies and electrical/gas/water utility companies. In other words, this sector is not disaggregated enough to accommodate the equation we are assuming, although these firms are conducting substantial in-house R&D.

On the basis of this assumption, we can construct a measurement scheme for a national R&D effort in the following way (Kodama, 1987; Yuzurihara, 1986): Given

Eij : i-th industry's R&D expense into j-th objective R&D, and let

pij : the share of the i-th industry in the total R&D expense for j-th objective,
where

$pij = Eij/\Sigma i \; Eij$,

then, pij is supposed to be the probability distribution over the possible alternative technical approaches to j-*th* objective R&D.

Let
Hj : the entropy of the j-th objective R&D,
then, it can be calculated by the following formula:

$Hj = - \Sigma i \; pij \bullet \log 2 \; pij$.

Since the data base is available every year since 1970, we can calculate the entropy values for each year and for each objective. Thus, we can produce *entropy dynamics* for each R&D category. Subsequently, the time-series entropy value shows us how the uncertainty is removed through development of a national effort. In a national R&D effort, which challenges unexplored fields of knowledge, it is very uncertain which industrial technology is indispensable for the national program to overcome the difficulties. But, if knowledge is accumulated in the progress of a national effort, it gradually becomes certain which technology is essential for problem-solving and which is marginal.

Therefore, generally speaking, if a program proceeds well as expected, the entropy value drops gradually until the program can be terminated. However, when unexpected incidences occur in the progress of a national program, it again becomes uncertain which technology can meet emerging and newly-formulated performance criteria, hence its entropy increases again. In other words, as the entropy decreases during the execution of a program, the innovation pattern shifts from the fluid to the specific.

Prototypical patterns of entropy dynamics

Although there are various types of national R&D programs, generally speaking, we can divide them into the following two categories: *mission*

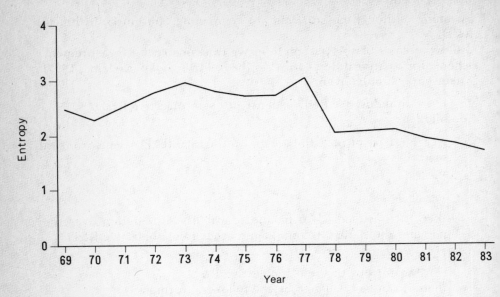

Figure 8.1 Entropy values of environmental protection

programs, where the mission is clearly stated and easily defined; and *generic programs*, which are typically multi-objective and which are designed to promote the mobilization and networking of actors, the development of infrastructure, the diffusion of technical knowledge and so on.

Among those five programs in the data base, 'environmental protection' is obviously a type of mission program, and 'information technology' is a type of generic program.[4] Therefore, let us describe, first of all, the patterns of entropy dynamics of the two prototypical R&D programs, in order to test the hypothesis set forth in the preceding sections. The entropy values of the two programs are shown in Figures 8.1 and 8.2. Clear-cut trends throughout the years studied are apparent.

The entropy value of environmental protection continued to decrease after some fluctuation in the earlier periods. In other words, this program exhibits the process of decreasing entropy. We can interpret from this trend that the uncertainty is being removed concerning which industrial technologies should be developed to overcome environmental problems. This indicates that we have been able to solve the environmental problems one by one, by appropriate applications of technologies. However, whenever a new problem appears and becomes visible, such as the rise in global temperature caused by global carbonation, the entropy may tend to rise again.

On the other hand, entropy of the program for information technology appears to follow an almost monotone increasing curve, at

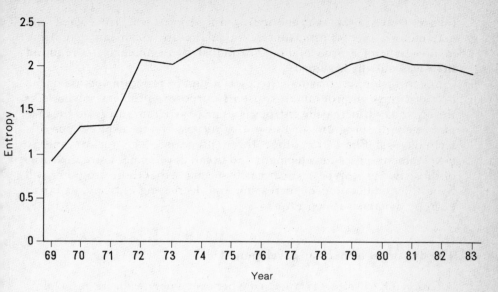

Figure 8.2 Entropy values of information technology

least up to 1976. The saturated or gradually decreasing curve follows thereafter. In other words, we are becoming more uncertain about which technologies are essential for information technology. This is a reflection of the fact that more industrial sectors are utilizing information technology and are thus making R&D investments in this technology. However, this is also a reflection of the fact that more industrial sectors are producing important innovations in this field and that the contributions to innovation are not limited to only electrical machinery and communication/electronics equipment manufacturing.

By making a comparison between these two prototypical programs, we can draw the following tentative conclusions regarding the entropy dynamics. Some mission programs may indeed be looked upon as problem-solving processes, because they are clearly focused on particular devices or technical systems such as environmental protection, weapon systems, etc. However, it is also quite clear that there is a wide range of national efforts including 'Biotechnology', 'new materials', 'information technology', etc., that are not of this nature.

In programs of the generic type, the launching of a national program influences industrial R&D behavior. Industry might enter research fields which it would have never explored without the influence of a national program. By expanding the range of research, industry might develop new products triggered by this expansion. Therefore, in generic programs growing entropy may not always be the sign of program failure. That is, as far as a generic program is concerned, growing entropy may indicate success or advances. It could mean, for instance, that the involvement of a broader range of industrial technologies is required than was initially assumed.

In conclusion, decreasing entropy is a sign of program success in the case of a mission program, because its purpose is problem-solving. On the other hand, increasing entropy is a sign of program success in the case of a generic program, because its purpose is to explore possible technologies. Since the other three programs, i.e. nuclear energy development, space development and ocean development, are mixtures of those two prototypes, we can easily speculate that those programs will have the combination of increasing and decreasing entropy, as far as entropy dynamics is concerned.

The dynamics of nuclear development

A national R&D effort is launched whenever a new scientific principle is discovered which would fulfill one of the missions which the government is supposed to be responsible for. Nuclear development is a typical case of this sort. Therefore, the process of nuclear development can be interpreted as the process of demonstrating the technical and economical feasibility of utilizing the newly discovered scientific principle.

Entropy values of nuclear development from 1969 through 1983 are shown in Figure 8.3. As shown in the figure, the entropy values fluctuate

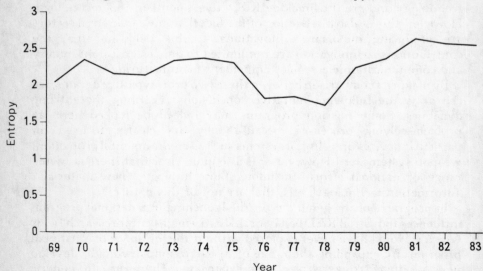

Figure 8.3 Entropy values of nuclear development

but stay stable until 1975. However, they drop drastically during 1976–8. They began to increase rapidly during 1979–81 and remain high until the present. The chronology of major events related to nuclear development is as follows:[5]

1975: *The Second R&D Plan of Nuclear Fusion* was published.
1978: Operation of the reprocessing plant was stopped because of an accident in the vaporizer.
1979: The Three Mile Island accident occurred in the USA.
1983: Operation of the reprocessing plant stopped again.

As far as commercial power generation by nuclear plants is concerned, we can trace back the number of plants constructed and the operating ratio of these plants. The change in operating ratio is shown in Figure 8.4. From 1970 to 1975 the operating ratio decreased constantly, reflecting early troubles, which is a common phenomenon observed in product development. However, it began to increase after 1978.

The accumulated capacity of power generation by nuclear plants is shown in Figure 8.5. As is shown in the figure, the capacity began to increase drastically from 1974 and leveled off around 1981.

Based on these observations, we can make the following interpretations. During 1975–8, the number of nuclear power plants increased and the overall operating ratio was enhanced. In other words, the commercialization of nuclear energy progressed significantly. Therefore, those industrial sectors which have direct relevance to the construction of nuclear reactors increased their R&D investment. The

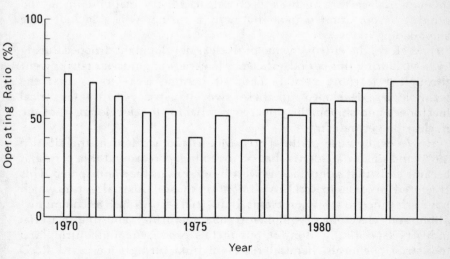

Note: The width of the bar is proportional to the number of power plants

Figure 8.4 Change of operating ratio in nuclear power plants

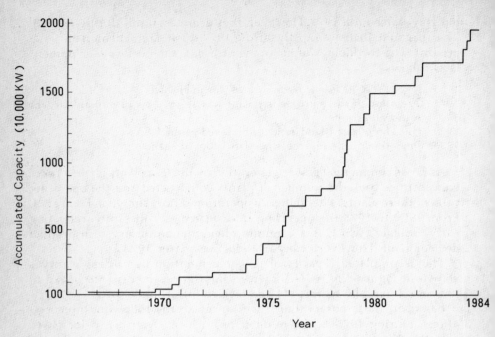

Figure 8.5 Accumulation of nuclear power generation capacity

intramural R&D investment of nuclear development was concentrated in industrial sectors such as electrical machinery manufacturing and other transportation equipment manufacturing, which includes the shipbuilding industry.

Therefore, the entropy value of nuclear development dropped during 1976–8. During this period, efficiency in generating nuclear power went through a learning period. Thus, it became clear to us that the technologies developed in these two industrial sectors (electrical machinery and shipbuilding) were essential for the development of the nuclear power industry.

However, because of the Three Mile Island accident in the USA in 1979, and similar accidents that occurred in Japan around this period, it became clear that safety factors were more serious than anticipated. This triggered increases in R&D investments in those industrial sectors which have relevance to safety problems. Industrial sectors such as communication and electronics equipment manufacturing, and the material industry (specifically, non-ferrous metals product manufacturing and industrial chemicals/chemical fibers manufacturing), increased R&D investment drastically. Therefore, the entropy value began to rise in 1979. In other words, it became uncertain which industrial technology was critical for the safe operation of nuclear power plants.

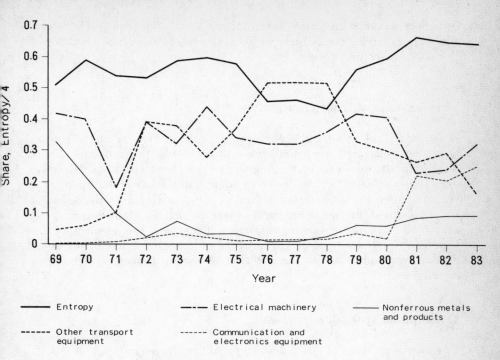

Figure 8.6 Major industries' share in total R&D for nuclear development

In order to show a more detailed analysis, the shares of several major industrial sectors out of the total intramural R&D expenditures for nuclear development are shown in Figure 8.6. Electrical machinery's share stayed high throughout the period with a gradual decline since 1981. The share for other transportation equipment increased substantially from 1976 to 1978, but dropped drastically from 1979 until the present.

By contrast, the share for communication and electronics equipment stayed at a low level of investment until 1980, but increased drastically in 1981 and has remained high since then. The same is true of the share for industrial chemicals, although its increase since 1980 was less dramatic than that of the communication and electronics equipment sectors.

The behavior of non-ferrous metals product manufacturing is worth mentioning. Its share was very high early in the 1970s, but decreased gradually through the mid-1970s. Then, its share started to slowly increase again after 1979. In other words, the technology in this industrial sector has become important again, but for different reasons.

In conclusion, this cyclic behavior of entropy values was brought about by unanticipated events, such as accidents. However, it was natural because the purpose of the program was to test the feasibility of utilizing a new scientific principle. And recognizing the existence of the unexpected composes a most essential part of social learning. Therefore, the cyclic behavior can be interpreted as the most visible manifestation of the social learning process.

The dynamics of frontier programs

Another typical national R&D effort is in programs where a new frontier is to be cultivated by mobilizing all available technologies. Space development and ocean development are examples of this kind. These are driven by the basic human desire to go high in the sky and deep into the sea. However, through the development of national efforts, the objective is transformed into more practical purposes such as satellite communication and exploitation of rare resources. Therefore, the program of this type can be thought of as the process of realizing long-term human dreams and indirectly as the meeting of more immediate technology development.

Dynamics of space development

The entropy values of space development are shown in Figure 8.7. As is shown in the figure, the entropy value dropped sharply in 1971 and rose

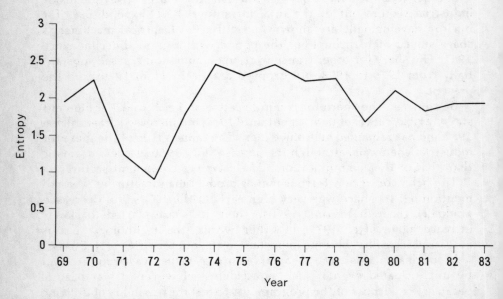

Figure 8.7 Entropy values of space development

Table 8.3 Comparison of specifications of rockets

Names of rockets	No. of stages	Length (m)	Diameter (m)	Weight (ton)	Types of fuel
M-3C	3	20.2	1.41	41.6	solid fuel for all stages
M-3H	3	23.8	1.41	48.7	solid fuel for all stages
M-3S	3	23.8	1.41	49.5	solid fuel for all stages
N-I	3	32.6	2.44	90.4	liquid for 1st liquid for 2nd solid for 3rd
N-II	3	35.6	2.44	134.7	liquid for 1st liquid for 2nd solid for 3rd

from 1973 to 1976. Then, it decreased gradually from 1977 to 1979. The Japanese history of launching satellites is as follows:[6]

Until 1975, the purpose and the mission were confined to testing rockets and to scientific investigations on the universe, respectively. However, since 1975, Japan has started to launch satellites for practical uses. For this purpose, the development of the N-series rockets began, as shown in Table 8.3.

Since 1981, Japan has started to develop the N-II series rockets, a scale-up of the N-I rockets. The usage of launched satellites also changed. Until 1977, usage was confined to scientific investigations. Since 1977, however, they have been used for telecommunication, broadcasting and weather forecasting. In 1979 and 1980, however, Japan failed to put the satellites into the right orbit.

Based on these observations, we can formulate the following interpretations. In entering the development of the N-series rockets in 1975, and in the transition from N-I to N-II in 1981, the launching stations and related facilities had to be redesigned. Therefore, during those years, R&D investment was concentrated on these industries, such as the shipbuilding industry. This is reflected in the sharp decrease in entropy during the few years which precede 1975, and the shallower drop during the few years before 1980.

Since 1977, satellites for practical uses such as telecommunications, broadcasting and weather forecasting have been launched and tested in space. Therefore, communication and electronic equipment manufacturers started to increase their R&D investment. Thus, we can observe a gradual increase of entropy in the years which precede 1977.

The failures in 1979 and 1980 demonstrated to the industries that some key component technologies such as the apogee motor and the satellite separation device were not yet established. Thus, uncertainty increased and this was reflected by a small increase of entropy after 1980. In fact, this triggered interest in those industries, such as motor vehicles manufacturing, which could supply the needed technologies.

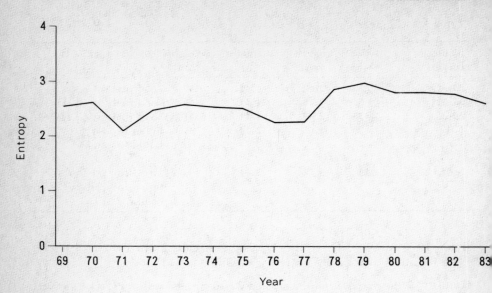

Figure 8.8 Entropy values of ocean development

Dynamics of ocean development

The entropy value of ocean development is shown in Figure 8.8. It dropped sharply in 1971, and rose during 1972-3. It started to increase in 1978 after its gradual decline during 1974-7.

The Japanese history of ocean development is as follows:

Japanese ocean development focused on the desalinization of sea water from 1970 to 1975. The major event in ocean development was the International Ocean Exhibition which was held in Okinawa in 1975.

In 1974, the exploration of ocean resources was added to the research agenda of the program. But it was not until 1978 that the items on this research became more specific, with the addition of, for example, the development of undersea uranium recovery technology, and the development of ocean power generation systems.

Based on these observations we can make the following interpretations. Since the early Japanese ocean development program focused on desalinization of sea water, only mechanical technology was important. Hence the high concentration of investment by the ordinary machinery manufacturing industry progressed and it brought the entropy decrease in 1971. However, the Ocean Exhibition stimulated the interest of the other industries, such as the shipbuilding industry, which can supply construction technology needed for sea architecture. This caused the entropy increase from 1972 to 1973.

But, after 1975, desalinization projects were completed and development then focused only on the construction technology for sea architecture. Therefore, R&D investment became concentrated in a few industrial sectors, such as iron/steel manufacturing and shipbuilding. This led to the decline of entropy during 1974-7.

However, around 1978, some specific projects, such as the application of remote sensing to ocean investigation, recovery technology for extracting uranium from the sea, ocean power generation and over-the-ocean communication using satellites, were identified as new projects of the ocean development program. This aroused a wide range of interests from many industrial sectors, and it caused the increase of entropy after 1978.

In both cases, we can find that the cyclic behavior of entropy dynamics was caused by the phase shifts of the programs. In the case of the space program, the development can be divided into the following three phases: development of rockets, launching of satellites and redesign of key components. In the case of the ocean program, the development can be divided into the following three phases: desalinization of sea water, construction of sea architecture and exploitation of sea resources. Whenever we have a phase shift, the entropy value rises, and the uncertainty is increased. Newcomers join the development programs and increase their R&D investment drastically to respond to the uncertainty factor.

In conclusion, the cyclic behavior is a manifestation of how the dream is realized a step at a time, by articulating the specific uses of the developed technologies.

A derived taxonomy of national R&D efforts

The dynamics of national R&D efforts is formulated as the changes of fluidity in identifying both the demand and the supply of these R&D programs, i.e., their performance criteria and the technical approach to meet these criteria. By using entropy as the measure of this fluidity, we can produce several patterns of entropy dynamics. This measurement enables us to establish a new scheme of taxonomy for national R&D efforts, as shown in Table 8.4.

As far as the time-shape of entropy dynamics is concerned, we obtained the following three patterns: the pattern of increasing entropy; that of decreasing entropy; and that of cyclic behavior of entropy. In a national program of the generic type, the entropy value follows the pattern of increasing entropy, because its purpose is to explore the relevant industrial technologies as widely as possible. On the other hand, in a program of the mission type, the pattern of decreasing entropy is

Table 8.4 Derived taxonomy of national R&D efforts

Category	Sub-category	Entropy Dynamics	Generated by	Examples
generic type		increasing		information technology biotechnology (*) new materials (*)
intermediate	new science	cyclic behavior	supply side	nuclear development high energy physics (*)
	new frontier	cyclic behavior	demand side	space development ocean development
mission type		decreasing		environmental protection defense R&D programs (*)

(*) estimated by the author without the measurement of entropy dynamics.

exhibited, because its purpose is to solve problems as efficiently as possible.

However, in many programs which are both generic and mission types, the entropy value fluctuates and exhibits cyclic behavior. In this category there exist the two types of national programs: one is the program in which a newly-discovered scientific principle is to be exploited for specific purposes; and the other is the program in which a new frontier is to be cultivated by applying available technologies.

Although both types of national programs of the intermediate type exhibit a cyclic behavior of entropy dynamics, the mechanisms of generating this behavior show a clear contrast. In a program of new science, cyclic behavior is generated by the occurrence of unexpected incidents, because its purpose is to verify the feasibility of utilizing this new scientific principle. In other words, it is brought about by the changes in the supply side of the program. On the other hand, in a program directed toward a new frontier, this behavior is generated by the shift in the goals of the program. In other words, it is brought about by changes in the demand side of the program.

Another way of interpreting the taxonomy described above is derived from the phase model, of R&D activity. In this model, we can divide the development of the national program into two phases: the *definition phase* and the *implementation phase* (NASA, 1968). In the implementation phase, the problems are well defined. Therefore, there is a lower degree of uncertainty regarding which industrial technology is essential for the program. Thus, R&D investment is concentrated in specific industries, and hence the entropy value tends to drop in the implementation phase.

On the other hand, in the definition phase, the R&D effort has to be placed on identifying both the target of the development and the essential technologies needed to be developed. Therefore, a diverse range of industrial sectors becomes involved in the program and a variety of companies invests in R&D. Thus, the entropy value tends to rise in the definition phase.

On the basis of this phased model, programs of the generic type are supposed to be composed solely of the definition phase, while those of the mission type are composed solely of the implementation phase. Thus, they generate either the monotone increasing entropy or the monotone decreasing entropy patterns.

In a program of the intermediate type, however, these two phases alternate as the national program progresses (Schmoch, Grupp *et al.*, 1988). Thus, the cyclic behavior of entropy dynamics is observed in these types of programs. This phenomenon can be best described by the term *'national program cycle'*. Our analysis shows that this alternating pattern occurs because of external dynamics, such as unexpected accidents, or because of the internal dynamics of the program, such as scaling-up for development.

Policy implications

Once we recognize the existence of the three patterns of entropy dynamics, i.e., the pattern of increasing entropy for generic programs, the pattern of decreasing entropy for mission programs and the pattern of cyclic behavior for programs of the intermediate type, then we can draw several policy implications in terms of policy formulation, policy management and international relations.

As far as policy formulation is concerned, the recognition of entropy dynamics leads to a new formulation of the national R&D effort as the identification process of critical industrial technologies. This formulation of a national R&D effort might lead to a clearer understanding of the justification for government support for R&D efforts. In the mission program the government's task is to reduce the entropy, while it is to enhance the entropy in the generic program. And the cyclic behavior is a sign of social learning or of realizing expectations.

As far as policy management is concerned, it is always a problem to determine when a national program should be terminated. The answer might be that we can terminate government support when the entropy stops changing, i.e., it stops increasing in a generic program and it stops decreasing in a mission program. In the program of the intermediate type, we should support a program as long as its entropy has a chance to fluctuate. In any case, the entropy measure can be a powerful tool for decision-making concerning the termination of government support.

As far as cooperation is concerned, whether it be domestic or international, it should be aimed at exploring all the possible options.

Thus, we come to a new scheme for international cooperation which is quite different from conventional schemes such as cost-sharing and/or task-sharing. This new scheme might be called *'option-sharing'*, because it shares the alternative technical options.

Because of the fluid characteristics of the early stage of a national R&D effort, no one and no country is certain about the performance criteria and the optimum technological approach among possible alternatives. Therefore, an effective and constructive role of international co-operation is to share all the possible candidates. Only with international cooperation can we explore all the possible alternatives.

Moreover, this scheme of cooperation might solve the common dilemma between international cooperation and national sovereignty. This scheme allows each nation to make her own decision concerning which option will be taken. But the information about which option is optimal is shared among the participating countries, because the judgment about optimality can be drawn only after all of the possible alternatives are tried and only by comparing these alternatives.

This sharing will be encouraged further by the free flow of researchers among countries and by allowing individual researchers to choose freely the research options in which he is interested to pursue in his research career. After it becomes certain which option is optimal, the national programs are terminated and the researchers will go back to their own countries. Thus all knowledge, including the know-how developed through being engaged in the optimal program, will be automatically brought back by these researchers to all of the participating countries.

In conclusion, only with a option-sharing scheme can we play a positive-sum game in the days when the movement toward protect-ionism movement places us in danger of playing a negative-sum game[7]. It might also be an important conceptual breakthrough for us to be able to realize techno-globalism in the present world, where a sentiment of techno-nationalism widely prevails (Reich, 1983).

Notes

1. The author would like to express thanks to Dr Yoshiki Morino for his valuable advice and his help in preparing some materials, and also to Mr Gerald Hane and Mr Orland Camargo for their efforts in correcting his English.
2. Comments made by Allen E. Puckett (Chairman and Executive Officer of Hughes Aircraft Company) at the First US-Japan Conference on High Technology and International Environment, organized by US National Academy of Sciences (at Santa Barbara, California, on 16–18 August 1985). It is documented in the *Japanese Scientific Monthly* (1986), vol. 39, no. 1, p. 12.
3. Statistical Bureau, Prime Minister's Office of Japan, *Report on the Survey of Research and Development*.

4. The Government of Japan, *White Paper on Telecommunications; White Paper on the Environment*.
5. The Government of Japan, *White Paper on Nuclear Power*.
6. The Government of Japan, *White Paper on Science and Technology*.
7. Opening speech by Harold Brown (former US Secretary of Defense) and summary statement and recommendations at the Second US-Japan Conference on High Technology and International Environment, 9–11 November 1986. It is documented in the *Japanese Scientific Monthly* (1987), vol. 40, no. 2.

References

Abernathy, W. (1978), *The Productivity Dilemma*, The Johns Hopkins University Press, pp. 68–85.

Abernathy, W. and Utterback, J. (1978), 'Patterns of industrial innovation', *Technology Review*, June/July p. 40.

Kline, S. (1985), 'Innovation is not a linear process', *Research Management*, Vol. 24 no.4, pp. 36–45.

Kodama, F. (1986), 'Technological diversification of Japanese industry', *Science*, vol. 233, 18 July, pp. 291–6.

Kodama, F. (1987), 'Dynamics of national R&D program' in *Research on Socio-Economic Aspects of Energy Systems*. Reports of Special Project Research on Energy under Grant-in-Aid of Scientific Research, Ministry of Education, Science and Culture, pp. 163–8.

Kodama, F. *et al.* (1986), *The Innovation Spiral: A New Look at Recent Technological Advances*, presented to the Second US-Japan Conference on High Technology and the International Environment, Kyoto.

NASA (1968), *Phased Project Planning Guideline* (NHB 7121.2).

Nelson, R. (1977), *The Moon and the Ghetto*, W.W.Norton & Company Inc., pp. 105–25.

Oshima, K. and Kodama, F. (1988), 'Japanese experiences in collective industrial activity: an analysis of engineering research associations' in H. Fusfeld and R. Nelson (eds), *Technical Cooperation and International Competitiveness*, Rensselaer Polytechnic Institute, School of Management, New York, pp. 93–103.

Pavitt, K. (1984), 'Sectoral patterns of technical change: towards a taxonomy and a theory', *Research Policy*, vol. 13.

Pavitt, K., Robson, M. and Townsend, J. (1989), 'Technological accumulation, diversification and organization in UK companies, 1945–1983', *Management Science*, vol. 35, no.1.

Reich, R. (1983), 'Beyond free trade' *Foreign Affairs*, vol. 61, no. 4, pp. 773–804.

Rosenberg, N. (1988), 'Civilian spillovers from military R&D spending: the American experience since World War II' in H. Fusfeld and R. Nelson (eds), *Technical Cooperation and International Competitiveness*, Rensselaer Polytechnic Institute, School of Management, New York, pp. 167–87.

Schmoch, U., Grupp, H., *et al.* (1988), *Technikprognosen mit Patent-indikatoren*, Verlag TÜV Rheinland Gmbh, Köln.

Yuzurihara, M. (1986), *Structural Analysis of Big Projects*, dissertation paper submitted to Department of Arts and Sciences, Saitama University.

Part III
Organizing Technical Change

9 The internationalization of R&D—an interpretation of forces and responses

Jon Sigurdson

Introduction

This chapter attempts to provide an overview of some major changes which can be identified in the globalization of research and development activities. Throughout the paper there is a focus on companies as major agents of change. Simultaneously, there is an indication that company-specific comparative advantage is becoming a more relevant concept than the traditional nation-specific comparative advantage, when discussing changing trade patterns. The chapter starts by indicating system shifts in the global economy which point to the emergence of a 'network economy' in which internationalized 'knowledge companies' will play an increasingly important role.

Then follows a discussion on the increasingly important role of joint research and strategic alliances which enable and support a continued globalization. The change of companies into knowledge organizers connotes company networks in which central research facilities and other core activities will become increasingly imperative in combination with joint research and international strategic alliances. The chapter concludes with a brief discussion of the present global rivalry among nations before indicating analytical tools which are required in order to understand better the changing international R&D situation, and to be able to formulate relevant policy guidance for nations and companies.

System shifts in the global economy and the internationalized R&D system

Changes in the R&D system—by nations and by companies, and internationally by both categories of actors—cannot easily be understood without considering major changes in the global economy. One brief interpretation for the period after the Second World War, drawing on the analysis of a French economist, Charles-Albert Michalet, will be given before moving on to describe the changing character of the R&D system.[1]

Immediately after 1945 the world economic system was influenced by rapidly increasing exports where the nation-state had a very strong control and where the national comparative advantage was a dominating factor. Then followed, in the 1950s, a period when countries were not only exporting goods but also exporting units of production. Thus the controlling agent started to shift from the nation-state to companies which were 'multinational' in character (MNCs) and which soon started to influence and dominate a new international division of labour. It can be said that the MNCs began utilizing the national comparative advantages for their own benefits.

A third stage followed when financial resources became equally or more important for companies than production facilities. Then MNCs *and* banks became significant agents of control and change, rather than national companies. The emerging powerful actors were to a considerable extent escaping the control of the nation-state. Today we have a situation where company strategies for financial and industrial operations go together. Michalet argues that control of networks and the time element in operations is now becoming more essential than company control of resources inside a specific nation.

An ongoing reaction to the present situation is found in the continued change of the global economy which, according to Michalet, can be characterized as a 'network economy'. Access and control of knowledge is now becoming more important than finance, and obviously R&D resources play a very central role for many categories of enterprises. The successful companies will, again according to Michalet, increasingly be networking companies rather than traditional MNCs controlling products and markets, a change which is also supported by the analysis in this chapter. In this new situation we may envisage the re-emergence of regulation in a national or international context which can be termed 'mixed economy'.

The various stages are itemized in Table 9.1 below. This is a simplistic presentation which overlooks the simultaneous existence of all four systems when we look into the situation of different countries and different industrial sectors. The situation is further modified by institutional characteristics which provide some countries with greater possibilities than others of maintaining national regulation of companies. However, for certain industrial sectors, like the electronics industry and increasingly so in the car industry, the indicated changes are evident in a global context.

The proliferation of strategic alliances—or inter-firm agreements— can be seen as an indication of the need to regulate the environment in

Table 9.1 System shifts in the global economy

System	Form	Agent	Regulation
International trade	Export	Nation-state	International division of labour (ex *ante*)
International production	Foreign direct investment	MNCs	International division of labour (ex *post)*
Globalization	Finance	Banks + MNCs	Escaping state control (?)
Network economy	Knowledge	Network company	Mixed economy + Re-regulation

which the companies operate. When the companies are under cut-throat competition they have to regulate in order to stabilize the situation. The same holds true for the nation-states, at least the big ones—or cluster of small and medium ones, like the EC. Thus we may see the emergence of a world mixed economy—in the words of Michalet. He argues that the inter-firm agreements and alliances are building up what could be called a new regulation of the world markets. In this perspective he regards it possible that in the future an increasing number of networks will mix private and public actors on the model of European arrangements like *Esprit* and *Eureka*.

Given the indicated shifts in the global economy I will discuss the ensuing changes in the R&D system. Traditionally it has been commonplace to view the system as consisting of two major components: (1) the infrastructure composed of universities with their departments and research institutes, and various categories of national research institutes, most of which are mainly financed through state budgets; (2) the corporate central research laboratories and development activities within the company divisions, mainly financed by the private sector. It is now possible to identify three more layers in the R&D system. First, research consortia have emerged as an intermediate layer—ultra-structures—to be further discussed later on, between companies on one hand and universities and research institutes on the other (see Figure 9.1).

Many of the activities of the R&D Framework Programs within the European Community naturally belong to the category of ultra-structures.[2] The same is true for the Japanese research consortia which have served as an inspiration for similar efforts both in Europe and in the USA. Strategic alliances—among companies—are of a similar nature but come into existence usually without the direct support of national or international agencies.[3] Finally, it is also possible to identify the emergence of global science programs—which could be designated

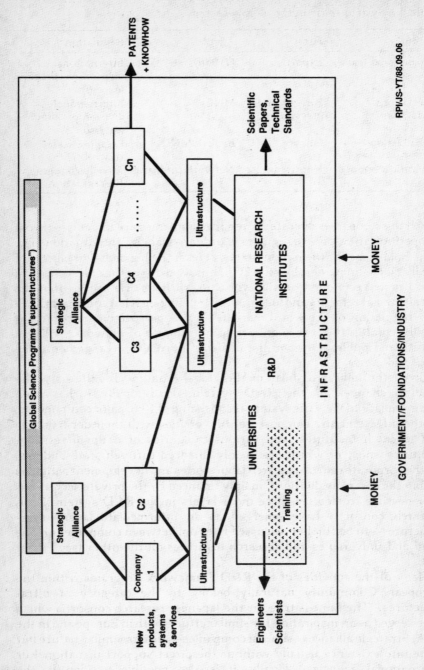

Figure 9.1 R&D system—networking

superstructures. These are attempts to organize science on a global scale and are evident in AIDS research, meterology and certain environmental research activities. The Japanese proposal for a Human Frontier Science Program could possibly be included. Although such superstructures have in the past been geared to efforts for organizing scientific activities, they may in the future encompass endeavours to organize industrial research on a global scale.

When considering the five different layers it becomes evident that the science and technology system is becoming increasingly internationalized which limits the possibilities of pursuing nationalistic policies—at least for the small and medium countries. The universities and the research institutes will remain under national control. Company research is increasingly influenced and controlled from outside the national borders. Many ultrastructures are still national but the Framework Programmes in Europe rapidly shift the centre of gravity to the Community. Strategic alliances are in the European context usually international which is obviously also true for global science programs.

Before discussing the newly emerging elements in the R&D landscape I would like to emphasize the basic differences between joint research (ultrastructures) and strategic alliances. The latter are generally initiated or dominated by companies. The former are consortia consisting of companies and institutions with a fairly large number of participants with the aim of sharing the knowledge which is produced by the consortia. Outside the sphere of EC joint research consortia are almost always national in character.

Joint research and strategic alliances

Joint research for the development of industrial technologies is a fashion word among government planners in all industrialized countries. The attempt at organizing private industries and government agents into consortia with substantial state subsidies started with the research associations in the UK some 70 years ago. At the introduction in Japan some 40 years later, the concept drastically changed to limit the membership and duration of such associations. The engineering research associations, as the original form of research consortia are known as in Japan, underwent gradual changes as the country climbed the technological ladder.[4] After an intermediate period of focusing on intermediate technologies the core is now on long-term research or development projects which often have more than a smattering of basic research included. Simultaneously, the forms of organization and finance have multiplied and the initiative for establishing joint research has been widely diffused throughout the Japanese administration.

The Japanese concept of joint research was not politically visible in Europe until the early 1980s. It has since then strongly influenced, or at least supported, the national initiatives and those of the European Commission to establish multitudinous forms of joint research. These include national programs such as Alvey for information technologies in the UK, Verbundforschung in Germany, and many of the components within the EC R&D Framework Programme. Also included in the category of joint research are various forms of research linking industry directly to the academic sector. This is exemplified by the newly created engineering research centers in the UK which partly draw on the inspiration of centers established by the National Science Foundation in the USA, as well as genetic engineering centers in Germany.

Thus, it is possible to identify two different trends in joint research. One is the establishment of research consortia which have the aim of revitalizing groups of companies in technologies of critical importance. The other is the more recent establishment, within the academic community, of new research centers/groups which are to have direct and close links with industrial firms. The latter resemble much more the new orientation of joint research in Japan. The former may be an indication that European countries and firms are in a catching-up and restructuring phase which has already been completed in Japan.

I will finally discuss the different functions which research consortia are expected to fulfil. It is vital to differentiate between explicit objectives and undeclared, but generally understood, objectives. The former generally state technological or scientific criteria which are usually more or less fulfilled. However, the creation of linkages and networks are generally a more important objective although rarely expressed. The awareness as such, among a group of companies, to embark on broad technological development and initiation of new research activities within companies may occasionally be more important—if the research consortium is able to achieve the correct timing.

The objectives naturally differ among companies and one special relation inside consortia, justifying special attention, is that between supplier of equipment, and producer of products using such equipment. Demand articulation is, in such instances, an important element as the transfer of knowledge, inside the consortium, from the producer to the supplier facilitates correct decisions with regard to specifications and introduction in the market. The existence and timing of the VLSI Project in Japan which fostered close relations between VLSI makers on one hand and equipment makers such as Nikon and Canon may partly explain why these companies, and not Zeiss and Leitz in Europe today, are global manufacturers of wafer-steppers, used in the production of integrated circuits.

Research consortia are usually subsidized by governments, or by the European Commission in the case of EC projects. Occasionally the participants in a consortia may *de facto* form a regional cartel for the joint development of certain key technologies or products. This appears to be the case for the proposed Joint European Sub-Micron Silicon Initiative (JESSI) and its sister organization—Sematech—in the USA. Both have been formulated and implemented in order to meet the challenge of Japanese competitors. However, the technological and market leadership of Japanese companies makes it extremely difficult for the US and European efforts to be successful.

Occasionally, the consortia may extend to an even larger group of partners when the joint theme is a technology which will lead to standardization of systems or interfaces. Thus, we can identify a spectrum of joint research consortia varying from those consisting of only a limited number of partners to those having a very large number of members. The number of participants can be explained by looking at the assumed or real benefits related to costs accruing to each member. In a joint technology development project the benefits will decrease with an increasing number of participants to share the costs. Thus, we may see many partnerships with only a few members and not so many with four to eight members. However, there appear to be many consortia with a fairly large number of members (see Figure 9.2). Such consortia are generally concerned with standardization or long-term research, the results of which are considered important but cannot immediately be appropriated.

Different options may still exist for companies although the general trend is towards increasing levels of cooperation. One possibility is to engage in narrow specialization and find a niche in which the company is able to maintain its dominance. Another possibility is to let or make the national government enforce different kinds of legal protection by

Benefits/Costs
(Number of consortia)

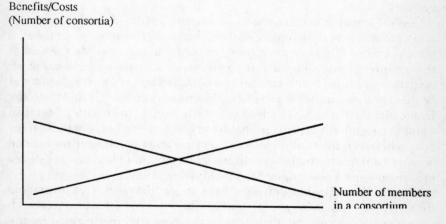

Number of members
in a consortium

Figure 9.2 Number of consortia members related to benefits/costs

restricting access to the domestic market, by special protection of important assets like intellectual property which can occasionally be enforced world-wide, or regulations for certain products such as drugs.

However, for expanding areas in the spectrum of sophisticated manufacturers cooperation in the form of joint research and strategic alliances will remain in order to:

1. improve efficiency;
2. reduce costs/risks for the individual company and consequently, in most instances;
3. reduce the development time (product cycle) by providing more resources.

It is obvious that strategic alliances fall into several different categories and I want to suggest that they should be analysed with regard to actors, geographical circumference and purpose. In many instances a strategic alliance will have to be analyzed with regard to more than one angle. Many strategic alliances are constituted by two companies. However, they often involve a larger number of companies and they may include other actors such as government institutions.

Here we can see an overlap between company-dominated alliances and government-influenced alliances. The latter may more correctly be identified as joint research projects/programs or research consortia. A similar dichotomy can be found when discussing the range of alliances. Company-dominated alliances are today more often than not inter-national in character. However, when traversing into research consortia we find structures which are usually limited by the national borders—or supra-national borders like those of the European Community. Finally, I would like to point out that alliances also meet very diverse targets such as joint marketing and standardization for future telecommunication systems.

Several research centres have, during the 1980s, initiated studies on strategic alliances or company partnerships and a number of data bases have subsequently been developed, to be discussed towards the end of this chapter. I will illustrate the emergence of partnerships based on statistics contained in the data base constructed by the Centre d'Etudes et de Recherches sur les Enterprises Multinantionales (CEREM) of the Universite de Parix-X. The leading researcher, Lynn Krieger Mytelka, argues that in both organizational form and content a distinction can be drawn between the traditional joint venture and the joint venture which is also a strategic partnership with the latter having a focus on knowledge production and knowledge sharing (Mytelka, 1989).

Mytelka distinguishes between three major functions: (1) agreements that involve knowledge production in a broad sense (choice of research priorities, joint pre-competitive research, joint engineering or develop-ment activities); (2) goods production (including licensing, subcontracting and joint ventures); and (3) commercialization of goods or services whether jointly produced or not. A fourth category covers those agreements that were global in nature, that is, they involve at least two of the above functions as well as exchange of equity. Drawing on the data base, Mytelka has compiled the following statistics (see Table 9.2).

The table shows that all types of inter-firm agreements have increased during the period which would indicate that knowledge sharing is only one category of an increasing interaction among companies.

There is a considerable overlap in objectives between joint research consortia and strategic alliances, some of which may be complementary. However, there is one basic difference in our knowledge of the two categories of research cooperation. The former are always known although all details may not have been revealed. The latter are rarely known outside the circles of participating companies, unless the formation of the partnership has been publicly revealed. However, there can be no doubt that both strategic alliances and joint research are increasing both in numbers and in significance, and they provide a weighty underpinning for an emerging network economy and are increasingly catching economists' attention.

Networking, company central research facilities and other core activities

A noted Japanese economist, Ken'ichi Imai, argues that future industries will be characterized by the accumulation of know-how related to industrial technology which has been built up not only by the company which uses that technology to produce products (Imai, 1983). What is

Table 9.2 Distribution of inter-firm agreements* by function, 1980–5

Year	Knowledge	Production	Commercial-ization	Global†	Total
1980	11	12	6	2	15
1981	15	13	10	10	31
1982	17	16	15	24	58
1983	24	25	31	41	97
1984	36	37	36	57	131
1985	47	39	51	58	149
TOTAL	150	142	149	192	481
Percentage	31.2	29.5	31.0	39.9	100

*Includes only agreements to which at least one European-based firm is a party
†Agreements which involve two or more of the preceding functions and including equity joint ventures.

equally, if not more, important is the process of accumulation of the required industrial technology through feedback between manufacturers and the makers of machinery which incorporate the technology into equipment and devices. This view supports the earlier observation about the role of demand articulation within the Japanese VLSI project.

Such an approach has characterized the development of industrial technology in Japan for the past couple of decades. Thus, Imai points out that the production plants in Japan do not rely on a specific technology but on a system in which production technology is gradually improved in response to requests by users and in cooperation with machinery makers. So, a company anxious to promote technical innovations can regard its organization for achieving such an objective as a large system which reaches far beyond its corporate walls and includes related machinery makers and users. In the past it has been taken for granted that the size of the company is a major factor when considering the efficiency of 'large-scale technologies'. However, Imai states that:

the factor determining the effect of technical innovation is the size of the 'system' related to the process of acquiring knowledge for the development. At the same time, the efficiency depends on how well know-how and information are transmitted and transferred.

Imai goes on to argue that if Japanese companies are achieving good results in the new phase of technical innovations it is because of the scale and economy of their systems and the efficiency with which know-how is transferred.

More recently Imai has identified the characteristics of different types of networks which are utilized by companies in Japan (Imai, 1988). There are in his classifications three important categories of networks. First, there are networks for the procurement of raw materials and the marketing of raw materials. Besides procuring raw materials from various markets, Japanese industries are closely linked with a system of contractors which supplies the specific machines and sophisticated technology and equipment necessary, while associated firms within the own company group form the basis of the distribution network structure.

Second, there are networks for organizing the small and medium-sized subcontractors which are utilized to manufacture and supply equipment. Location of such subcontractors is usually close to the major company controlling the production.

Third, there are also networks which involve research and these are of particular interest in the context of the presentation contained in this chapter. Such networks involve relations between the research structure of the company, on the one hand, and government research institutes and university departments/institutes on the other. The second network has in the past been the most important as it has had the most direct impact on the international structure of manufacturing. However, Imai argues that the third network is now gaining in importance. Thus we can possibly, in the future, view the international structure for research and development—dominated or influenced by companies—in the same light as we today contemplate the international structure of manufacturing.

There is a consensus that industrial R&D activities are expanding, becoming more important and consequently more strategic. This will also lead to changing emphasis on R&D functions. There are several indications that the role of basic research, controlled by companies, will increase in importance. The rapid expansion and proliferation of central research laboratories in Japan during the 1980s is an indication that 'basic research' is assuming a more central role than has previously been the case.

To clarify the situation it is important to distinguish among different categories or approaches for basic research. Professor Hirazawa distinguishes between pure fundamental research, basic research which may be partly scientific, partly technological, exploratory (seeds) research and mission-oriented basic research. He argues that all categories are increasing in importance which partly explains the proliferation of central research laboratories in Japan.[5] Hirazawa considers time to be a major explanatory factor. He argues that the ability to find and 'select' critical knowledge is essential. When developing complex technology systems it is seldom possible to identify all the necessary knowledge elements in the early stage. Thus, basic research capability has to remain on-tap to solve problems, occasionally of a fundamental nature, and we may see the basic research function becoming increasingly integrated with other R&D activities (Hirazawa, 1989).

The changing character of the Japanese industrial R&D system may have extensive consequences for the other major industrial regions. However, there has until recently been little analytical support, outside Japan, to substantiate the fact that basic research is contributing to the success of Japanese companies. Mansfield has the following to say:

Japanese firms tend to be quicker and more economical than U.S. firms at developing and introducing new products and process, but this advantage seems to exist only among innovations based on external technology.

Whereas U.S. firms put more emphasis on marketing start-up, they put much less emphasis on tooling, equipment, and manufacturing facilities than do Japanese firms.

Applied R&D in Japan which focuses more on processes than in the United States, seems to have yielded a handsome return; but there is no evidence that the rate of return from basic research has been relatively high in Japan. (Mansfield, 1988)

However, we may in the coming years have reason to look very differently at basic research in Japan. Nikkei High Tech Report argues that Japan must, in the coming years, transform itself from the world's fabrication centre to a creative intellectual production centre (Nikkei High Tech Report, 1988). Thus, the country's research industry, with the possible cooperation of national research organizations and also universities, may play an instrumental role in such a transformation.

The article notes that the current investment boom in research differs from the earlier one by aiming directly at lessening the dependence on outside technology. The present burst is centered around a variety of competing high-tech industries almost always linked to overall corporate strategy. A considerable share of new research activities is aimed at diversification into new business fields. Many companies have linked up with university laboratories in cooperative research agreements. As a consequence, many corporate laboratories are, according to the article, becoming independent and are transformed into research units operating under their own directives.

It appears that many companies view their basic research as an important 'economic' activity in itself. In a Nikkei Sangyo Shimbun article in mid-1987 it was reported that Hitachi is separating its basic research wing and relocating it in Saitama prefecture, north of Tokyo, the reasons apparently being 'a desire to clarify that the research centre is a separate organisation from the business side' (Sakakibara, 1988).

The ability to adjust to a rapidly changing situation in markets and for products is likely to require a different balance between decentralized and central resources for R&D or rather among different functions of R&D. I would in this context like to introduce a still unfamiliar view on the two faces of R&D. In a recent article Cohen and Levinthal argue that 'R&D not only generates new information, but also enhances the firm's ability to assimilate and exploit existing information' (Cohen and Levinthal, 1989).

The authors note that the role that R&D plays in learning has received little attention in the past because leading economists have previously assumed that technological knowledge which is in the public domain is a public good. A major reason for allocating resources to R&D, aside from generating innovations, would be to develop 'the firm's ability to identify, assimilate, and exploit knowledge from the environment—what we call the firm's 'learning' or 'absorbtive capacity', according to the authors.

They conclude that '(T)he observation that R&D creates a capacity to assimilate and exploit new knowledge sheds new light on a range of questions'. This would, for example, furnish clarification of why certain companies invest heavily in basic research in the obvious knowledge that most of this will rapidly leak into the public domain. The authors argue that firms may carry out basic research to enable them to identify and exploit potentially useful technological or scientific knowledge which is generated in universities or government laboratories. This could then give them an advantage over competitors in exploiting new technologies.

The new indicated perspective would imply, the authors say, that 'variables that influence the firm's incentives to learn should affect the incentives to conduct basic research'. The automobile industry is given as an example where manufacturing depends increasingly on fields that draw heavily on basic science including those related to microelectronics and ceramics. So, the authors expect that car manufacturers will expand their basic research efforts in physics and chemistry to evaluate and exploit new findings. Thus we can assume that the role of basic research, both in Japan and globally, is undergoing major changes and will become a major component of company network strategy.

De-coupling of company R&D from national systems

It has for the past decades been taken for granted that the location of production facilities of big multinational (multidomestic) companies could for many types of products and processes be located almost freely around the world. This is nothing new to the management of the companies but the results often come as a shock to governments or regions when they see production facilities being closed down. The location is based on economic and other considerations which are usually simple to understand although the exact timing of a corporate decision is difficult to predict. Certain types of processing are preferably done near the source of raw materials but production costs are changing the location criteria.

Labour-intensive production, which in the past included many types of assembly, is preferably done in countries or locations where labour costs are low—other conditions being equal. However, the increasing level of automation which is partly motivated by quality considerations, reduces the significance of low labour costs. Finally, location of production facilities is increasingly decided by closeness to the market. Such a closeness may in itself be a distinct advantage but the location in the market may often be required by national governments. Such demands which were prevalent in the developing countries have now become widespread within the EC and the USA to force Japanese companies to produce abroad rather than export.

The location of research and development activities have in the past only marginally been influenced by the location of production facilities and most company R&D activities have until recently been concentrated in the 'domestic' country of an MNC. However, it is today possible to discern a new situation for R&D within industrial companies. It may in fact be possible to identify a de-coupling of company R&D activities from nations, similar to de-coupling of production. There are two major reasons. First R&D has become increasingly important in many companies, and ranges from 5 to 15 per cent of sales of high technology companies—like those in computers, telecommunications and pharmaceuticals. This may in fact mean that R&D expenditure constitutes 15–45 per cent of the value added in such companies.

Second, conditions for research and access to resources for carrying out research varies widely around the world. Given the considerable amounts involved a relocation of research may in the long run considerably improve the competitive position of a company. In a study of internationalization of R&D in US multinational companies before 1973 the following four kinds of foreign R&D units were identified.[6]

1. Technology Transfer Units (TTUs): to facilitate the transfer of the parent's technology to the subsidiary, and to provide local technical services;
2. Indigenous Technology Units (ITUs): to develop new products for the local market, drawing on local technology;
3. Global Technology Units (GTUs): to develop new products and processes for world markets;
4. Corporate Technology Units (CTUs): to generate basic technology for use by the corporate parent.

Westney notes, in a more recent study, that each type of unit has distinctive linkages with the local subsidiary, the parent organization and with local sources of technology (see Figure 9.3). Naturally the strength

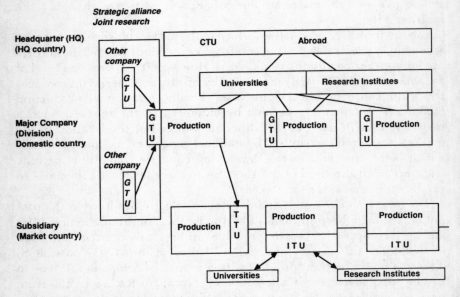

Figure 9.3 Location pattern for R&D in a multinational company

of the ties with the local centres of science and technology varies across the four roles. Westney states that the ties are virtually non-existent for a TTU, stronger for an ITU, stronger still for a GTU and strongest for the CTU.

I will now try to illustrate the present situation by using a couple of recent surveys as well as various news items. I will start by identifying some of the reasons why foreign companies decide to establish research facilities in Japan (Inoue, 1987). In late 1987 the *Japan Economic Journal* reported that 'since 1986 nearly 20 U.S. and European chemical, pharmaceutical and electronics giants have formed R&D centres in Japan or announced such plans to do so in the future'. Ciba-Geigy A.G. was one of the European companies.

The report mentions that a major goal of these Japan-located projects envisaged by most foreign institutions was to acquire sophisticated applications technology in close contact with Japanese industries. It is mentioned that Imperial Chemical Industries (PLC) completed a laboratory in Tsukuba in early 1987 with the objective of improving its technology in engineering plastics and opto-electronics products, including display devices and interconnectors. The reporter also mentions that Deutche Bank will open a five-storey high-tech 'incubator' to house about 30 German research labs. The article ends by stating that some Japanese companies, such as Takeda Chemical Industries, viewed the location of research facilities of its competitors, e.g. Ciba-Geigy, as a 'considerable threat'.

A year earlier the same journal had the following to say about the location of Japanese research centres abroad (Hasegawa, 1986). The reporter, Hasegawa, notes that Japanese research and development are being created one after another in the USA and technologically advanced nations. He says that the aim is to collect the most up-to-date information on technology and production for manufacturers. The centres should also be seen as Japanese corporate countermeasures to growing moves in the USA to clamp down on the easy outflow overseas of information and technology. In a more recent article we learn that the attitude towards locating R&D overseas has changed considerably during the past couple of years (Inoue, 1988). The report is based on a survey on Japanese corporate R&D investment abroad. Almost all of the 177 companies surveyed had significantly stepped up R&D efforts in the preceding 18 months—primarily in the USA and Europe. Altogether 23 of the then existing 66 foreign research centres (owned by 58 companies) had been established during 1987 or 1988. Even more remarkable is the fact that 37 more companies were contemplating new overseas R&D centres and another 53 indicated that they would establish such facilities in the future.

Most of the new research centers would be located in the USA and Europe but some companies disclosed that they were opening R&D

centers in South Korea, Taiwan and China. Among the new R&D centers established in Europe is the one by Canon, Inc., in England and another one by Aisin Seiki Co.—the auto parts manufacturer associated with Toyota—at Sophia Antipolis in the south of France. In this research and academic city near Nice the company will carry out development on automotive and new engineering. In addition, it will also seek new technologies for both energy and advanced information systems. Aisin Seiki already has four laboratories in the USA and Europe but the new centre in France is the first research centre operated as a locally incorporated entity (Okazaki, 1986).

Following on the establishment of the research centre in France, Aisin Seiki has decided to establish a new centre in Ann Arbor Technology Park, Michigan. It will integrate its Comet Laboratory in Detroit and its Comet UC-D office in the mechanical engineering department of th University of California at Davis into the new institute. The new center will conduct research on future car technologies, focusing mainly on motor configurations to be used in the twenty-first century (Nikkei News Bulletin, 1988).

There are four major reasons for moving R&D overseas, according to the survey report. First, companies want to be close to their customers. Second, companies wish to have access to new foreign technology. They see this 'as a way to maintain the momentum in the new products' development race'. Third, more and more companies are also stressing the benefits of hiring foreign researchers, 'as a way to give new stimulus to their R&D teams'. Fourth, some firms argued that their foreign R&D investment was partly motivated by stronger interest in basic research. This is true for the new NEC research centre to be established in Princeton, in May 1989, where the company intends to conduct basic research on telecommunications technologies. Dr Uenohara, vice president of R&D at NEC, is also considering setting up another research institute in Europe—subject to the availability of competent staff (Hasegawa, 1988).

Japanese companies are also forging relationships with Western universities in order to launch research and development facilities and underwrite scientific and technical projects (the *Japan Economic Journal*, 1988). The reason given is that companies want to conduct research nearer to the potential markets for their products and at the same time take advantage of the generosity of the academic institutions. In contrast to the criticism that often accompanies direct investment by the Japanese, these companies have been readily welcome on the campuses. Kobe Steel Ltd., for example, in late 1988 established its first overseas research institute at the University of Surrey. The company plans to establish research for work on resin-based composite materials.

The revealed pattern closely supports the early findings of an extensive survey of a group of US companies. The investigator, Ronstadt, found an evolutionary pattern of foreign R&D investment. He concluded at the time that economic reasons existed for US companies to pursue R&D abroad and such investments made those companies more competitive than they would have been otherwise (Håkansson and Laage-Hellman, 1984; Ronstadt, 1978). An evolutionary pattern of relocating research abroad has been confirmed by investigations of the Swedish industry.

In the early 1980s firms in the Swedish mechanical engineering industry had 36 per cent of their R&D abroad compared with 14 per cent on average (Swedenborg, 1982). Some six years later the average share appears to have increased considerably. According to a survey of 20 of the largest engineering and chemical enterprises, in Sweden, approximately 23 per cent of all industrial R&D is done outside Sweden (Håkansson, 1989). Håkansson notes that Swedish companies have been very active in acquiring companies abroad which he sees as a major explanatory factor for the considerable increase in Swedish industrial R&D activities.

A similar pattern to that revealed for Sweden is likely to exist for other small, highly industrialized, countries with large multinational companies, such as Netherlands and Switzerland. The share of R&D abroad may for the time being remain at a lower level in countries like Germany and France. It may be worth noting that the stock of foreign direct investment owned by Swedish companies in 1985 amounted to 9 per cent of GDP. The figures for Switzerland and the Netherlands are much higher, 48.9 per cent and 35.1 per cent respectively, while the figure for West Germany was below 10 per cent (CTC Reporter, 1988). The discussion has so far centered only on the industrialized countries although they interact closely with the other parts of the world economy. In order to understand better the global dynamics of R&D it is important to identify the outside forces which are fanning the fire of innovation in industrialized countries.

The global rivalry and the changing trade pattern

Economists often argue that there is one major way of understanding technological differences between countries. This point of view, adopted in the standard neo-classical theory of international trade assumes that all countries are on the same production function (Sveikauskus, 1983). Calculations can then determine the relative abundance of those inputs associated with science and technology versus other input factors.

In September 1979 the United Nations held its conference on Science and Technology for Development in Vienna which followed a similar UN conference some 15 years earlier. There were great expectations that science and technology, mainly generated and controlled by the advanced countries, could be made available for the developing countries. Very little of these expectations have materialized and I will attempt in the following to provide an analytical framework to explain why such expectations have little relevance in our present political and institutional system. It is surprising that hardheaded politicians would ever have supported such idealistic and altruistic notions.

In a paper published in 1979, Krugman maintains that there are substantial differences in the production possibilities faced by different countries (Krugman, 1979). He argues that advantages in innovation and lags in the diffusion of knowledge are the basic influences which permit incomes to be higher in the industrialized world than in developing nations. Consequently, it is in the interest of the industrialized countries to maintain a superior ability for massive and rapid innovations.

Such a view illustrates the potential economic significance of innovation in advanced countries, since the generation of new technologies in industrialized countries and their diffusion to the rest of the world then essentially determines the world income distribution and world economic development. From an economist's point of view it is necessary to have data from many countries in order to carry out such an analysis. However, more important is an understanding of certain characteristics of a global R&D system.[7]

Competition now covers a broad range of manufacturers and services. There are many reasons for this including the convergence of relative factor endowments in communication and transportation and maturation of economies. Thus, an advanced industrial country is faced with competition from three origins—other industrialized countries, new industrializing economies (NIE)[8] and developing countries.

There are two momentous relations which strongly influence both companies and governments. The first relation is the ongoing vertical change between developing countries, newly industrializing economies (NIEs) and the industrialized countries. Many of the developing countries are successful in building up an increasingly efficient and export-oriented industry which to a considerable extent is based on labour-intensive production methods and increasingly successful transfer of technology (see Figure 9.4). The success of this evolutionary process in less developed countries (LDC) is greatly influencing the conditions for the continued industrialization of the NIEs. As a consequence the newly industrialized countries have been forced to restructure their industries and initiate aggressive developments in high technology sectors at an earlier date than would otherwise have been the case.

The technological progression of the NIEs will naturally erode the headway previously enjoyed by the industrialized countries. They are then forced into long-lasting restructuring of their industries and rapid technological transformation in order to maintain the competitiveness for their domestic companies (see Figure 9.4). We will illustrate this with

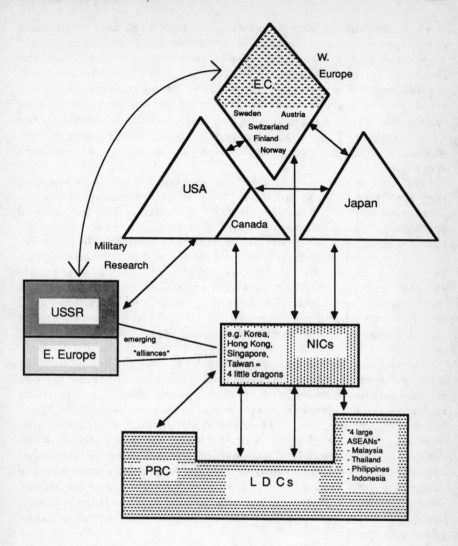

RPI/JS-YT/88.09.05

Figure 9.4 Triad rivalry and technology competition

information which indicates the emergence of Korea as a technological power. Already in 1987 a commentator in Japan had the following to say:

Korea has nearly caught up with Japan in the field of high technology, primarily by applying Japan's own methods for achieving the top rank—a strong work ethic, close co-operation betwen government and industry, and long-term investment plans that ignore short-term profit considerations. (Takahashi, 1987)

As a consequence, Korean products such as VLSI devices and high consumer electronics such as VCRs are competing in the world market where Japanese companies have dominated. At the same time the changing relations between the various layers also provide new possibilities and complementarities. The second dynamic relation—which may be more immediately important for Europe today—is that within the Triad structure which consists of the USA, Japan and West Europe.[9] This triad structure today controls most of the global expenditure on R&D activities—outside the planned economies.

I will now differentiate among different types of products and how they have affected trade relations. First, there are products from the primary sector which consist mainly of minerals and agricultural products. Minerals cannot be mined if they do not exist within the national boundaries which decide the national advantage. The comparative advantage of agriculture is directly related to the factor endowment and today everyone is aware that we would have a very different trade pattern if import markets were not controlled through numerous mechanisms. Such a situation is disadvantageous to many developing countries and other countries which are naturally well endowed—and is also detrimental to the interests of consumers in the industrialized countries.

Second, the manufactures of the secondary sector can be simplistically classified in simple labour-intensive products such as shoes and textiles, complex labour-intensive products like ships and sophisticated products such as digital telephone exchanges or video tape recorders (VTR). There has been a considerable shift in the trade pttern for simple labour-intensive products which at first favoured the NIEs and now the developing countries. The response of the advanced industrialized countries has been to concentrate on fashion products for which the design and short-product cycles are essential. As fabric per se has become less important, the successful industry, in countries like Japan and Italy, has put increasing emphasis on fashion appeal—the intangible value-added component.

A Japanese analyst, Makino, argues that the textile industry in Japan is increasingly relying on the services offered by fashion designers as it continues to churn out new products (Makino, 1988). Makino sees this as a perfect example of secotertiary-sector industry which combines the tangible goods (clothing) and intangible services (fashion).

A similar shift has taken place for complex labour-intensive products which is now favouring the NIEs and to some extent the developing countries. The response has been to focus on design-intensive products like ice-cutters and cruise-liners in the area of shipbuilding.

Third, the sophisticated manufacturers have not been unaffected. The indicated shifts in the trading pattern have forced the industrialized countries to exit from many industrial sub-sectors and concentrate on more sophisticated production. Thus, in most industrialized countries the industrial structure has changed in direction of more industries which are R&D-intensive which partly explains the long-term increase in R&D expenditure.

Finally, services have increasingly become an important element in international trade. The simple tasks like sea transportation have been taken over partly by developing countries while more sophisticated services in finance, telecommunications, trans-ocean optical fibre networks are almost completely controlled by the industrialized countries.

At the same time the globalization of markets for many such products have intensified and forced companies to shorten the product cycle, improve the product and incorporate more and new functions. This is to a considerable extent done by companies in industrialized countries in order to maintain the comparative advantage *vis-à-vis* the NIEs, to which we will return later on.

All these measures have contributed to raising the R&D expenditure. Shortening the product cycle increases the design and development costs unless such costs per each unit produced can be reduced through increasing the number of units produced. Improving the product in order to stay ahead will usually increase the development costs and the same effect comes from incorporating more functions into a product. Spiralling development costs are evident in the car industry where a new model may require 500 million dollars or more. Other examples of very large R&D costs can be found in telecommunications equipment, IC manufacture as well as aircraft manufacture.

There are two more factors, aside from the increasing R&D-intensity, which forces companies to reconsider their capability and start looking for alliances. One is the increasing risks which are associated with major development projects like a new car model, a new aircraft or a new digital telephone exchange system. Thus, in an increasingly number of instances it has been seen as desirable to share not only the R&D costs but the risks associated with a project. The other is the increasing complexity of large development projects which require competence and research which are only to be found in other companies. These three factors together have to a considerable extent been responsible for the very substantial increase in joint research and strategic alliances which has taken place over the past two decades.

New tools of analysis

This presentation has indicated that the balance of power is definitely shifting from nations to global companies which is most evident for small and medium nations. What is true in the industrialized world is even more so among the countries in the Third World which in many ways appear to be outside the mainstream of hectic innovation in the increasingly sophisticated industrial sectors.

There is a world-wide trend to privatize R&D and global companies are playing an increasingly important role in this process. The result is that '(C)ompany mergers in Europe will bring together the research resources of the European countries' (Dickson, 1989). These are the words of Michael Heseltine, Britain's former defence secretary, when he addressed members of the Save British Science organization in November 1989. Furthermore, he argued that '(T)en years from now Europe will not think in terms of national research programs, for the simple reason that such programs will not be able to match in scale or sophistication the American or Japanese challenges'. These comments provide a strong underpinning for a shift from national policies to European policies for science and technology. However, such changes are not limited to Europe but affect the global system as discussed in this chapter.

This raises a number of questions. What is the future role of nations in formulating national programs? Should national programs provide an input into international programs in science and technology? How should the roles between global companies and national governments be defined? There are many other questions which also demand answers. Some answers depend on an improved understanding of changes in a global system for science and technology, while others have a strong political connotation. Companies have emerged as increasingly important actors establishing wide S&T networks and integrating various S&T activities to serve their strategies. Joint research and strategic alliances are important indicators of this new situation. This suggests that we need S&T indicators which clearly reveal structural changes in various parts of an S&T spectrum. The use of data bases on patents and papers partly testifies that structural changes can be revealed through bibliometric analysis. This is most clearly shown in the earlier chapter on laser research by Anders Granberg in this volume.

Given the increasing importance of structural changes in which companies are involved it appears highly desirable to establish data bases which in considerable detail cover company-specific activities in science and technology and do not rely only on indirect evidence. The beginning of such data bases exists in the research projects which have focused on strategic alliances and now exists in several places. However, those data bases are still fragmentary, with little differentiation between significant and not so significant alliances. Furthermore, they are seldom comprehensive and rarely provide long time series, assuming that such coveted data bases existed it is still necessary to refine the analysis in order to define policies at the national and international level. Only then would it possible to understand the character and dynamics of the international science and technology system and suggest efficient ways of intevention (as is to be discussed in the following chapter).

Notes

1. The following comments are based on a paper by Charles Albert Michalet, 'The changing forms of the internationalisation process' and his comments presented at a seminar, organized by the working group on Oligopolies and Hierarchies, Paris, 23–23 April 1989.
2. Ultrastructures are networks for communications or collaboration and are similar to the characteristics of a matrix organization. Thus ultrastructures are organizationally superimposed over an existing infrastructure linking different competences within that structure. The ultrastructures can have widely different forms and life-spans. Their most important function is to enable—through a communication network—an optimal use of competence within a system in order to identify and treat strategic R&D problems. (This definition above has been extracted from Stankiewicz and Granberg, 1986.)
3. A strategic alliance is a long-term agreement between two or more companies with the explicit aim of joint production, or sharing, of knowledge. Strategic alliances may also include joint production and commercialization although knowledge sharing and/or joint production of knowledge is central. Thus, strategic alliances are different from mergers, acquisitions, licensing which are usually dominated by one partner. Joint ventures may occasionally be akin to strategic alliances.
4. See, for example, Sigurdson (1986) which provides a brief historical overview.
5. Ryo Hirazawa, Dept. of General Systems Studies, University of Tokyo. His views are best expressed in 'Arantana jidai o mukaete no kiso kenkyu sushin no kangaekata' (Ways of thinking about the promotion of basic research in meeting the new age), June 1988, 25 pp.
6. This information has been extracted from Westney, 1988. The original has appeared in Ronstadt, 1984.
7. Chalmers Johnson has recently argued that basic differences in the institutional set-up has to be considered when negotiating the trade issues between Japan and the USA (see Johnson, 1988).
8. NIC, which stands for Newly Industrialized Countries, is used interchangeable with NIE. The latter has come into vogue in order to alleviate the political sensitivity of China with regard to Taiwan and Hong Kong.
9. The concept has become widely used after the publication of Ohmae Ken'ichi (1985), *Triad Power—The Coming Shape of Global Competition*, London.

References

Cohen, W.M. and Levinthal, D.A. (1989), 'Innovation and learning: the two faces of R&D', *Economic Journal*, 99, pp. 569–96.
CTC Reporter (1988), 'The process of transnationalization in the 1980s', no. 26.

Dickson, D. (1989), 'Heseltine urges new technology policy for Europe', *New Scientist*, 2 December.

Håkansson, H. and Laage-Hellman, J. (1984), 'Developing a network R&D strategy', *Journal of Product Innovation Management*, vol. 7, no. 4.

Håkansson, H. (1989), '23% av kostnaderna for FoU i utlandet', *IMIT Nytt*, 1989. This news item is based on the study *Forskning och Utvecklaing i Utlandet* (Research and development abroad), Stockholm School of Economics, Stockholm, November 1988 (draft version).

Hasegawa, Y. (1986), 'Counter to technology controls', *Japan Economic Journal*, 13 September (downloaded from Nikkei Telecom Database).

Hasegawa, Y. (1988), 'Japan firms expand R&D overseas', *Japan Economic Journal*, 17 September, p. 55.

Hirazawa, R. (1989), *Technology Management in Leading Japanese Companies—Technoscience Approach* (seminar paper).

Imai, K. (1983), 'Japan's industrial society: technical innovation and formation of a network society', *Journal of Japanese Trade and Industry*, no. 4, pp. 43–8.

Imai, K. (1988), *Technological Change in the Information Industry and Implications for the Pacific Region*, Discussion Paper no. 130, Inst. of Business Research.

Inoue, Y. (1987), 'Foreign firms set up research beachheads', *Japan Economic Journal*, 14 November (downloaded from Nikkei Telecom Database).

Inoue, Y. (1988), 'Japanese firms rapidly increase global research and development', *Japan Economic Journal*, 24 September (downloaded from Nikkei Telecom Database).

Japan Economic Journal (1988), 'Firms extend global research to reach labs', 31 December, p. 46.

Johnson, R.R. (1988), 'Conflicts of similarities', *Speaking of Japan*, Nikkei Telecom Database (NIMA22EU.TXT, pp. 14–19).

Krugman, P. (1979), 'A model of innovation, technology transfer and the world distribution of economics', *Journal of Political Economy*, vol. 87, pp. 253–66.

Makino, N. (1988), 'The changing corporation', *Journal of Japanese Trade & Industry*, 1 November, Nikkei Telecom Database (NIMA24IT.TXT, pp. 45–50).

Mansfield, E. (1988), 'Industrial innovation in Japan and the United States', *Science*, vol. 241, September 30.

Mytelka, L. (1989), *Crisis, Technological Change and Strategic Alliance* (seminar paper).

Nikkei High Tech Report (1988), 'Japan nurtures a "research industry" while moving into the intellectual service', 25 April, Nikkei Telecom Database (NIMA21RD.TXT, pp. 60–3).

Nikkei News Bulletin (1988), 'Aisin to establish research institute in the US', Nikkei Telecom Database (NIAP30.TXT, p. 12).

Okazaki, M. (1986), 'Japanese companies tap foreign brain power by establishing overseas R&D', *Nikkei High Tech Report*, 11 August (Nikkei Telecom Database).

Ronstadt, R.C. (1984), 'R&D abroad by US multinationals' in R. Stobaough and L.T. Wells Jr. (eds), *Technology Crossing Boarders: The Choice, Transfer, and Management of International Technology Flows*, Harvard Business School Press, Boston.

Ronstadt, R.C. (1988), 'International R&D: the establishment and evolution of research and development abroad by seven US multinationals', *Journal of International Business Studies*, no. 9, pp. 7–24.

Sakakibara, K. (1988), 'Basic research dominated by corporations', *Japan Times*, 15 May, Nikkei Telecom Database (NIMA22EU.TXT, pp. 42–6).

Sigurdson, J. (1986), *Industry and State Partnership in Japan—The Very Large Scale Integrated Circuits (VLSI) Project*, Discussion Paper no. 168, Research Policy Institute, Lund.

Stankiewicz, R. and Granberg, A. (1986), *Långsiktig Teknisk Forskning i Sverige, Vasttyskland och Japan* (Long-term technological research in Sweden, West Germany and Japan), STU-information 531-1986, Stockholm.

Sveikauskus, L. (1983), 'Science and technology in the United States foreign trade', *Economic Journal*, 93, pp. 542-54.

Swedenborg, B. (1982), *Svensk industri i utlandet. En analys av drivkrafter och effekter* (Swedish industry abroad. An analysis of influencing forces and effects), Industrins Utredningsinstitut, Stockholm.

Takahashi, M. (1987), 'Korea's growing high tech capabilities threaten Japanese industry', *Nikkei High Tech Report*, 9 March, Nikkei Telecom Database (NIMA21RD.TXT, pp. 4-7).

Westney, D.E. (1988), *International and External Linkages in the MNC: The Case of R&D Subsidiaries in Japan*, Working Paper Y#1973-88, Sloan School of Management, M.I.T.

10 A vision of S&T policy in a resource-conscious society

Helmar Krupp

Introduction

From a static point of view, the system of technology-oriented research, technological development and the utilization of technology is being exploited by the neo-corporatism of business and public administration. We experience an economization of politics. The primary function of technical innovations appears to be the increase of work and capital productivity, helped by marketing, the creation, maintenance and extension of markets and consumer needs. This system has strained to such an extent the natural resources, which are either still available at no cost (air, water) or are underrated (soil, fossil energy), that considerable, even global damage to the ecosphere has resulted (increase of carbon dioxide and decrease of ozone). This damage already appears to be reducing welfare and will probably continue to do so even more in the long term.

From a dynamic point of view, the system of science, technology and business seems nevertheless to be able to register these damages, to draw them to public attention, and within the political system, to bring about environmental protection measures. To date, however, these measures have been greatly delayed and are still insufficient. Thus, the task of the coming decades will be a more reasonable exploitation of natural resources as the third factor of production (after work and capital) through an increase in their productivity (the saving of resources). This high priority task will have to be accomplished through government-induced innovation of context conditions within areas of infrastructure such as energy supply, traffic and transport, city planning, etc.—in other words, through re and not de-regulation. In the long run, in view of the threats to the environment and of the increasing external costs of our life-style, fundamental discussions as to the goals of society will be imperative to ensure a sustainable future with an increase in welfare rather than an increase in the gross national product.

There are a number of vital and still unanswered questions, concerning the more distant future which should be addressed:

1. Will the rate of the ecologizing of the existing economy be sufficient to prevent catastrophic ecological damage?
2. Will it be possible to establish a better-balanced relationship with the not yet industrialized countries without serious sacrifices to the industrialized countries—e.g. new international economic order—and will the social learning of the latter be able to cope with the ecological problems?
3. How will our society cope with such major risks as damage caused by the media and advertising, the fragility of values and finally, individual and social access to the generic basis of man and nature?

Objectives

This chapter focuses on two major themes.

1. First it outlines the institutional system within which the applied natural sciences and technological research (and development) in the Federal Republic, as well as the genesis and exploitation of technology, take place. This system covers suppliers (the research and development institutions), as well as customers and sponsors, in particular public administration and business. This system is embedded in an international context which sets physical, economic and political context conditions, among others.
2. Second, the chapter identifies the interests of society which instrumentalize this system.

Both of the above themes are first treated from a static perspective in the next section. However, fundamental research in, for example, high energy physics, as well as theoretical sociology and philosophy, are not taken into consideration. The following section discusses the particular environment risks which require radically changed context conditions in research, development and technology. This section also includes a description of the possible and the required reactions of the system of research institutions, and of development and utilization of technology in accordance with the new context conditions. This naturally leads to a section which includes a discussion of long-term social goals. Finally, an attempt is made to provide a techno-historical context of the present situation.[1]

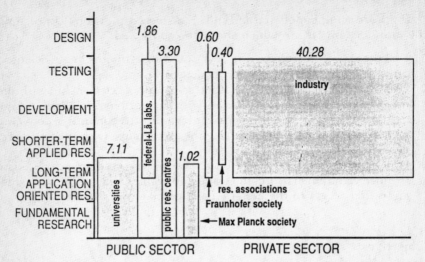

Figure 10.1   The R&D structure in West Germany, 1987 (H. Grupp, H. Krupp, 1987, p. 17)

The present research structure and its orientation

The activities and legal status of West German research institutions can be graphically arranged in a two-dimensional diagram (see Figure 10.1). The steps of the so-called vertical technology transfer from research to application are indicated along the ordinate; the distinction between public and private status is shown along the abscissa. The figures represent the annual expenditure on research and development in billions of dollars; they are proportionate to the area of the rectangles.

While universities, the Max-Planck-Society, and to some extent the public research centres, are primarily involved in fundamental research and long-term application-oriented research, the Fraunhofer Society, research associations (AIF) and in particular industry are concentrating on short-term application-oriented R&D. This is indicated by the position of the rectangles in the figure.

The Fraunhofer Society, supported by public funds, develops new, cross-sectoral technologies and promotes their diffusion into various sectors of industry. Complementary to these activities, the research institutions of the AIF work on specific technologies for their particular industrial sectors. Through their industry-oriented projects, the Fraunhofer Society and the AIF, as well as industry's own research and development capacity, serve directly the interests of the particular sponsoring business sector. Parts of the public research centers are already now tied to business, and are likely to be even more so in the future.

In universities too, attempts are being made to strengthen ties to industry. Certainly, the funds given by industry to universities in research contracts respresent only a small percentage of overall university research expenditure. However, in certain fields of natural sciences and technology, and in particular in technical universities, this percentage is still sufficient to determine to a large extent the direction of the work undertaken. Both the public administration and the universities are anxious to strengthen further the ties between university and industry, not only through individual projects, but also through multi-client projects, for example, and through so-called science parks.

These remarks demonstrate that (1) in non-university research institutions in particular, West German public and semi-public research is tied primarily to the interests of business. The individual research institutions have their specific clientele, and thus, research supply is tailored to their demand; and (2) the interrelationship between public administration and industry is so close that even those projects and programmes which are solely government-sponsored and carried out primarily in public research centres and the Fraunhofer Society serve to a great extent the interests of industry.

The institutions which are shown in Figure 10.2 generate the technical potential which in turn is instrumentalized for their own particular purposes by industrial enterprises and the public administration through technological genesis.

To illustrate more clearly how technology supply through research and development on the one hand, and technology demand on the part of the public administration and industry on the other are brought together, a four-sector model of final demand has been used (see Figure 10.2). Most research, development and technological potential is polarized into four sectors. The rationale for each sector can be formulated as follows:

1. The consumer goods sector is based on needs which can, to a great extent, be stimulated and manipulated (fashion, cosmetics, prestige and throw-away goods etc.). The growing satiation of the market increases its potential supplier control. Through marketing strategies, a car can for example be elevated from a functional means of transportation into a prestige-giving, recreation instrument which plays a significant role in social behaviour (Jochem, *et al.*, 1976), and causes high external costs (Grupp, 1986). This development is being encouraged by the current pricing policy in the transportation sector. The television, once a means to satisfy curiosity, a need for information and entertainment etc., is now a significant and addictive behavior determinant. Current media policies (liberalization) further this development. Here too, there are resultant high, if hard to quantify, external costs.

type	examples	mediation of supply / demand
consumer goods - short-lived - long-lived	food, cosmetics,clothes...... home,furniture,cars......	wants / needs / marketing
investment goods	buildings, machines......	economic rationale
public procurement	buildings, office equipment, vehicles...... ⋮ armament, space vehicles......	administration, legitimation, prestige......
infrastructure/ meritorious goods	energy environmtl. protection traffic/transport city renewal telecommunication medical treatment ⋮ culture	public - organisation and articulation of demand - regulation of <u>systems</u>

Figure 10.2 Structure of technology supply and demand

2. The investment goods sector is largely determined by economic rationale. Apart from adding to production capactiy, it serves primarily to increase productivity. Thus, for example, through automation of production, time is saved and rejects and costs are reduced. In this sector, a demand-pull on rationalizing technology is articulated and satisfied through direct linking with technical supply potential. Because of its high export ratio this sector, in particular, is subject to the pressures of international competition.

3. The public procurement sector includes a great variety of products ranging from office equipment and cars up to armaments and space vehicles. The complex rationale for these products will be treated below.

4. The infrastructure and meritorious goods are particularly significant in the context of this paper. As is indicated in the third column of Figure 10.2, energy supply or transportation, for example, form large, indeed transnational subsystems, so that demand and supply require preparatory measures on the part of the public administration to help articulate and organize the market; these measures constitute their physical, economic and legal context conditions (regulations).

The government of each industrialized country intervenes these days in the fourth sector of infrastructure and meritorious goods primarily through:

1. Its own production, as in the case of waste and water disposal, public health;

2. Production in public enterprises such as electricity plants, water and gas supply, coal mining, crude oil refining, the national railway system;
3. Public procurement within for example, public health, the construction industry, crude oil refining, telecommunication and the national railway system;
4. Subsidies and transfers of property within such areas as electricity, gas, water, nuclear fuel and the mining industry;
5. The regulation of both access to markets and market size, as in the case of the coal, iron and steel industries, agriculture, energy production and transportation; and
6. The regulation of prices, as in the case of agriculture, the coal, iron and steel industries, within the national railway and postal systems, electricity.

As a function of the classification criteria used, and at 1986 prices, the fourth sector share of the gross domestic product is found to range from 690 to 900 billions of DM per annum, representing from 43 to 49 per cent of GDP (Schwitalla, 1988). The largest contributions (over 20 billions DM p.a.) come from the following sectors: energy and water supply, mining, the chemical industry, crude oil refining, the construction industry, transportation and telecommunications.

In the fourth section it is shown that innovation in infrastructure is an absolute prerequisite to the overcoming of environmental risks. On the other hand, most of the damage to the environment emanates from the areas being discussed here. Furthermore, the existing and considerable public intervention facilitates government-imposed, environmentally-oriented, innovative re-regulation rather than de-regulation.

The natural sciences, technological research and development and the genesis and utilization of technology together form a system in which public and private research and development institutions and sectors of the domestic economy are closely intertwined. The interaction between the public administration and business in the genesis of technology is apparent in research and technology policy. The instruments of this policy are:

1. Direct, project-oriented aid to research capacity in industry as well as well as in public and semi-public research institutions; the most heavily supported fields include electronics, data-processing, telecommunications, new materials, genetic engineering, nuclear energy, space flight, armaments, etc.
2. Indirect aid through subsidies to whole sectors of industry, for example to small and medium-sized enterprises.
3. Institutional aid to public and semi-public research establishments.
4. Technology-oriented regional support; examples include new technology based firms, the establishment of science parks, the

technopolis concept, joint projects between universities and industrial enterprises.

Since the financial and thus personnel resources in these areas are several times greater than those available to fundamental research, and since these resources are relatively easily obtainable, by far the largest share of the research capacity in West Germany (80 per cent—education excluded) goes toward the instrumentalizing of research and development for applications in the four sectors referred to.

This closely interwoven system of research, public administration and business finds its motivating justification in such goals as: (1) growth of the economy; (2) creation and maintenance of jobs; (3) ensuring of international competitiveness; (4) guarantee of technological progress; and (5) socio-technological innovation. These motivating justifications lead to ideologies which push the macro-economic cost/benefit considerations, technology assessment, national and international public welfare into the background. This indeed is what is presently happening in the case of the support of manned space flight (Krupp and Weyer, 1988). An international comparison shows that while the social-political relevance of manned space flight is still debated in the USA, it is questioned less in the Federal Republic and hardly at all in countries such as France, Japan and the USSR. Other examples of rationally deficient policies are exemplified by such projects as commercial supersonic transport, the fast breeder and the magnetic train. In these instances, technology assessment is still practically non-existent in West Germany.

As a further example, government programmes to speed up the diffusion of automation in production and in offices neglect the fact that these programmes may aggravate unemployment problems and that prematurely-introduced products, deficient interface compatibility, poor-conceived organization and workplace concepts etc. cause high learning costs. The programme evaluations currently under way are finding it difficult to quantify these aspects. In the competitive, international technology push, there is little time left for concepts of social and environmental compatibility or 'humanization of work' so that technological genesis and diffusion take on a quasi-deterministic character from the point of view of both management and the work force. It is therefore desirable that despite the pressure of international competition, there should still be room for better-balanced development planning.

International networking leads to the suspension of rules of competition in the interests of the strategic technology push. In order to assure their major projects against a change in government, national industrial consortia coordinate internationally when they apply for development funding to their governments (or to the European Community) and simultaneously wave the international competition flag. This is observable in such areas as sub-microelectronics and manned space flight.

Further characteristics of the system are as follows: 'alternative' directions in research and technology, and policy making are down-played; technology assessment is denounced as technology arrestment and the very expression 'alternative energy sources' is given negative connotations. Particularly in the case of major national projects, assessment committees tend to degenerate into self-serving interest groups, and program definition, execution and evaluation take place in a homogeneous environment biased against alternative options. Such situations appear to be common occurences in socialist countries as well.

It is possible to conclude that the system of research institutions business/public administration, from a static point of view, is a tight complex of interwoven interests. These include industry, business associations, banks, political parties and government departments together with the attendant research and development capacity. This system serves the economy is so far as it ensures profit. Technological innovation is desirable only to the extent that it serves the system. Environmental protection is considered to constitute a restriction to the system, and has consequently won little support in the past. An indicator is the annual volume of investment in environmental protection measures as compared to the overall volume of investment. Even today, the annual outlay for alcohol and advertising is considerably higher than the outlay for environmental protection—both investments and operating expenses.

Through the systemic networking, science and technology may eventually make considerable contributions to technological innovation but, is at the same time, damaging the environment. However, science and technology have, in addition, the potential to forecast risks to the environment at an early stage and to meet them technologically, given favourable political context conditions. In the following section, the way in which such a transformation could come about is outlined.

An ecology perspective for the economy

Industrialization, economic and population growth, as well as social and individual behaviour, lead to, the ever-increasing burdening of the environment. The areas which are thereby threatened cover a wide spectrum, from the poisoning of local drinking water (coming from refuse dumps, industrial plots or river bank sediment) to damage of regional forests, to global carbon dioxide (CO_2) increase and ozone (O_3) reduction in the atmosphere. An indication of the growing acceleration of this global development is given by Figure 10.3. It shows that at any

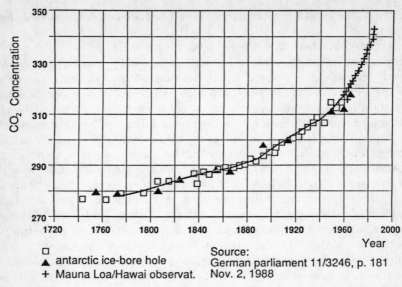

Figure 10.3 Changes in an atmospheric concentration of carbon dioxide

latitude, as of the middle of the next century at the latest, a significant change in climate may occur.

A particular qualitative danger to the environment results from nuclear energy generation. It is not simply the risk of major accidents as in Chernobyl; far more relevant from a statistical point of view is the ubiquity of the processes through which radioactive material can be released into the environment: mining of uranium minerals, isotope separation, fuel production, reactor use, fuel reprocessing, waste disposal, transport processes, terrorist and military misuse. The risk potential is increasing with the increase in the nuclear energy share of the world-wide energy supply, and, moreover, at an accelerating rate as technologically lesser developed countries as well as 'political trouble spots' gain possession of the technology. A change-over from nuclear fission to nuclear fusion would change the situation quantitatively but not qualitatively.

This chapter is concerned only with risks to the environment. The restriction is not as narrow as it may initially appear as risks to the environment are at least for the next few decades strongly linked to energy consumption. This in turn is dependent on the kind of energy technologies that are used, on transport technologies, on urban renewal methods and styles of living. Thus, although this chapter confines itself to environmental risks, the material which it covers, and in particular, the ensuring options for action open to the policies of the infrastructure sector, affect roughtly 50 per cent of the gross domestic product (GDP).

The networking of interests in the system of research institutions/ business/public administration have nevertheless not prevented the serious and ever-increasing damage to the environment from being registered and integrated into the system so that, indeed, tentative measures towards the reduction and prevention of the damages as well as new context conditions for the future genesis and exploitation of technology are beginning to be worked out.

At first, it was fundamental research in fields such as geophysics, chemistry, biology and medicine in universities and in institutions such as the Max-Planck Society, as well as international counterparts, that provided scientific knowledge on ecological damage. Then governmental laboratories and the public research centers entered the scene, at times at the explicit request of government departments. Today, the scientific discussion is also taking place in many specialized publications and associations and is being supported by such institutions as the German Research Foundation (DFG) and the Volkswagen Foundation. Finally, trade magazines and even the mass media are taking over the task of further spreading and popularizing the critical information.

This present state of affairs should not obscure the fact that still today, and not just as several decades ago when the re-thinking process began, it takes exceptional personal courage, financial and professional security and special niches in research institutions to carry but critical environmental research and publish the results. This is because personnel departments, hiring committees and expert committees at sponsoring institutions as well as the publishers of scientific journals tend seriously to hinder changes of paradigms. In contrast to some US professional associations, the West German counterparts do not provide legal help to their members in cases of conflict. Still today, the publicizing of new ecological damage is opposed by the perpetrators and their interest groups. They can count on support from scientific consultants and contract research to such an extent that hardly any scientific institution remains untarnished by the suspicion of the conflict of interests.

Thus, the confusing ambiguity of the ecological discussion results partly from the complexity of ecological systems, partly from the difficulty of formulating a clear-cut path of action from the scientific results, but also from the ready availability of scientists to the various interest groups involved.

The Green movement has emerged from a great many, highly heterogeneous causes and political processes and has manifested itself locally through a variety of citizens' action committees and nationally through voter migrations. This movement can take a large share of the credit for the widespread dissemination of the environmental research results beyond the confines of the system of research institutions/industry/ public administration. It is thanks to this movement that it is now possible to talk of the beginning of a fundamental change of consciousness.

In the wake of the 'Greens', all the other parties and all governments have come up with demands—at least in their programmes—for the reduction of threats to the environment. The turning into law and subsequent execution of specific measures vary considerably depending on the polluting material and industrial sector involved; overall, not nearly enough is being done.

Lack of positive action in the areas of waste dumping, nitrogen oxide (NOx) emission, heavy metal accumulation, drinking water and food protection, ecologically compatible agriculture, industrial chemicals etc. is obstructing what success has been achieved in the reduction of both industrial sulphur dioxide (SO_2) emissions and pollution in communal sewers. for example. The long list of deficient action areas is in itself an indication of the extent to which pollution abatement is lagging behind the development of the polluting potential. What makes the situation worse is that due to economic growth, in particular in less and underdeveloped countries, individual national measures are frequently over-compensated on a national as well as on an international level, so that the environmental risk is becoming greater both nationally and internationally.

Since the perception of environmental risks is increasing, the question arises as to how these risks can be translated into terms of economic-political calculations and measures. Liberal economists argue that the markets in sectors for consumer and investment goods should be able to react to the change that has taken place in environmental consciousness, since it can be reflected in changed consumer and buyer preferences. Goods that are ecologically compatible will be given preference, whereas the demand for goods that are harmful to the environment or polluted should be dropped. The fact is, however, that sufficiently risk-free substitutes for many needed items are either not available at all, or not available in sufficient quantities at comparable prices. This is true for foodstuffs, synthetics, biocides and cosmetics, for instances. And behavioral patterns and the advertising industry obstruct such changes in preferences.

More serious is the fact that most of the burden on the environment develops in the fourth sector, the area of infrastructure, where changing consumer demands are not sufficiently organized, articulated or capable of being implemented. This is true for example, in the cases of regenerative energy production, more efficient public commuter traffic or heat-insulated construction. Here, innovation through governmental regulations is needed in order to bring about a reduction in risk.

In order to quantify the present ecological damages, external costs of technologies have been estimated. External costs and external benefits are those effects which occur outside the market. Three examples are used to illustrate the possibilities and limitations of such calculations.

The total external environmental costs of cars in comparison with other means of transportation amounts to almost DM 100 billion per year (Grupp, 1986; see Table 10.1).

The total of the external costs which are caused by air pollution are estimated to be in the region of DM 10–50 billion per year (Hohmeyer, 1988; see Table 10.2).

The external costs (1982 prices) of nuclear generated electricity amount to 0.1 to 0.2 DM/kWh (electric) and of fossil fuel electricity, 0.04 to 0.09 DM/kWh (electric); the external benefits of electricity generation through, for example, wind energy amount to about 0.9 DM/kWh (electric). Wind energy is therefore now socially profitable. The major contributions to the external costs of fossil fuel electricity, for example, seem to ensue primarily from:

damages to the environment	0.1–06. DM/kWh(electric)
surcharges for the exploitation of non-renewable resources	0.2 DM/kWh(electric)
publicly supplied goods and services, R&D subsidies	0.001 DM/kWh(electric)
monetary subsidies, accelerated depreciation	0.003 DM/kWh(electric)

As is indicated by the range of estimates given above, these calculations (Hohmeyer, 1988) are quite hypothetical; nevertheless, they can serve as a relevant basis for action. It becomes apparent from these examples that production methods, goods and services of the infrastructure and indeed, of all other sectors too, will have to be reassessed and reassigned priority after inclusion of their external costs. In the same way, production methods in the investment goods sector should be forced by environ-

Table 10.1 Estimated external costs for means of transportation (West Germany, 1986, shares and total costs)

Damage	Air Traffic	Railway	Ship	Road	Total %
air pollution	2	4	3	91	100
noise	26	10	0	64	100
land use	1	7	1	91	100
construction and maintenance	2	37	5	56	100
accidents	1	1	0	98	100
Sum of external costs in 10^9 DM/a	2	14	2	68–77	85–95

Source: Grupp, 1986

Table 10.2 Environmental degradation costs in West Germany (1988, estimates)

Damages to	Total quantified damages (1,000 mio. DM/a)
Flora	6.03–9.09
Fauna	0.09
Man (health)	1.62–40.35
Materials	2.23–4.00
Climate	0.06–0.11
Total (by addition)	10.03–53.64
Total (using error statistics)	31.84±19.45

Source: Hohmeyer, 1988

mental protection laws to be innovated in the future, so that the materials cycles are closed to the maximum extent.

As the above examples show, the external costs represent a considerable percentage of the GDP, so that economic growth will have to be confronted with the accumulated costs of damages to the environment in order to obtain a more representative measure of our welfare (Leipert, 1987). Quantitative indications for such new welfare calculations are given by (a) the necessary costs of repairing ecological damage; and (b) the 'real' costs of natural resources, which, in the case of fossil fuel, we owe to the accumulated utilization of sun energy obtained within geological periods of time (Odum, 1988).

Just as fossil energy carriers cannot be regenerated, several other damages to the environment are irreversible. This includes changes in the mineral composition of the soil to 'acid rain', the dying-out of species and chronic illnesses, for example.

Methodologically, the most ambitious attempt at such a social reassessment of technologies is technology assessment, which tries to assess all impact dimensions and all technological alternatives available (Jochem, 1988a and further literature mentioned in his bibliography). However, technology assessment may fall short of high expectations, since the results tend to present somewhat fragile *post-factum* signals likely to disappear in informational noise. Nevertheless, technology assessment should be supported, if only to encourage more rational technological discussions—since, given the manifest failure of expertocracy, recourse to a widespread democratic decision-finding would appear to be unavoidable.

In concluding the ecological perspective it is essential to mention the following three dimensions:

1. Many of the reaction paths causing damages to the environment have not yet been adequately understood (the dying of forests; health

damages such as allergies, respiratory diseases, radiation cancer, etc.; carbon dioxide accumulation and ozone reduction in the atmosphere, etc.).

2. The quantifications of external costs, cost/benefit ratios, opportunity costs and so on, as well as their translation into presumed complete models technology assessment are extremely deficient.
3. The evidence of the many causes of ecological damage and of the extent of that damage seems to be quite sufficient to warrant the designing of preventive measures and the setting of priorities of action.

Is a reorientation possible?

A fundamental problem is caused by systemic interdependency. An individual agent, be it an industrial enterprise or a community, can adopt only limited environmental protection measures if it wants to avoid economic repercussions. Thus, contextual measures which effect society as a whole are required.

There are many hindrances, even if ecological reforms are genuinely supported by the ruling majority:

1. The differentiation of tasks of the various governmental departments is a stumbling block to integrate problem-solving in the case of larger problem complexes such as drinking water, foodstuffs, dying forests, energy, transportation, construction. Departmental egotism, party clashes, competition between the state and the federal governments, sector-specific lobby pressure from industry and industrial associations all interfere with rational problem-solving.
2. Due to gaps in scientific knowledge, and the problems of social cost/benefit accounting, the diverging interest groups can equip themselves with equally diverging expert opinions, so that action-relevant signals tend to be cancelled out in informational noise.
3. Even when all of the scientific problems have been solved, the vested interests of the large industrial sectors (automotive, chemical, road construction) can obstruct, or at the very least, delay such legal action as the imposition of speed limits, the ban on propellant gases, emission limits.
4. A further complicating dimension is found in the international context where the European Community, GATT and international industrial competition are powerful forces. The pressure to have to coordinate on an international level can delay the decision-making process to an extraordinary degree and by invoking threats to competition, opponents are in a position to disrupt it seriously.
5. Even after regulations have become law, the execution of the

regulations can in fact be prevented through pressure of interest groups, as commonly happens in the enforcing of traffic regulations. Laws concerning the environment frequently contain weak clauses such as those pertaining to economic feasibility, which makes it possible to suspend them in many cases.

Although the obstacles are extraordinarily great, it appears that an ecologizing of the economy is, at least in principle, possible, in so far as the system of R&D is able to identify risks to the environment and to develop ecological technologies. At least in principle, it seems possible to regulate the utilization of technologies through context conditions so that ecologically beneficial technologies could prevail over those that are ecologically harmful. Through adequately innovative context conditions, future technological innovations to increase work and capital productivity would be supplemented by innovations to increase the productivity of the natural resources (resource-saving).

The rate of this development is determined to a greater extent by the functional implementation of context conditions than by the technological possibilities. In the final analysis, the technical constraints are in no area the real obstacle. Because of the complexity of larger systems such as energy and transportation, and because of the time required for development and testing of larger innovations and the pertaining costs, as a general rule, an introductory phase of roughly one or two generations (25–50 years) must be reckoned with. Given the rate of increase of environmental risks much required re-regulation can in all likelihood no longer be delayed.

Whereas it is frequently argued from a systems standpoint (for example, Ronge, 1986) that systemic self-referentiality and the corresponding consolidation of interests between the public administration, business and technology would thwart an ecologizing of the economy and technology, the system nevertheless seems capable of producing its own reforms. Competition on all levels—science, technical development, companies, interest groups, government departments, political parties, states, the public domain—and their cross-linkages through the media tend to dissolve irreversible consolidation of interests. This correlates with the fact that Japanese innovations in the area of environment and energy in the past decade have led to measurable competitive advantages (Grupp, 1987b).

What concrete steps will have to be taken? In the long run—with a time horizon extending late into the next century—the most important tasks in the infrastructure sector are the following changes:[2]

1. regenerative energy production, primarily through the use of solar energy, with nationally and regionally varying contributions from water, wind, geothermal energy, biomass etc.;

2. the closing of industrial material cycles by the recycling of waste materials and the minimizing of residual emissions;
3. construction norms which minimize loss of energy and encourage the utilization of passive solar energy, not only in detached buildings, but also through the exploitation of integrated energy supply concepts for groups of buildings and town districts (co-generation, district heat);
4. integrated transportation concepts which reduce the use of the car in commuter traffic and relieve the roads of long-distance traffic; the further development of local public transportation, a shift to the train, bicycle paths, etc.; the tunnelling of long-distance traffic; noise protection. While governmental bodies and the pertinent scientists occupy themselves primarily with the pros and cons of de-regulation concepts, more emphasis should be given to the development of welfare cost concepts which would most likely point towards the necessity for re-regulation (Becher *et al.*, 1988).

In the coming decades, what is of vital importance on the priority scale is exhausting the potential for a more rational use of energy with a possible increase in the productivity of primary energy by a factor of 5 to 10 (Jochem, 1988b). The available technological potential is to a great extent already cost-effective in many sectors. At the same time, the load on the environment would be greatly relieved.

The regulatory, or re-regulatory, instruments required to reach the goals consist primarily of:

a. innovative norms and rules in such areas as machine licensing (more efficient use of energy, noise abatement, etc.); the setting of maximum emission levels; speed and acceleration limits for motor vehicles; the insulation of buildings; the technical construction of waste dumps; electricity costs (at least linear, if not progressive rates);
b. levies (taxes), subsidies and transfer payments, for example, levies on activities and goods which burden the environment; subsidies for the introduction of energy and environment saving products and processes; transfer payments between air polluters and those affected;
c. information campaigns concerning the existing potentials for increasing the productivity of natural resources, and motivation campaigns to encourage more resource-conscious consumer behaviour (as has been shown by the changes in behaviour concerning nutrition and smoking, informative symbolic politics can be very effective);
d. research, development, demonstration and pilot projects and trans-national agreements concerning the stationing of solar energy plants and energy transportation grids.

The scientific discussion concerning effective and cost-effective re-regulation measures has to consider the multiplicity of parameters and their effects. It also has to consider the difficulty in forecasting them, still poorly developed (Becher *et al.*, 1988), so that future re-regulation policies will require a high degree of monitoring evaluation and periodic readjustment.

Such re-regulation might, on the one hand, hamper the intensity and rate of innovation with regard to conventional products, processes and services; on the other hand, it could open up considerable resource-saving innovation potential, as in Japan in the 1970s. The supreme economic goal of capitalism, to obtain profits, need not be negatively affected, since the restricted exploitation of environmental resources could be compensated for by the innovative deployment of work, capital and technologies.

Is such a re-regulation politically feasible? The international experience of the past decade seems to indicate that the chances for resource saving re-regulation correlate with

1. a high GDP per capita as in the OECD countries (poorer countries give a lower priority to the saving of resources; thus, the richer countries are all the more obliged to implement new resource policies);
2. high local or regional ecological damage (as in Japan);
3. sufficient organization and articulation of public opinion on the part of those who have been negatively affected or who are at risk (at the earliest in the USA);
4. particular regional factors such as, for example, the large supply of solar energy in California, wind energy in Denmark, water energy in Canada and geothermal energy in Southern Italy.

Of late, there are two additional encouraging factors:

1. The example provided by Japan through early re-regulation with regard to the more rational use of energy and environmental control which has led to an edge in international competition (Grupp, 1987) indicates that re-regulation interests are compatible with those industry.
2. The growing global risk to the environment is encouraging a concerted international effort and is eliminating, at least gradually, the counter free-rider argument.

Nevertheless, the counter-interests are strong and it is not possible to predict whether the rate of extent of the ecologizing process will be sufficient to prevent major future damages; or whether a sustainable future is realizable and could offer the not yet industrialized countries sufficient qualities of life.

Estimates as to energy supply and environmental pollution seem to indicate that given the present rate of population growth, behavioural patterns and established technologies, an equalization of prosperity between industrialized and non-industrialized countries will not be possible without untenable damage to the environment. On the other hand, changes in behavior and technical innovations in the industrialized countries are not inconceivable, so that, as has already been pointed out, consumption of primary energy, for example, could be reduced to a fraction (perhaps even 20–10 per cent) of its present level (Jochem, 1988b). Should it be possible to bring about this through re-regulation in the industrialized countries, and finally, in the not yet industrialized countries as well, then a common ecological sustainable future cannot be ruled out.

Basically, not only the capitalist system, but also other economic and social systems appear capable of such a change, provided they are given stringent ecologically-oriented context conditions. In view of its social consensus behaviour, Japan could quite well turn out to be the leader in the field. Applied research would continue to serve primarily industry and politics, but thanks to new context conditions, with a reduced potential for damage.

Our society needs a welfare-oriented political discussion of goals which balances and, through innovative context conditions, operationalizes differing and to some extent conflicting goals such as economic growth (GDP), welfare growth, the protection of resources, the reduction of inequities, the humanization of working life, socially acceptable technologies, a new international economic order and so on. Science should take up the challenge, even if it means jumping over the shadow of its own traditional reticence as to the discussion of social norms.

Innovative context conditions would change the direction of demand-pull and technology-push at the four sectors of final demand towards a more sustainable regime, and the contribution of science and technology to society accordingly.

Technical determinism versus social constructivism

Over a period of millenia, the processing and manufacture of materials and the development of machines and power have successively been converted into tools of industry. Informational feed-back led to self-controlled, automatic production methods, in the processing of materials and the production of chemicals, and finally to automatic information processing and computer-integrated manufacturing (CIM). As the key dates in Table 10.3 indicate, the innovation phases have become progressively shorter.

The last step in mankind's exploitation of nature has been provided by genetic engineering, through which our very essence can be radically

Table 10.3 Major human phases of innovations

Type	Date	Innovation
Materials	– Paleolith	building materials, clothing, adornment, ceramics ...
	– 3000	pyramids, bronze, iron, glass ...
	+ 1884	artificial silk
Force	– 4000	wheel, plough
	– 2300	lever
	– 240	pulley
Energy	+ 500	water, windmill
	+ 1665	steam engine
	+ 1822	electric motor
	+ 1956	commercial nuclear reactor
Information	+ 1623	mechanical computer
	+ 1938	binary computer
	+ 1941	programmable computer
Genetic	+ 1944	genetic code
engineering	+ 1953	DNA double helix
	+ 1972	cloning
	+ 1980/1	transgenic mouse

altered and likewise economically instrumentalized. The risk engendered by genetic engineering could well be even greater than that caused by the present destruction of the environment.

Put into a historical perspective, until recently, this evolution was presented primarily as a quasi-deterministic event documented by inventions and inventor literature. Through the isolating of individual technical trajectories, it is possible to gain a more precise understanding of this evolution. Such trajectories include:

1. the micro-miniaturization of mechanics, electronics, optics and biology and their mutual fusion, which come under labels such as opto-electronics, fiber optics, biochips, etc;
2. the informationization of automats and feed-back robots into 'robots with artificial intelligence'; the extension of these notions leads to a wide range of developments up to the automatic sequencing of human DNA with very different interfaces between machine and man;
3. the steady improvement in materials, expected to continue in the future, with regard to strength, durability, formability and substitutability;
4. the technization of the individual household through electrical and electronic equipment and telecommunications.

Parallel to this quasi-deterministic approach, the evaluation of social innovations along various trajectories (Bijker *et al.*, 1987) becomes apparent. These include social systems which modify or control the quasi-deterministic innovations. Figure 10.4 provides a simplistic overview which indicates that social configurations contain different competing projects with unpredictable outcomes.

When the Battelle Institute took over the electro-photographic copying process from its inventor Carlson, from a techno-economic standpoint it appeared to be in a hopeless competitive position as compared to other technologies and suppliers. The subsequent techno-economic 'break-through' was achieved not only by the further technical development, but also by the Xerox marketing strategy based on leasing.

Today, it is hard to predict which technology will go into the making of the chips of the future containing as many as one billion transistors. The West German joint project BESSY, developed by the Fraunhofer Society, is working on X-ray lithography, while the ambitious European consortia project, Joint European Submicron Silicon Initiative (JESSI), envisages several competing technologies.

Quasi-deterministic approaches tend to prove their worth with hindsight whereas *ex-ante*-oriented models seem to demonstrate the indeterminate character of the future. Deterministic and constructivistic approaches converge in neo-corporatistic models, according to which industry and public administration form configurations which bring about economic and technical changes which ensure the stabilization of major sectors (Janicke, 1986; Ronge, 1986). The manned spaceflight program, for example, has no cost-effective scientific techno-economic use, and serves only national prestige and the arming of the atmosphere. Industry with vested interests and the corresponding government agencies have instituted the programme through political advertising, and keep it stable in the face of governmental and public opinion change through a network of international contracts (Krupp and Weyer, 1988).

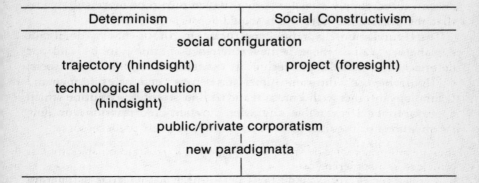

Determinism	Social Constructivism
social configuration	
trajectory (hindsight)	project (foresight)
technological evolution (hindsight)	
public/private corporatism	
new paradigmata	

Figure 10.4 Relations between technological and social innovations

As this example shows, social constructivism is present; nevertheless, the prevailing, (even) international configuration has considerable determination power, at least temporarily. According to Olson (Olson, 1982), such national entrenchments may become so stable that only catastrophes can break them up. However, there are indications as in the case of single-issue citizen groups over the present decade that these governmental-industrial complexes are becoming vulnerable in the face of new paradigms. It is not that a particular paradigm which has long been dominant is at some point in time replaced by another; there are at any given time a number of paradigms competing with differing majorities and minorities (Fleck, 1935) and some always manage to impose themselves temporarily over others. This is true not only on the level of individual projects, where at any particular time, alternative problem-solving, alternative projections for the future, and differing risk-assessment make the formation of varying configurations possible. This applies equally to more ambitious programmes such as future scenarios heavily reliant on nuclear energy, as opposed to those which are based primarily on renewable energy sources. For traffic systems, the strongest competitors in a car-dominated scenario are the supporters of public commuter transportation and high quality combination-transport. The tenacity of entrenched paradigms as opposed to new ones can be at least partially attributed to the fact that existing interest groups are better able to assert themselves than those in the formative stage. However, electrical power companies, for example, have an advantage over the multifarious and heterogeneous 'environmental protection industries'.

The persistence of present-day techno-industrial subsystems has its economic *raison d'être* in existing, and in the case of electricity supply, extremely high investments (several hundred billions of DM in the Federal Republic alone), and the desire to profit from lower costs for as long as possible. In the case of wide-area solar energy utilization, other, decentralized supply structures might turn out to be more suitable so that the present-day structures would depreciate.

Thus fundamentally, the constructivism thesis has a dominant explanatory value; there is nevertheless something to be said for deterministic models of technical trajectories within rigid social configurations. At the same time, social constructions of science and technology interact with a natural and techno-scientific evolution which appears to be irreversible and where extensions, revisions or new formulations of theories or processes embody their predecessors:

thus, quantum mechanics is a further development of classical mechanics, the last contained as a borderline case;
new projects on electricity production from fossil fuel add, integrate and improve older processes (fuel gasification).

The social embedding of this evolution as well as specific trajectories or projects and the setting of priorities are, however, not deterministic; they constitute a social construction, even if they are often politically invincible.

The discussion on the genesis of technology can be summed up as follows. Our socially organized technology, although pervaded by natural scientifc-technical evolution, serves socially-immanent constructed goals which result from controversies and compromises among partial goals of political subsystems.

As far as our social future is concerned, the most crucial aspect is whether our self-destructive universal economism can be controlled through self-limiting context conditions made possible through a process of social learning and to which individual and group behavior can adapt.

Notes

1. I would like to thank my colleague Gerhard Becher for his support.
2. The following list is based on relevant ISI work, *inter alia* (ISI, 1988).

References

Becher, G. *et al.* (1988); *Der Einfluß wirtschafts- und gesellschaftspolitischer Rahmenbedingungen auf das Innovationsverhalten von Unternehmen*, ISI project 10 485 0, commissioned by Bundesminister für Wirtschaft, Karlsruhe.

Bijker, W.E. *et al.* (eds.) (1987); *The Social Construction of Technological Systems* (New directions in the sociology and history of technology), MIT Press, Cambridge, Mass.

Fleck, L. (1935); *Entstehung und Entwicklung einer wissenschaftlichen Tatsache: Einfuhrung in die Lehre vom Denkstil und Denk Kollektiv*, Basel Benno Schwabe and Co., 1935; Suhrkamp Frankfurt 1980.

Grupp, H. (1986); 'Die sozialen Kosten des Verkehrs', *Verkehr und Technik*, 9 and 10.

Grupp, H. and Krupp, H. (1987); 'An International Perspective on Science and Technology in the Federal Republic of Germany', Proceedings of the Symposium *Research in the Federal Republic of Germany*, Tokyo, 19 November 1987.

Grupp, H. *et al.* (1987a); *Spitzentechnik, Gebrauchstechnik, Innovationspotential und Preise—Trends, Positionen und Spezialisierung der westdeutschen Wirtschaft im internationalen Wettbewerb*, TÜV Rheinland, Köln.

Grupp, H. *et al.* (1987b); *Technometrie: Die Bemessung des technisch-wirtschaftlichen Lei-stungsstands. Enzyme, Genetechnik, Solargeneratoren, Laser, Sensoren, Roboter in der Bundesrepublik Deutschland, Japan und den Vereinigten Staaten*, TÜV Rheinland, Köln.

Hohmeyer, O. (1988), *Social Costs of Energy Consumption*, Springer, Berlin/Heidelberg 1988; now also available in German from the same publisher.

ISI (1988); ISI director of publications valid as of April 1988.

Jänicke, M. (1986), *Staatsversagen, die Ohnmacht der Politik in der Industriegesellschaft.* Piper München-Zürich.

Jochem, E. (1988a), *Technikfolgenabschatzung am Biespiel der Solarenergienutzung.* Peter Lang, Frankfurt.

Jochem, E. (1988b), Möglichkeiten zur Eindämmung der Klimaänderungen, Enquête-Kommission des Deutschen Bundestages 'Vorsorge zum Schutz der Erdatmosphäre', hearing on June 20, Bonn.

Jochem, E. *et al.* (1976), *Die Motorisierung und ihre Auswirkungen.* Schwartz Göttingen.

Krupp, H. and Weyer, J. (1988), 'Die gesellschaftliche Konstruktion einer neuen Technik, Legitimationsstrategien zur Durchsetzung der bemannten Raumfahrtals Biespiel', *Blatter fur deutsche und internationale Politik* 9 and 10/1988 Köln.

Leipert, C. (1987), *Folgekosten des Wirtschaftsprozesses undvolkwirtschaftliche Gesamtrechung.* Project report ISSN 0256 -7296, WZB, Berlin.

Odum, H.T. (1988), 'Self-organization, transformity, and information', *Science,* **242**, p. 1132–1139.

Olson, M. (1982), *The rise and decline of nations,* Yale University Press.

Pinch, T.J. and Bijker, W.E. (1984); "The social construction of facts and artefacts", *Social studies of science,* **vol 14**, 3, p. 339–441.

Ronge, V. (1986), 'Instrumentelles Staatsverständnis und die Rationalität von Macht, Markt und Technik in Hartwich', Hans Herman: *Politik und die Macht der Technik,* Westdeutscher Verlag Opladen, p. 84–101.

Schwitalla, B. (1988), *Abgrenzung des Einfluß bereichs innovationsfordernder Maß nahmen unter umwelt- und energiepolitischen Nebenbedingungen.* ISI Karlsruhe (unpublished manuscript).

Index

(Figures in italics indicate an article by the author so annotated. The word *passim* after an entry means that the subject is referred to in scattered passages throughout the pages indicated. 'n' means that the item annotated is referred to in a note.)